Contemporary
Sports
Reporting

About the Author

Douglas A. Anderson is professor and director of the Walter Cronkite School of Journalism and Telecommunication at Arizona State University. He is author or co-author of six books, two of which have gone into subsequent editions: *A "Washington Merry-Go-Round" of Libel Actions; Contemporary Sports Reporting; Electronic Age News Editing; Contemporary News Reporting; News Writing and Reporting for Today's Media;* and *Writing the News.* He also has written more than sixty academic articles, papers, book chapters, and workbooks. His articles have appeared in academic and professional publications that include *Journalism Quarterly, Newspaper Research Journal, American Journalism, Grassroots Editor, APME News,* and *Journalism Educator.* His teaching specialties are communication law, editing, and reporting. He is a former daily newspaper managing editor and sports editor. Professor Anderson holds a Ph.D. in journalism from Southern Illinois University, where he was a graduate fellow.

Contemporary Sports Reporting

SECOND EDITION

Douglas A. Anderson
Arizona State University

Nelson-Hall Publishers
Chicago

Project Editor: Dorothy J. Anderson
Text Designer: Corasue Nicholas
Cover Painting: *Basketball II* by Nancy Wieting

Library of Congress Cataloging-in-Publication Data

Anderson, Douglas A.
    Contempory sports reporting / Douglas A. Anderson.—2nd ed.
      p. cm.
    Includes index.
    ISBN 0-8304-1288-3
    1. Sports journalism—History—20th century. I. Title.
PN4784.S6A5   1994
070.4'49796–dc20

92-10948
CIP

Manufactured in the United States of America.

10 9 8 7 6 5 4 3 2 1

™ The paper used in this book meets the
minimum requirements of American
National Standard for Information
Sciences—Permanence of Paper for
Printed Library Materials, ANSI
Z39.48-1984.

To my wife, Claudia,
and my daughters, Laura and Mary

Contents

Preface

David Shaw, media critic for the *Los Angeles Times*, was correct when he wrote that "the times—and the nation's sports pages—they are a changin.'" We still read about "frosh phenoms," "sophomore sizzlers," "junior jumping jacks," and "sterling sinewy seniors," but hyperbolic references and cliches are found less frequently.

On pages that not long ago were filled almost totally with play-by-play accounts and features on major sports, we now find first-person stories by athletes as they suffer through preseason training camps, comprehensive in-depths about athletic department budgets, how-to pieces on buying skiing equipment, detailed coverage of litigation, and descriptive accounts of poetically nimble gymnasts.

Contemporary Sports Reporting examines the changes that have occurred on the nation's daily newspaper sports pages. It explores coverage philosophies of small-circulation and large-circulation newspapers. Mainly, though, it presents examples of and comment on newspaper sports stories. Throughout, it provides instruction on the techniques of good sports reporting. The book dissects coverage of revenue-producing sports and non–revenue-producing sports. It discusses how to interpret and use significant statistics to strengthen stories. It examines scoring procedures and common terms used in the non–revenue-producing sports—sports that many writers do not cover regularly.

In addition to examining coverage of sports, the book presents effective writing styles for features; discusses types of columns and provides examples; looks at how ratings and all-star teams are compiled; examines the explosion of off-the-field sports reporting, focusing on investigations by the National Collegiate Athletic Association; and explores the techniques necessary for in-depth reporting. The text closes with chapters on designing sports pages and legal considerations. In the appendix are guidelines from the *Associated Press Stylebook and Libel Manual* that are helpful to sportswriters and editors.

Contemporary Sports Reporting was written for those who want to be sportswriters or editors. The book provides an overview of sports writing basics. Much of the advice is given by working reporters and editors. Thus, the book provides a realistic survey of an exciting, changing field. *Contemporary Sports Reporting* could be of value to experienced sportswriters, too, particularly those who have not covered some of the sports discussed or those who enjoy examining good work by their colleagues around the country.

The scope of the book is limited primarily to newspaper coverage of college and high school sports that receive attention in most regions of the country. Most sportswriters, especially those just entering the field, seldom cover professional sports. Thus, references to the pros are minimal.

When the first edition was published, John Riggins was starring for the Washington Redskins; Georgia's Herschel Walker had bolted to the fledgling United States Football League; and the University of Alabama was trying to adjust to life after Paul "Bear" Bryant.

The second edition has been revised and expanded:

- *Updated examples throughout.* The examples are from a variety of newspapers: metropolitan dailies, small-circulation dailies, and campus dailies.
- *New chapters titled "Courtrooms and Boardrooms" and "In-Depth Reporting."* The new chapters reflect significant developments on sports pages during the past decade. No longer is coverage devoted almost exclusively to heroes: high-scoring basketball players; swift, elusive running backs; and fence-rattling baseball sluggers. Those stories, of course, remain the staple of sports coverage. But, on many days, coverage centers upon NCAA investigations, contract negotiations, astronomical salaries, trials, and drug revelations. Sportswriters increasingly are dealing with stories previously handled only by reporters on the news side. In addition, sportswriters often are called upon to probe subjects in depth by writing articles that go beyond basic news stories.
- *Several new sections within chapters.* For example, sections have been added that examine the historical evolution of sports writing styles; that discuss innovative sports reporting outlets such as *USA Today's Baseball Weekly*; that explore the emergence of women sportswriters and the challenges they face; that present the functions of college sports information offices and the roles of sports information directors; and that look at the expanded use of informational graphics to supplement stories.

- *An increased emphasis on first-person accounts.* For example, Chapter 3, "Precontest Coverage," features the day-by-day pregame coverage by *Omaha* (Neb.) *World-Herald* sportswriter Lee Barfknecht as he prepares for a Nebraska-Colorado football game; Chapter 4, "Football," features a full Saturday on the job as Barfknecht covers the Nebraska-Colorado game and files his stories afterwards; Chapter 5, "Basketball," features the preparation and game coverage by the *Las Vegas Review-Journal*'s Bruce Pascoe as he travels to Las Cruces, N.M., to report on the UNLV–New Mexico State game; and Chapter 18, "In-Depth Reporting," contains advice from Suzanne Halliburton of the *Austin* (Texas) *American-Statesman* as she and her colleague, Shelly Sanford, put together an award-winning series on eating disorders among female athletes at the University of Texas.
- *Suggested exercises at the end of each chapter.*
- *An expanded appendix that contains Associated Press sports style rules.*

Several individuals supplied story examples, consented to interviews, and provided valuable advice. I owe the following special thanks: Lee Barfknecht, *Omaha World-Herald* sportswriter, who kept a diary of his work leading to and during a Nebraska-Colorado football game; Suzanne Halliburton, *Austin American-Statesman* sportswriter, who shared her secrets for first-rate investigative and in-depth work; Dave Lumia, sports editor of *The Mesa* (Ariz.) *Tribune*, who described the decision-making process of page design at his newspaper; Ben McConnell, assistant art director/graphics editor at *The Dallas Morning News*, who presented the strategies necessary to supplement stories with informational graphics; and Bruce Pascoe, *Las Vegas Review-Journal* sportswriter, who kept a diary of his work leading to and during a UNLV–New Mexico State basketball game.

I also wish to thank others who consented to interviews or provided narrative or examples that were valuable to the production of this second edition as well as those who supplied examples that were used in both the first and second editions: Paul Borden, *The Clarion-Ledger*, Jackson, Miss.; Mark Brand, Arizona State University; Penny Butler, *The Arizona Republic*; Steve Campbell, *The Dallas Morning News*; Bob Clark, *Eugene* (Ore.) *Register-Guard*; Rick Cleveland, *The Daily News*, Jackson, Miss.; Tracy Dodds, *The Orange County* (Calif.) *Register*; Bruce Farris, *Fresno* (Calif.) *Bee*; Howard Finberg, *The Arizona Republic*; Pete Goering, *Topeka* (Kan.) *Capital-Journal*; Melanie Hauser, *Austin American-Statesman*; Terry Henion, *Omaha World-Herald*; Bob Hentzen, *Topeka Capital-Journal*; Bruce Itule, Arizona State University; Mike Kelly, *Omaha World-Herald*; Joe McGuff, *Kansas City* (Mo.) *Star*; Gail Maiorana, *The Mesa Tribune*; Charlotte Porter, Associated Press; Stu Pospisil, *Omaha World-Herald*; Steve Schoenfeld, *The Arizona Republic*; Buck Turnbull, *Des Moines* (Iowa) *Register*; Paul

White, *USA Today*'s *Baseball Weekly*; and Jeff Wohler, *The Oregonian* in Portland.

It should be noted that some of the sports reporters and editors mentioned in this book have moved to other jobs. References to these journalists, however, remain within the context of their jobs at the time their articles were published or at the time they were interviewed for this book. Also, in several instances I refer to findings based on a national survey of sports editors. These findings were contained in an article I researched and wrote for *Journalism Quarterly*, ''Sports Coverage in Daily Newspapers.''

The sports information office at Arizona State University was particularly helpful in providing numerous examples of statistics for various sports. The campus daily at Arizona State, the *State Press*, provided most of the photographs.

Credit for typing much of the manuscript goes to Marian Buckley and Fran Mularski of the Auxiliary Resource Center in the College of Public Programs at Arizona State University.

I also would like to extend my appreciation to two professors who reviewed the proposal for this second edition and who offered insightful, concrete suggestions: Sean McCleneghan of New Mexico State University and James Stovall of the University of Alabama.

I am indebted to my editor at Nelson-Hall, Dorothy Anderson, with whom I worked on this edition as well as the first. A diligent and kind overseer, she polished my writing and helped to keep the book on schedule.

Most of all, though, I would like to thank Joel Horn, a talented graduate of the Walter Cronkite School of Journalism and Telecommunication at Arizona State University. Joel, the recipient of several national collegiate writing awards, was the prototype college journalism major; he balanced his studies with work at the student newspaper and with internships and part-time jobs at daily newspapers and ASU's sports information office. Joel gathered some of the material—including much of the background on enforcement practices of the NCAA—for this second edition, and he contributed sections on *The National, USA Today*'s *Baseball Weekly*, the challenges faced by women sportswriters, and the work of sports information directors. The assistance of Joel, one of my former students who has a bright future, was invaluable.

Acknowledgments

For permission to use printed material and personal quotations, I wish to thank the following: pp. 21-22, The Associated Press, used by permission of The Associated Press; p. 31, Reprinted with permission of *The Arizona Republic*; p. 32, Reprinted with permission of *The Phoenix Gazette*; pp. 33-34, Reprinted with permission of the *Daily Kent Stater*; p. 35, Reprinted with permission of *The Arizona Republic*; pp. 49-52, Lee Barfknecht, the *Omaha* (Neb.) *World-Herald*; p. 53, Reprinted with permission of *The Arizona Republic*; pp. 53-54, Reprinted with permission of the *Austin* (Texas) *American-Statesman*; pp. 55-56, Reprinted with permission of the *Omaha* (Neb.) *World-Herald*; p. 63, The Associated Press, used by permission of The Associated Press; pp. 64-66, 68-69, 71, Source: National Collegiate Athletic Association; pp. 75-77, Lee Barfknecht; pp. 78-79, Reprinted with permission of the *Omaha* (Neb.) *World-Herald*; pp. 86-91, 94, Source: National Collegiate Athletic Association; pp. 95-98, 102, Bruce Pascoe; pp. 98-102, Reprinted with permission of the *Las Vegas* (Nev.) *Review-Journal*; pp. 110-13, Reprinted with permission of *The Dallas Morning News*; p. 114, Reprinted with permission of the *Omaha* (Neb.) *World-Herald*; pp. 119-25, Reprinted with permission of *The Fresno* (Calif.) *Bee*; pp. 130-32, Reprinted with permission of the *Omaha* (Neb.) *World-Herald*; pp. 137-40, Reprinted with permission of the *Austin* (Texas) *American-Statesman*; pp. 147-50, Reprinted with permission of *The Arizona Republic*; pp. 156-58, Reprinted with permission of the *Topeka* (Kan.) *Capital-Journal*; pp. 163-66, Reprinted with permission of Tribune Newspapers (Arizona); pp. 172-76, Reprinted with permission of *The Des Moines* (Iowa) *Register*; pp. 183-86, Reprinted with permission of *The Arizona Republic*; pp. 187-90, Reprinted with permission from *The Daily Northwestern*; pp. 190-92, Reprinted with permission of the *State Press*, Arizona State

University; pp. 193-94, Reprinted with permission of the *Colorado Springs Gazette Telegraph*; pp. 195-99, Reprinted with permission of *The Phoenix Gazette; pp.* 203-05, Reprinted with permission of the *Topeka* (Kan.) *Capital-Journal*; pp. 205-07, Reprinted with permission of *The Arizona Republic*; pp. 207-09, Reprinted with permission of the *Omaha* (Neb.) *World-Herald*; pp. 209-11, Reprinted with permission of *The Kansas City Star*; pp. 211-12, Reprinted with permission of *The Arizona Republic*; pp. 219-26, Reprinted with permission of the *Omaha* (Neb.) *World-Herald*; p. 232, Reprinted with permission of *The Arizona Republic*; pp. 234-35, Source: National Collegiate Athletic Association; pp. 237-38, Bruce Pascoe; pp. 238-45, Reprinted with permission of the *Las Vegas* (Nev.) *Review-Journal*; p. 241, The Associated Press, used by permission of The Associated Press; pp. 251-54, Reprinted with permission of the *Austin* (Texas) *American-Statesman*; pp. 255-59, Reprinted with permission of the *State Press*, Arizona State University; pp. 267-70, Dave Lumia; pp. 271, 280, Adapted from a book in progress, *So You're in Journalism Graphics: Now What?*, by Ben McConnell; pp. 301-18, The Associated Press, used by permission of The Associated Press.

SECTION I

Introduction to Sports Reporting

It is not uncommon for readers to turn first to the sports sections of their newspapers to find the details of how their favorite basketball teams fared.

(Photo by Irwin R. Daugherty)

CHAPTER ONE

Trends in
Sports Reporting

On a cool, crisp November Friday night in Shickley, Nebraska, excitement runs high. The high school's eight-man football team is unbeaten; the Longhorns are the pride of this small community. Windows of downtown businesses are whitewashed with slogans: "Take State"; "Go Longhorns"; "Ambush the Roosters."

Milligan, another small town down the road, is the opponent. Its prep football team is also unbeaten. Eight-man football. Who really cares? At least a handful of daily and weekly newspaper sports editors in South Central Nebraska care. They have sent reporters and photographers to cover one of the area's big games.

The morning following the contest, fans and players from both towns read the story in the *Hastings Tribune*. It begins:

> SHICKLEY—Milligan erupted for 22 second-quarter points to stun Shickley 40-8 in a battle of eight-man undefeated football powers here Friday night.
> Visiting Milligan (population 323) and homestanding Shickley (population 371) played before a crowd of 1,500.

Professional teams that draw from hundreds of thousands of area residents sometimes use gimmicks such as "poster night" and "bat night" to draw crowds. But in many small towns, such as Shickley, high school teams play before crowds larger than the combined populations of the competing communities. So it is in thousands of burgs across America on Friday nights. Almost everyone seems to have an interest in the local team. Most of these games will not be covered extensively—if at all—by radio or television. Fans turn to newspapers for details.

Interests of readers, of course, spread beyond accounts of high school games. Sports sections, depending on the season, contain stories and statistics about college, professional, and recreational sports. In addition, information on dog racing, auto racing, horse racing, harness racing, cycling, sailing, rowing, bowling, new coaches, player trades, and road races can be found.

A study published in *Newspaper Research Journal* concluded: "To adequately serve its various constituencies, the sports section needs to provide balanced coverage to a wide range of sports and sports-related topics."

Roots of Sports Coverage

By mid-nineteenth century, newspapers and magazines were devoting space to sports coverage. But it was in the post–World War I years that sports writing started to evolve rapidly. The decade of the 1920s often has been described as the "Golden Era of Sports." Flowery, romantic, overblown prose dominated sports pages of the day.

The longtime sports editor of the old *New York Herald Tribune*, Stanley Woodward, examined the evolution of sports writing styles in a book published in 1949, *Sports Page*. He wrote that reporters of the 1920s "wallowed in jargon, florid phraseology and mixed figures. Even the best of them fell into line. It was the day of Jack Dempsey, Babe Ruth, Earl Sande, Red Grange, the Four Horsemen and such."

Indeed, possibly the best remembered sports lead paragraph was written by Grantland Rice in 1924. He began his story about the Notre Dame–Army football game with these words:

> Outlined against a blue-gray October sky, the Four Horsemen rode again. In dramatic lore they are known as Famine, Pestilence, Destruction and Death. These are only aliases. Their real names are Stuhldreher, Miller, Crowley and Layden. They formed the crest of the South Bend cyclone before which another fighting Army football team was swept over the precipice at the Polo Grounds yesterday afternoon as 55,000 spectators peered down on the bewildering panorama spread on the green plain below.

That lead paragraph probably would not get by any sports editors today, but it remains a classic. Rice, a Phi Beta Kappa graduate of Vanderbilt, who majored in Greek and Latin, was known primarily for the verse he used so often in his writing. But, he also could craft straightforward leads in a style that would dominate sports pages in later decades. For example, here is

Rice's lead paragraph, written in 1923, on the Jack Dempsey-Luis Firpo fight:

> In four minutes of the most sensational fighting ever seen in any ring back through all the ages of the ancient game, Jack Dempsey, the champion, knocked out Luis Angel Firpo, the challenger, just after the second round got under way last night at the Polo Grounds.

By the middle of the twentieth century, sports writing had evolved into the "On-the-Button" school, according to Woodward—a style that left "the hooray-hooray business to the radio announcers and yet refuses to make a career of sneering." Woodward continued:

> The giants of our crafts, such as [Grantland] Rice, [W.O.] McGeehan and [Westbrook] Pegler, were the founders of this school. In its establishment something was taken from each of them. Rice contributed rhythm and euphony; Pegler a grumpy and grudging curiosity for fact, and McGeehan a certain twist, in the likeness of Anatole France, which could make an ordinary sentence interesting.

Woodward wrote that Rice, McGeehan, Pegler, "and others of their caliber were the pioneers of modern sportswriting."

Clearly, writing styles on the nation's sports pages have been evolving since the 1920s. The dominant flowery, gushy prose of the 1920s and 1930s gave way gradually to a more streamlined style during the World War II years and after. Woodward wrote that the war made sportswriters temper their "regard for the nobility and intrepidity of individuals who were operating only as athletes."

Newspaper accounts in the 1950s and 1960s often featured play-by-play reporting and statistics. In general, however, today's sports writing strikes a balance. It is not as flowery as that of the 1920s, nor is it as nuts-and-bolts as that of the 1950s and 1960s. At many newspapers today, reporters strive for a blend: a writing approach that goes beyond bare-boned statistics but, at the same time, steers clear of overblown prose. Today's writing is literate, but it is not ornate.

Author Jerome Holtzman quoted Walter (Red) Smith, one of the most respected sportswriters ever, in a book published in 1973:

> I won't deny that the heavy majority of sportswriters, myself included, have been and still are guilty of puffing up the people they write about. . . . I've tried not to exaggerate the glory of athletes. I'd rather, if I could, preserve a sense of proportion, to write about them as excellent ball players, first-rate players. But I'm sure I have contributed to false

values—as Stanley Woodward [sports editor of the *New York Herald Tribune* who hired Smith in 1945 from the *Philadelphia Record*] said, "Godding up to those ball players."

Smith might have indeed occasionally published lavish pieces about athletes, but he was known primarily as a gifted wordsmith. Holtzman wrote that Smith, who spent much of his career at the *New York Times*, was "most likely, the best sports columnist-reporter in the history of American journalism."

Today's Sports Pages

The nation's newspapers are responding to the interests of their readers. A national survey of daily newspaper sports editors found that sports are given considerable attention, according to an article published in *Journalism Quarterly*. Eighty-nine percent of daily newspapers devote all or parts of two or more pages to sports each day; nearly one-third provide all or parts of four or more pages.

Other survey findings:

■ Football, basketball, and baseball are covered most extensively. Still, there is a growing awareness of the need to cover so-called minor sports, women's sports, and participation sports.
■ Despite the emergence of women's sports and participation sports— along with the continuing attempts to upgrade coverage of them—the majority of space still is devoted to men's competitive athletics.
■ The amount of space devoted to professional sports, college sports, high school sports, and participation sports varies with circulation. Smaller circulation newspapers generally place more emphasis on high school sports.

No longer are readers choked by cliches and superlatives in every sports story. Sportswriters have declared war on jargon. This is not to say that all sports page stories are "negative," but there has been and continues to be a movement against too much "cheerleading."

Cliche- and jargon-riddled stories such as the following used to be found routinely on sports pages:

Coach Gary Richardson's giddap Broncos enjoyed another wild and woolly victory here Saturday as City College rolled over Metropolitan State 115-69 in a classic cardiac cage thriller.

It was a scorcher from the outset as City College tickled the twines with 23 field goals on 41 attempts enroute to a 54-31 halftime advantage.

Sophomore sensation Bob Johnson, the smooth-winged gazelle-type performer from Riverdale, scored the first eight points the run-gun go-go Broncos put on the scoreboard. He led the winners with 23 counters.

But Johnson was not the only top-notch Bronco on the hardwoods. There were a host of others who played yeoman roles in the sterling triumph.

Included were the likes of Dan Higgins, the diminutive, hustling guard; Frank Yost, the lanky 6-6 junior forward; Jack Jensen, the towering 7-0 postman; and Mark Koch, an experienced hand in the backcourt.

And then there was Dave "the belly" Kelly, who dropped in three straight feathery 15-footers during the closing minutes of the opening canto to put the game on ice.

Coach Richardson bubbled with enthusiasm as he discussed his team's gallant effort. "I thought we really took it to them tonight," he exclaimed. "I think when push comes to shove, this team can really make things happen."

Howard Williams, a leaping 6-8 forward, led the losers with 31 points. An All-America candidate with a 26-points-per-game average, Williams dazzled the crowd with outside shooting accuracy and strong inside moves.

"Williams is a fine player," coach Richardson said. "But I thought we defensed him well in the first half. Yes sir, we really got after him."

Fortunately, one would have to look long and hard to find many stories in the 1990s so filled with jargon and cliches.

The Evolution of Sports Coverage

Wick Temple, Associated Press general sports editor, told the AP sports editors at a convention in Minneapolis on the eve of the 1980s that the gradual transition from promoting sports through lavish praise to covering sports had not been easy. *Editor & Publisher* magazine quoted Temple:

> Sportswriters were cheerleaders for so long that coaches and players have come to expect newspapers to be a source of scrapbook material for them. . . . It is going to take another decade for sports reporters to gain acceptance as journalists and put an end to the conception that they are publicity men and women.

In another article in *Editor & Publisher*, John Consoli quoted Bill Dwyre, sports editor of the *Los Angeles Times*, who said: "Some of the old-time sportswriters were excellent, but sports then were portrayed as fantasy imagery." Dwyre said many sportswriters "were boosters for the teams they covered." However, "somewhere along the way, journalism was introduced to the sports pages."

Also quoted was Will Grimsley of the Associated Press. According to Grimsley: "Sports writing has undergone a change. Sportswriters used to be hero worshippers. They used to sit in the press box and actually cheer when the team they were covering scored. Today, we have a more cynical, more penetrating breed of sportswriter. I think this is better for the fan."

Penn State football coach Joe Paterno does not think that most sports-writers are cheerleaders. At an AP Sports Editors annual convention in Washington, D.C., Paterno said he had "gotten uptight over whether anything I say will be twisted to embarrass me." According to an article in *Editor & Publisher*, Paterno said: "There's an anti-hero attitude today. Sports reporters are always trying to find chinks in the coach's armor politically, financially, any way they think they can make a story. I recall telling a reporter once he ought to write more about the positive things that happen, and all he did was look at me and say, 'But that's not the way it's done anymore.' "

David Shaw, media critic for the *Los Angeles Times*, in a comprehensive article about the evolution of sports coverage, said sports writing in earlier eras consisted primarily of adjectives, scores, and statistics, some-times called "meat and potatoes" reporting. Shaw wrote, however, that "the times—and the nation's sports pages—they are a-changin', and it is now no longer sufficient to write sports stories by the numbers . . . or by the cliches."

Shaw said sports writing "is in a state of flux, moving in one direction but still being tugged backward." He said the biggest change in sports pages has been "the coming of sociology . . . and the concomitant shift . . . away from its traditional image as the toy department of the newspaper."

The *Times* reporter labeled the change "more evolution than revolution." He credited *Philadelphia Daily News* sports editor Larry Merchant with pioneering "acerbic, trenchant, iconoclastic reportage" in his sports sections as early as 1957. Shaw also cited the impact of *Sports Illustrated*, founded in 1954, and television. *Sports Illustrated*'s blend of "literacy and leisure" has spilled over to daily newspapers, and television's increasingly comprehensive sports coverage has forced newspaper reporters to go beyond bare-boned statistics and play-by-play reporting.

Not everyone agrees that the movement from statistics, profuse praise, and play-by-play to more sociologically probing reporting is good. Michael Novak, author of *The Joy of Sports: End Zones, Bases, Baskets, Balls, and the Consecration of American Spirits*, wrote in *Columbia Journalism Review* that he wanted to escape the "mundane world of everyday" when he read the sports pages. He said, "The human spirit . . . is starved for good reporting of strong narrative forms. Sportswriters are storytellers. They should tell truthful yarns." Novak contended that "the most damaging effect of television (on sports reporting) has been its enervation of newspaper writers and their editors. On occasion, one cannot see the televised game. Then it is almost impossible to find out in the papers the drama of the game itself. The writers take for granted that their readers have seen the game; they write about everything else."

Bob Broeg, sports editor of the *St. Louis Post-Dispatch*, wrote in the *Bulletin*, a publication of the American Society of Newspaper Editors, that sports writing "has gone from verse to worse, which really isn't right or even correct. But it has changed from purple prose with paeans to almost complete locker room coverage in which what the athletes say has replaced what they do."

Shaw concluded that most of the nation's daily newspaper sports pages seem "to be suffering from a kind of identity crisis . . . vacillating uncertainly between the old and the new."

David L. Smith, assistant managing editor and executive sports editor of the *Dallas Morning News*, outlined what he saw as "the evolution of good sports sections." Smith's article, published in the *Bulletin*, listed the following:

■ More opinion and analysis.
■ Better mix of shorter and longer stories, with emphasis on the short.
■ More graphics, charts/data and fact boxes.
■ Movement away from all-agate pages.
■ Greater use of "The Second Look" package. (Smith described a Second Look column as "an accumulation of tidbits, trends, quotes and other items that need repeating and emphasis." He said such a feature, "if handled properly, is a quick read, light and breezy yet full of information.")
■ Stronger concentration on pre-event coverage.

Smith, who is one of the country's best-known sports editors, wrote: "TV, particularly since the advent of cable, lets the viewer and sports fan sit in his or her chair and select from all sorts of programs. Our sports pages must provide that person with a similarly full selection."

Recommendations for Improvements

Several themes emerged in a survey that asked sports editors for recommendations on how to improve daily newspaper sports coverage: the need to tighten writing even more by continuing the war on cliches and jargon; the need to use better and brighter graphics (sports pages are tailor made for large, dominant, action-filled photos); the need to place more emphasis on coverage of local events; and the need to include a locally written opinion column.

Craig Reber, sports editor of the *Columbus* (Neb.) *Telegram*, said the sports emphasis at small- and medium-circulation dailies and weeklies needs to be on local and area events. He said, "That's where the real sports are: The guy who builds his own canoe, the old-timer who was a basketball 'barnstormer' in the 1920s and 1930s, the local who was a big star at state 'U' who is now playing pro basketball in Europe, local park board meetings, and recreation softball stories."

Lynn Houser, sports editor of the *Kendallville* (Ind.) *News-Sun*, called for more art (especially local pictures), better attention to layout and grammar, more emphasis on women's sports and features, and "less play-by-play reporting."

The sports editor of the *Meadville* (Pa.) *Tribune*, Patrick Rini, cited a deficiency in women's sports coverage and coverage of non-revenue sports. "We must reduce play-by-play of professional sports, especially in papers where box scores are used," he said. "This would open some space for other material. With the amount of attention the other media give big-time sports, and with the amount of television watched, newspapers must respond to coverage wants of nonrevenue sports."

Bob Snider, sports editor of the *Scottsdale* (Ariz.) *Daily Progress*, viewed coverage of nonrevenue sports differently. He said: "With more sports than ever before—and often less space—concise, yet informative writing is mandatory. When deciding how much space to devote to a topic and when to staff an event, editors need to look more closely at how many readers really want to know. Unfortunately, this means even less coverage for 'minor' and women's sports."

The survey certainly revealed that most sports editors think writing quality has improved during recent years, but Tim Flowers, sports editor of the *Arkansas City* (Kan.) *Traveler*, said too many sportswriters continue to "write in jargon." He said: "That's fine if you're writing for the *Sporting News*, but not all readers of newspapers understand all the 'inside lingo.' A mother is more interested in what the coach thought of how her son performed than how many times he came down with a cross block."

While the sports sections of the nation's daily newspapers are growing increasingly more complete, better written, and better edited, there remains, according to some, a market for a national sports daily.

The Birth and Death of *The National*

When *The National* made its debut on January 31, 1990, it did so on the premise that the country longed for a daily sports newspaper. It also did so with a tremendous stockpile of talent, not to mention cash. Owner Emilio Azcarraga, a Mexican broadcasting mogul, initially indicated that he was prepared to subsidize the New York-based newspaper through five years of red ink. To commemorate the launch, he gave each of his three hundred employees—including some of the country's most gifted writers who had been lured by very high salaries—a gold coin worth $500.

But *The National*'s start-up could not have come at a worse time. America was in a deep recession. While the number of other vehicles available to advertisers—most notable cable television—was steadily increasing, many advertisers were cutting back on their ad budgets.

Although it quickly attracted 100,000 readers, due in some degree to considerable positive publicity at the outset, *The National*'s total circulation never exceeded 281,000—a growth rate not rapid enough for a newspaper that, according to *The National*, needed a circulation of 500,000 just to break even.

A Sunday edition was canceled after nine months. The plan to localize coverage in virtually every big-league city was abandoned. When the price of 50 cents a copy was raised to 75 cents in January 1991, circulation fell below 200,000.

The National also had logistical problems. The paper's ten regionalized editions were printed in the local areas and were distributed by Dow Jones & Co., owner of *The Wall Street Journal*, but waiting for late scores and stories reduced press runs and disrupted truck schedules.

"People were so demanding of late scores," Frank Deford, editor and publisher of *The National*, was quoted as saying in *Sports Illustrated*. "It would have been a piece of cake if we were *The Wall Street Journal* and all our games were played in the daytime."

On June 13, 1991, after sixteen months, 393 issues, and a reported $100 million of debts, *The National* ceased publication. Clearly, most of the employment opportunities for aspiring sportswriters are with daily newspapers. But the appetite of Americans for sports news is considerable; quality sports publications likely will continue to sprout.

Gannett's New *Baseball Weekly*

In December 1990, about the same time *The National*'s ship was taking on water, some of Gannett's top executives were bandying about the idea of publishing a weekly baseball newspaper. And on April 5, 1991, *USA Today*'s *Baseball Weekly* was born.

"Some of the chief executives in Gannett are big baseball fans, and they were having a discussion one day and said, 'You know, it seems like there's no real one place anymore that you can get all the baseball information that you'd like,' " said Paul White, editor of *Baseball Weekly*. "You know, one simple place on a weekly basis [where you can find] up-to-date, timely stuff. And they said, 'Hey, let's give it a try.' "

"[It was] very unlike Gannett. Not a lot of research. It was more of a gut reaction—'Let's go for it.' "

Each issue, priced at $1, features updates on each of the twenty-six major league teams, boxscores, statistics, minor league reports, and articles on collectibles, fantasy leagues, and baseball nostalgia. Unlike *The National*, *Baseball Weekly*'s circulation goals were modest. In fact, because of low production costs, *Baseball Weekly* needed a circulation of only 130,000 to 150,000 to remain in the black. In June 1991, circulation stood at 250,000, of which more than 30,000 came from subscriptions.

Baseball Weekly's production costs are reasonable because it uses eighteen of *USA Today*'s thirty-plus printing sites around the country. The papers are printed on Thursdays and go out on trucks with the Friday morning edition of *USA Today*. "There was virtually no expense, just a little bit of trucking involved," White said. "And the system that we know already works was in place, so it was pretty easy from that standpoint."

Because *Baseball Weekly* was able to keep down costs, advertising sales projections remained modest. Lack of advertising revenue was another primary cause for *The National*'s demise. "[We use] the same production facilities that *USA Today* uses, we're in the same building [in Arlington, Va.], we use the same composing room," White said. "We didn't need as much advertising to make a go.

"And one thing we've done well with is classified advertising. We have a very specialized audience. It's really easy to tell an advertiser what audience they're getting. . . . There's just so much of that kind of advertising right now in baseball with the collectibles [and] the fantasy leagues—that's a real big thing."

Although White said there is "a little bit" of competition for advertisers between newspapers and cable television networks, he said the types of advertising are different for each medium. "For instance, the advertisers you see on ESPN baseball telecasts are still a pretty high profile—the beers, the cars, the obvious ones that you've grown used to," he said. "Our advertisers tend to be a little bit different. We have a lot of big ads [from] the baseball card manufacturers, the memorabilia dealers [and] some of the equipment manufacturers.

"And one of the things I understand from our ad people is that they don't really feel like they've touched on everything they can do because we got such a late start in our first year that ad budgets were locked in. We just couldn't get into a lot of people's ad budgets. A lot of them said, 'Yeah, it looks like a decent enough [advertising] vehicle, but we've got nothing left to dole out this year.' "

White, who has been with *USA Today* since its inception in 1982, said in the coming years the editorial staff intends to fine-tune *Baseball Weekly*. Because the paper hits the newsstands each Friday during the season, it includes boxscores through Wednesday of that week.

"We've tried to be real responsive to fans," he said. "The one nice thing is it's a very active group of readers. These people are real interested in the sport. And they call, they write and they really make it easy for you to edit because they're constantly letting you know what they'd like to see more of [or] less of. They have good ideas.

"The one thing I've tried to instill in everybody here is we're all fans, too. Let's always think of it from that standpoint. Let's not think of it from a journalist's standpoint. As a fan, if we're traveling or sitting at home, how would we want to see this subject covered?"

In retrospect, White said, the publishers of *The National* made two glaring mistakes: "When they started out, they were in essence a daily *Sports Illustrated* in newsprint. You can't read that much. I don't care who you are. . . . Well, the readers told them that, and they began, despite the little ego blow to a lot of people I think, to respond to that. They were shortening things up, becoming a little more results-oriented.

"But the bottom line, and this is tied with the circulation, is that nobody wants to hear your excuses. When they get up in the morning, they want to know who won. And [*The National*] couldn't deliver late scores to most of the country."

Despite what happened to *The National*, White remains confident that America still longs for a daily sports newspaper, and that one day someone will try it again.

Preparing to Cover Sports

Journalism students interested in careers in sports reporting must realize that masterful use of the language and knowledge of style are as important on sports pages as on page one.

Joe Smekens, sports editor of the *News-Banner*, Bluffton, Indiana, said many young journalists he had dealt with had difficulty with proper usage and "had a tendency to stray away from the heart of a sports story." He said: "I feel that journalists should learn to adapt their writing standards to the type of environment in which they are working, which in some cases merely means to 'call it like it is' without getting flowery with words."

The sports editor of the *Sentinel*, Nacogdoches, Texas, Bill Griffin, said: "Not all journalists can be [Bob] Woodwards and [Carl] Bernsteins [*Washington Post* reporters who played a primary role in coverage of Watergate in the early 1970s]. Students should learn how to write first. Write, write, write. Describe, describe, describe."

The executive sports editor of the *Kansas City Star* and *Times*, Dale Bye, said that sports reporters need to know grammar. He said it should be "emphasized, re-emphasized, and re-emphasized." Bye also said: "Journalism majors need to have a fanatic appreciation for accuracy drummed into them from the first journalism course through graduation. This appreciation for accuracy needs to extend from the minutiae to the basic tenets of a story. Most particularly, I'm concerned with names and statistics."

Milton Cole, sports editor of the *Daily Hampshire Gazette* in Massachusetts, said sports editors need to "improve their knowledge of the language and acquire a reverence for it." He suggested that sportswriters work in straight news before moving to sports.

A working knowledge of the sport being covered also is a necessity. Cherie Bishop, sports editor of the *Daily Statesman* in Dexter, Missouri, said too many sports reporters are at a disadvantage because they do not understand sports. Several colleges and universities offer courses in sports reporting. But John Akers, sports editor of the *Ames* (Iowa) *Daily Tribune*, said he would like to see more courses, seminars, and workshops offered. "I would like to see professors criticize and compliment the field, rather than hold it in contempt."

Expanded Opportunities for Women Sportswriters

No longer is sports writing the exclusive domain of males. Indeed, the 1990s appear to hold much promise for women sports reporters. Most locker rooms—for many years considered male bastions—have been opened to both sexes for more than a decade, and there are more opportunities for women sportswriters and editors than ever before.

But aspiring female sports reporters should not let such a rosy picture taint their vision of reality; sports reporting still can be a tough business for women.

"It's so much better now than it was fifteen years ago," said Tracy Dodds, assistant sports editor for *The Orange County* (Calif.) *Register*, who added that she feels women are particularly good interviewers. "The general situation is improving. And just the fact that all the locker rooms are open makes it so much more workable. But that doesn't take away everyone's attitudes. So it's not like everything's fine now that the locker rooms are open. You still have to go in there and conduct yourself under such scrutiny that I can't even tell you.''

Dodds was a sports reporter for seventeen years before assuming her current position. She spent seven years at the *Milwaukee Journal* covering Big Ten Conference football and basketball, boxing, auto racing, and the National Basketball Association's Milwaukee Bucks.

At the beginning of the first year that Dodds covered the Bucks, she was not allowed in the team's locker room. She was forced to wait outside the locker room while her male counterparts were inside conducting interviews. Later, after the players had showered and dressed—and Dodds was an hour or so closer to her deadline—the players were ushered into an interview room set up specifically for women reporters. Dodds said the players grew tired of being asked the same questions in the interview room that they had just answered for the male reporters.

NBA locker rooms opened up in 1978, but women reporters still have problems gaining equal access. Ailene Voisin of the *Atlanta Journal-Constitution* has been an NBA reporter for ten years, eight of which were spent covering the Los Angeles (formerly San Diego) Clippers for the *San Diego Union* and the *Los Angeles Herald-Examiner*. Despite her years of NBA experience, Voisin still finds her credentials questioned from time to time. "Occasionally, a security guard at the front might try to stop me and bar me from going in, but invariably a coach, an assistant coach, or the public relations director will come out and tell them to let me in,'' she said.

Interview rooms still are used by many college and some professional teams for the expressed purpose of giving the media equal access to the players and coaches. In reality this gives the university or professional organization greater control over what the players and coaches say. Despite this fact, Dodds said interview rooms are sometimes the only way to handle media requests. "After a Rose Bowl game, an interview room is the only possible way with that many people. [The] Olympic Games, that's the only possible way—you need translators and you need security, all that stuff. There are times and places where interview rooms work best.''

However, daily beat coverage would be hurt if reporters were not allowed inside locker rooms, where reporters can speak one-on-one with a player or coach, Dodds said. Players and coaches are often more spontaneous with their answers to questions because they do not have a bank of microphones in front of them.

"First of all, you'd just give up on quotes after a hockey game or after a basketball game. Forget it, because it takes so much longer [hockey and basketball games usually are played at night, and reporters working for morning newspapers have to meet deadlines soon after a game has ended]. It inconveniences the players. They don't want to have to go through that. That adds an hour to their day. They don't want to add an hour to their day. And the quotes are so much more stilted [in an interview room]. If you can get someone inside and say, 'Gee, that was really quite a scene with that manager yelling in your face in front of 60,000 people,' . . . he's more likely to forget that you represent a million people.''

"Anyone who says access to locker rooms is unnecessary is naive and obviously is unfamiliar with professional sports reporting," said Voisin, who is NBA liaison for the Association for Women in Sports Media. "It's totally unrealistic to have separate interview rooms. You're dealing with time constraints after a game because of deadlines. And the immediacy of the players' reactions after the game often is crucial. You can't rely on a public relations director to bring the players into an adjacent room, because frankly it's a major inconvenience and I suspect [the players] would be less than accommodating.''

But do not think for a moment, Dodds said, that dealing with athletes gets any easier once you enter the locker room. When talking with aspiring women sports reporters, Dodds frequently compares a men's locker room to something many women are all too familiar with: "It's very much like when you walk alone past a construction site and twenty guys are whistling and making lewd remarks. How do you best handle that, go over and tell them off? You just don't even turn your head. The worst I ever do is look somebody in the eye and shake my head like, 'You are such a child.' It works much better.''

Voisin said she rarely has problems with NBA players. "Occasionally, a player will make a snide comment or something, but invariably when that happens one of the other players will intercede and actually tell him to behave himself.

"The players really comport themselves very professionally in the NBA. Part of it is they're trained that way. They have this rookie orientation seminar every year. The owners, the coaches, and general managers have all been very good about the whole issue. Pretty much, we've all been told that if there's ever an incident to go right to the commissioner with it.''

Despite her obviously strong feelings on the subject, Dodds said the locker room issue is "incredibly overblown and overrated." "It really is not a factor day-in and day-out," she said. "It is simply the issue that everyone uses as an excuse for why you [as a woman] shouldn't be doing this. It's an emotional issue, and it's an issue that causes you problems with your sources and the sources' wives, and it's really a sore subject with everyone. Plus, it is a subject that the general public can really latch on to for why women don't belong in this business.''

In 1990, Lisa Olson, twenty-six, who was covering the National

Football League's New England Patriots for the *Boston Herald*, was conducting a locker room interview with a player, Maurice Hurst. She was approached by four or five other players who surrounded her and made lewd comments and gestures while one of them exposed his genitals.

During the investigation that followed, it was reported that Victor Kiam, owner of the Patriots, had referred to Olson as "a classic bitch." He later spent $100,000 to buy full-page ads to apologize.

"Like anybody else, I was appalled," Voisin said. "I thought we'd moved beyond that. I just thought it was blatant harassment, and I feel bad that [Olson] was as young as she was, because who knows how any of us would have reacted at age twenty-five or twenty-six?"

Two months after the Olson incident, Sam Wyche, coach of the Cincinnati Bengals, barred Denise Tom of *USA Today* from the Bengals' locker room after a game. NFL Commissioner Paul Tagliabue fined Wyche $30,000, part of which was reportedly paid by the wife of a well-known NFL player to show her gratitude to Wyche for his efforts to keep women out of the locker room.

While understanding the rage that Olson and Tom must have felt, Dodds said the publicity surrounding the two incidents has been harmful to women reporters. "I have always, throughout my career, downplayed every incident. Handle it as quietly and as privately as possible. When you are able to do that, you are able to mend bridges and go on. When you have an incident like that, it hurts everything all the way around and it causes that emotional reaction to go rippling everywhere else. . . . Well, we just don't need it. It's just one more flare-up of something we're trying to downplay as much as possible."

Dodds, who began her fight for equal access in the 1970s, said there is a public misconception about the locker room issue. "People like to think it's about nudity and modesty, and it's not. It is about territorial rights. When I first started covering the Indianapolis 500 in 1972, I was not allowed in the garage area. . . . It was bad luck, just like green is bad luck. You never let a woman step foot into your garage. Nobody's getting dressed in there. There's a stupid car in there!

"The second year, I had to carry a letter saying, 'Tracy Dodds is a reporter. She'll be wearing badge number such-and-so,' because just having the badge wouldn't do it—somebody might have lent me theirs."

Dodds, who has worked for the *Houston Post* and the *Los Angeles Times* (she covered the National Hockey League's Los Angeles Kings for two seasons) in addition to the *Milwaukee Journal*, had some advice for young women pursuing sports writing careers: "You should take it one step at a time and not set yourself up for defeat by aiming too high, because the problem is, with the competition out here, a lot of times a woman will get a beat that she's not ready for. You get a woman in here who's bright and can write, but hasn't been out there, hasn't actually done it. They should start on preps and smaller colleges, and work some nights in the office to really understand the business inside and out, how it works.

"Instead, they're given [the NBA's Los Angeles] Lakers for a smaller paper. It happens. And, all of a sudden, it's just unbelievable—the types of judgment calls that you're called upon to make on your own, on deadline, out there by yourself. And the man standing next to you has come up through the business for many more years, and is much better equipped."

Voisin also stresses professionalism. "Do your homework," she said. "Make sure you're prepared for every event you cover. Familiarize yourself with as many sports as you possibly can to gain as much expertise as possible so that your judgment can't be second-guessed, because your judgment is always going to be called into question until you have established that you have an expertise in a particular area."

Opportunities in Sports Information Work

An increasing number of young men and women are pursuing careers in college sports information offices. Without question, the most helpful person to a sports reporter covering intercollegiate athletics is a sports information director. An SID is responsible for generating publicity and enhancing the image of the university in general and the athletic department in particular. Among other things, he or she suggests feature ideas, provides photographs, and arranges interviews.

Most SIDs have journalism degrees and possess both writing and public relations skills. The hours are long, the pay is relatively low, and the job is not glamorous, but most SIDs are quick to add that their jobs are satisfying and enjoyable. Sports information offices provide press releases and media guides for each sport that contain statistics and other relevant information such as rosters, player and coach biographies, stadium information, team records, and season summaries.

Mark Brand, the SID at Arizona State University, said that the keys to success for an SID can be summed up in two words: credibility and cooperation. "They go hand in hand, really," Brand said. "If you had to rank them, the number one thing would be to be credible. Credibility is everything in this business. If you don't have it, you're not going to be effective in your job and [the media] are not going to believe you.

"And a close second would be cooperation. If the reporter believes in you and your credibility, then the cooperation between the two is going to be much better, because we are a service office and we have to understand the needs of the media when a lot of times the administrators or the coaches do not. And we have to be a buffer, so to speak, between the two."

Clearly, while an SID is a reporters' biggest help, he or she may not be the best source for inside information. After all, an SID must be a "company man." "Sports information directors know when they can say things off the record and when they can't," said Scott Dupree, an assistant SID at ASU. "They're going to be looking after the department in general, whereas an assistant coach or an assistant athletic director may tip you off on something that the sports information director would rather you not know."

Brand and Dupree agree that it is their responsibility to make a reporter's job easier. "You have to have all of the pertinent information in the media guide, in a press release, in game notes—anything like that that you can provide to make their job easier," Brand said. "As an example, the game goes into overtime and the writer has ten minutes to finish what he had on his story. The outcome changes from the lead that he had, so he's really struggling. You've got to have information that you put together in a way that they can find it quickly, where it's in a book in the same place every year, so that year after year as a beat writer covers you he knows exactly where to look for the record section; they know where to look for the bios."

But some reporters do not pay attention to the material sent out by the sports information office. Dupree said, "My biggest pet peeve is when we send out releases and media guides and they call us up and say, 'What was ASU's record in 1988?' It's right in the middle of the media guide. Or, 'How much does Leonard Russell weigh?' Or, 'How many yards has [former ASU quarterback Paul] Justin thrown this year?' When they've got all this information that we give them, sometimes it makes you wonder if they ever look at it."

While sports information offices are valuable tools, reporters sometimes sidestep them and arrange interviews on their own. "Use us," Brand said. "That's what we're here for—to be a service, to be an intermediary between the coaches, the administrators, the student-athletes, and the media. . . . Hopefully, the SID will be cooperative and take the time to deal with [the media] and fill their needs. But sometimes if they don't ask [for help setting up interviews], that's when you can get into problems."

But be patient with the SID, Dupree said, particularly during football and basketball seasons. "Sometimes we get overwhelmed with work to do trying to keep up with a lot of reporters at once. Almost every sports information office is understaffed, and it's not easy trying to keep up with the demand, because every year there's more cable companies, more television, more newspapers, more magazines. Every year, there's more work to do."

Clearly, both sports information directors and sports reporters have demanding, yet generally enjoyable jobs. They must be good writers, effective gatherers and users of information, and knowledgeable about sports. They also must have integrity.

Ethics of Sports Reporting

Among the practices that led critics to accuse sports reporters of being "cheerleaders" was traveling with teams they covered without paying their share. The stereotype was firmly entrenched. Local sports reporter boards local team's bus or plane at the team's expense; sports reporter is treated to meals at the team's expense; once at the contest site, sports reporter gains free admission; sports reporter's team loses, but, in fairness to his friends (and benefactors), he couches his story with phrases such as "gallant effort," "herculean response," and "excellent game plan foiled." The sports reporter files his story, enjoys a postgame meal with "his" team, and rides home with his friends.

The question is logical: How can a reporter objectively and accurately report on a team when the reporter is practically part of it? Of course, some sports reporters are able to write objective, accurate stories under "freeloading" circumstances. But this practice raised eyebrows in the 1970s and 1980s.

The ethics of sports reporting was not of great concern until the 1970s. An awareness of newspaper ethics, in general, was revitalized in that decade as journalistic excesses during the Watergate investigation came under public scrutiny. The Associated Press Managing Editors Association, the American Society of Newspaper Editors, the Society of Professional Journalists, the National Conference of Editorial Writers, and the Associated Press Sports Editors were among groups that revised or implemented codes of ethics.

The realm of ethics is broad. It ranges from policies on accepting free gifts from sources to accepting complimentary tickets to games. It is, of course, difficult to articulate precise dos and don'ts concerning sports reporting ethics.

In 1975, the AP Sports Editors adopted its first code of ethics. That code began with this preamble:

> All favors stem from the simple fact that those with a money stake in attendance crave (and need) publicity. As a result, sports editors are placed in awkward situations—judging news on merit and also simultaneously being placed under pressure for space and placement above merit. The great majority of self-respecting sports editors have had their reputations sullied by the transgressions of those few who have demanded special favors, gifts, treatment, etc. The guidelines that follow are designed to place rational limits on favors of special treatment.

The code went on to place "rational limits" on APSE members under these numbered headings:

1. Travel, other expenses
2. Participation in outside activities that would create a conflict of interest or give the impression of one
3. Writers' groups (whose members should adhere to the standards of the Associated Press Managing Editors or the APSE)
4. Gifts and gratuities
5. Commercial ties
6. Communications equipment (provided by colleges and professional teams for which newspapers should be billed on a pro-rata basis)
7. Credentials, tickets
8. Outside employment
9. Use of merchandise or products
10. Miscellaneous
11. Summary

In 1989, in response to a survey in which members said that they wanted the organization's leadership to deal once again with the issue of ethics, the APSE decided to systematically re-examine the 1975 code. Steve Doyle, deputy managing editor/sports of *The Orlando* (Fla.) *Sentinel*, played a lead role in the process.

In 1990, at the APSE convention in Boston, the code was discussed extensively. "There was considerable debate," said Jeff Wohler, sports editor of *The Oregonian* in Portland. "Any time you discuss ethics, it's easy to get mired in a quagmire. Members asked the executive board to further refine the code."

Don Rawlings of *The Sporting News* and Doyle took on the task; they presented a revised version of the code at the annual meeting of the APSE in San Antonio in 1991. The new code was approved by the membership, but Wohler, who then was president of the organization, said that he thought the code should have included sanctions. "Still, it was an exercise to bring [the APSE] into the 1990s," he said.

The APSE adopted the following code:

1. The newspaper pays its staffer's way for travel, accommodations, food and drink.
   (a) If a staffer travels on a chartered team plane, the newspaper should insist on being billed. If the team cannot issue a bill, the amount can be calculated by estimating the cost of a similar flight on a commercial airline.
   (b) When services are provided to a newspaper by a pro or college team, those teams should be reimbursed by the newspaper. This includes providing telephone, typewriter or fax service.
2. Editors and reporters should avoid taking part in outside activities or

employment that might create conflict of interest or even the appearance of a conflict.

(a) They should not serve as an official scorer at baseball games.

(b) They should not write for team or league media guides or other team or league publications. This has the potential of compromising a reporter's disinterested observations.

(c) Staffers who appear on radio or television should understand that their first loyalty is to the paper.

3. Writers and writers' groups should adhere to APME and APSE standards: No deals, discounts or gifts except those of insignificant value or those available to the public.

(a) If a gift is impossible or impractical to return, donate a gift to a charity.

(b) Do not accept free memberships or reduced fees for membership. Do not accept gratis use of facilities, such as golf courses or tennis courts, unless it is used as part of doing a story for the newspaper.

(c) Sports editors should be aware of standards of conduct of groups and professional associations to which their writers belong and the ethical standards to which those groups adhere, including areas such as corporate sponsorship from news sources it covers.

4. A newspaper should not accept free tickets, although press credentials needed for coverage and coordination are acceptable.

5. A newspaper should carefully consider the implications of voting for all awards and all-star teams and decide if such voting creates a conflict of interest.

6. A newspaper's own ethical guidelines should be followed, and editors and reporters should be aware of standards acceptable for use of unnamed sources and verification of information obtained other than from primary news sources.

(a) Sharing and pooling of notes and quotes should be discouraged. If a reporter uses quotes gained secondhand, that should be made known to the readers. A quote could be attributed to a newspaper or to another reporter.

7. Assignments should be made on merit, without regard for race or gender.

Guidelines can't cover everything. Use common sense and good judgment in applying these guidelines in adopting local codes.

Exercises

1. Examine the sports sections of at least six daily newspapers for a one-week period. Do minor sports and women's sports receive an appropriate share of coverage?

2. Clip examples of cheerleading in sports stories. Do some sportswriters of the newspapers that you read regularly engage in more cheerleading than most of their colleagues?

3. Invite a panel of local sportswriters—men and women—to class. Ask them to discuss, among other things, what led them to become

sportswriters. Have the women faced obstacles that have not confronted the men?

4. Invite the sports information director from your school to class to discuss career opportunities in that field.

5. Discuss the code of ethics of the Associated Press Sports Editors.

Sportswriters often are on hand to capture the joy and drama of postgame victory celebrations.

(Photo by Henri Cohen)

CHAPTER TWO

Philosophies of Sports Reporting

Of the 1,611 daily newspapers published in America in 1990, only about 125 circulated more than 100,000. Hundreds of sportswriters work at the most widely circulated dailies in this country, but the vast majority work at non-metro newspapers.

Indeed, 1,343 daily newspapers (nearly 85 percent) have circulations of less than 50,000. The most typical American daily circulates between 10,000 and 25,000; more than 28 percent (459) fall in that circulation range. Most dailies are published in communities of 30,000 or less and often serve several surrounding counties. In addition, more than 7,500 weekly newspapers are published once a week in towns with populations generally less than 5,000.

Newspapers in all the above groups publish sports news, but the breadth and depth of coverage differ significantly among them.

Metropolitan Daily Sports Philosophy

Metropolitan daily sports staffs whose newspapers circulate throughout a state face a difficult challenge: They must fit national, regional, state, and local coverage into a limited number of inches each day. Many subscribers depend on metro dailies for all their print sports news. A metropolitan daily such as *The Arizona Republic* in Phoenix (circulation 330,000 on weekdays), for example, carries sports news for varied appetites.

The *Republic* provides:

- Coverage of events of national appeal and significance: professional basketball, with extensive coverage of the Phoenix Suns; professional football with extensive coverage of the Phoenix Cardinals; professional hockey; professional soccer; professional golf; and major league baseball, with extensive coverage of Cactus League spring training in Arizona.

■ Coverage of Arizona State University (located in Tempe, a Phoenix suburb) athletics, with emphasis on the revenue-producing sports: football, basketball, and baseball. Coverage also is provided for the nonrevenue men's sports: cross country, golf, wrestling, gymnastics, swimming, tennis, and track, as well as women's sports.

■ Coverage of athletics at the state's other four-year universities: the University of Arizona at Tucson and Northern Arizona University at Flagstaff. The emphasis, again, is on the revenue-producing sports, with some attention to the others, including women's sports.

■ Coverage of high school athletics. Primary emphasis is placed on the Phoenix metropolitan high schools, but at least line scores and box scores are provided for much of Arizona's prep competition. Coverage is given to both boys and girls, with emphasis on the major sports for boys.

■ Coverage of community college athletics.

■ Coverage of outdoor participant sports such as fishing, boating, and hunting.

■ Coverage (generally in agate type in list or result form) of golf, swimming, tennis, auto racing, bowling, archery, horse racing, dog racing, etc.).

The *Republic*, in addition to straight news and feature coverage, carries opinion and analysis columns by staff writers and editors. The columns generally focus on state athletics. Other metropolitan dailies, depending on the geographical sports tastes of readers, will likely follow similar patterns of coverage.

Nonmetropolitan Daily Sports Philosophy

Prep sports coverage is given considerable attention at most nonmetro newspapers. The *Colorado Springs Gazette Telegraph* (circulation 102,000) considers high school sports to be the heart of its sports section, according to staffer Terry Henion.

As is the case with many nonmetro dailies, the *Gazette Telegraph* devotes much of its space and staff to prep sports that draw the most fans, and presumably the most reader interest: football, basketball, and track. It also strives to give coverage to the non-revenue-producing sports: tennis, gymnastics, volleyball, wrestling, swimming, baseball, golf, and cross country.

"We generally try to make sure a summary of every local or area event gets on the agate page," said Henion. "And we attempt to cover at least three or four 'minor' events each week, concentrating on using a feature angle or human interest approach rather than a straight game story."

At the *Gazette Telegraph*, two or three pages of prep articles run daily; the stories and photos generally are packaged. Henion explained the rationale: "Packaging benefits our readers. They know immediately where to turn each and every day for high school stories. It also gives us the opportunity to produce some imaginative and bright layout schemes since the advertising department normally leaves the prep pages relatively wide open." The philosophy at the *Gazette Telegraph* is that it cannot give too much coverage to sports for more than fifty local and area high schools.

The *Hastings* (Neb.) *Tribune*, a paper that comes close to the "average" circulation daily, is typical of many of this country's newspapers. The *Tribune*, circulation 15,000, is published in a community of 23,500. It provides coverage for sixteen counties in south central Nebraska and north central Kansas. Three Hastings high schools (two public and one parochial), 60 area high schools, a private four-year liberal arts college, and a two-year technical community college compete for sports page space.

The *Tribune* provides wire service coverage of national sports—major league baseball, professional football, and professional basketball. It also provides wire service coverage of NCAA athletics, with emphasis on the Big Eight Conference (of which the University of Nebraska, University of Kansas, and Kansas State University are among the members). Professional sports such as hockey and soccer don't receive much attention; readers in the circulation area have little interest in them.

Sports editors and reporters at newspapers in this circulation category face a unique challenge: They must provide an overview of the most important national sports events, but the clear emphasis on coverage must be local. With limited space, the *Tribune* sports staff has to find a way to provide national coverage plus game accounts of major sports for the three local high schools, along with abbreviated (three or four paragraphs, with line scores) accounts of major sports for the remaining 60 area high schools. High school ratings, player profiles, and pregame stories are published each week. The liberal arts school, Hastings College, often receives votes for the top 20 in the National Association of Intercollegiate Athletics ratings for football and basketball. Thus, considerable space also must be devoted to local college coverage.

Community Weekly Sports Philosophy

Many residents of small towns subscribe to a statewide circulation daily and a regional daily. For sports fans in some smaller communities, such as Superior, Nebraska, however, this might not be sufficient. They subscribe to the metropolitan *Omaha World-Herald* for national sports coverage and for emphasis on University of Nebraska athletics; they subscribe to the *Hastings Tribune* for regional high school and college sports coverage. But neither of these papers—unless Superior High School happens to have one of the state's top prep teams—devotes more than a few paragraphs to Superior's athletic teams. Thus, people read the sports section of the weekly *Superior Express* (circulation 3,500) for accounts of Superior High School (boys and girls) athletic events. It might not be important to readers of the *World-Herald* or *Tribune* that John Lacey scored three points in last Friday's game against Fairbury; but it is of interest to Superior area readers who know John and his parents.

The *Express* provides coverage of all Superior games, as well as game and photo coverage for some neighboring smaller communities such as Nelson, Guide Rock, and Burr Oak, Kansas. The *Express* runs player of the week profiles of high school athletics, just as it carries line scores of grade school basketball games. It carries accounts of pee wee baseball games, junior high school volleyball matches, and eighth-grade girls track meets. One might even read that Henry Smith's eleven-year-old grandson, who lives in California, recently ran a 13.2 second, 100-meter dash in a grade school track meet there.

Though there is some overlap in sports coverage among newspapers of these three groups (particularly between the metro and nonmetro dailies), the papers should be viewed as complementing each other. Obviously, reporters for each should strive to write the most readable, comprehensive, literate stories they can. But they also must be cognizant of their readers' needs. The *World-Herald* cannot use valuable space to tell of Henry Smith's grandson, but the *Express* would not be fulfilling its mission if it failed to do so.

Campus Newspaper Sports Philosophy

Most college and university newspapers limit their coverage to campus teams. This certainly is the case at smaller colleges and universities that publish weekly papers. Some campus dailies at larger institutions, however, also cover local high school and area professional teams.

Still, no matter how large or small the college and its newspaper, the focus of sports coverage should be on campus athletics. More often than not, campus newspapers are not able to provide morning-after coverage. Thus, the best campus newspapers go beyond straightforward summary accounts of games on their sports pages.

Southern Illinois University's *Daily Egyptian*, a five-day-a-week tabloid that circulates 27,000 provides coverage of men's and women's athletics, coverage of major sports and nonrevenue sports, comprehensive precontest coverage, feature stories on campus athletes, coverage of intramurals, sports columns, features on SIU graduates playing in the pros, and occasionally wire service stories of particularly significant national sports events.

One is likely to see more coverage of professional teams at universities in metropolitan settings. Students find it tempting to get press credentials to professional sports events and to have the opportunity to interview some of the world's finest athletes. These reporters, however, should remember that most students do not read campus newspapers for 30-column-inch stories on professional athletes. Most would just as soon read about the starting safety on the college football team or about the all-conference athlete on the volleyball team.

High School/College Coverage Distinctions

Regardless of the type of newspaper—large daily, small daily, or weekly—reporters find similarities, as well as distinct differences, when covering high school and college sports.

Certainly, covering high school football is not as glamorous as sitting in a college stadium watching two of the country's best teams. Few high school facilities were constructed with the media in mind. If reporters are particularly brave, they can cover a prep football game perched precariously in a wobbly press box that is attached to an even wobblier light pole. Or, if the reporter chooses to walk the sidelines, he must spend most of the game down on one knee. If he fails to do so, there always is the chance a rabid fan, thinking that screaming "down in front" is ineffective, will leap the fence and physically put the reporter in a prone position.

Another problem with prep sports coverage, particularly during football season, is that the reporter often is subjected to the elements just like players, coaches, and fans. *Colorado Springs Gazette Telegraph* sportswriter Henion recalled a late November Friday when the state playoffs were scheduled in Boulder, Colorado. By noon, the temperature had climbed to 65 degrees; it was a beautiful Indian summer day. Two hours before kickoff, however, a Chinook wind, common to Boulder, blew in. The temperature quickly plummeted to 10 degrees. Then the snow came. Henion was stranded in Boulder until the following Wednesday—with only a light windbreaker on his back—when the game finally was played.

At kickoff, more than twenty inches of snow covered the ground around the field—and it still was coming down. The temperature was six degrees; the press box had no heat. The six writers covering the game, according to Henion, "fought over access to a light bulb on which to warm their hands."

Prep writers need to deal with more than physical inconveniences when covering high school sports, however. They need to realize they are dealing with boys—not yet young men—with fragile egos. Most sports reporters rationalize that a college athlete is reasonably able to take care of himself when asked pointed questions by journalists. This, however, is not necessarily the case with high school athletes.

Being cognizant of maturational and emotional differences between college and high school athletes should not translate to all-out "cheerleading" when covering prep events. But sports reporters need to be aware of the differences and should take them into consideration when writing game stories—particularly when using direct quotes. An unthinking, emotional outburst by a frustrated sixteen-year-old high school football player after a tough loss should not be the same "fair game" as a statement made by a reasonably composed and experienced twenty-one-year-old college athlete more accustomed to working with the press.

Many high school coaches insist that sports reporters arrange all interviews with athletes through the coaching staff. This might not be a bad practice for sportswriters to observe, even when it is not coaching staff policy.

Writing Style Differences

Writing approaches in morning (A.M.) and afternoon (P.M.) newspapers are different. Sports reporters for A.M. and P.M. newspapers cover the same games, which generally are played at night. Morning newspaper reporters must construct their game stories under tight deadline pressure and often do not have time to track down numerous players and coaches for direct quotations and interpretations of turning points. Thus, their lead paragraphs traditionally have been summary accounts that emphasize who played, who won, what the score was, and who starred.

Reporters for afternoon dailies have later deadlines and, thus, more time to develop story angles, analyze key plays, and talk with players and coaches. Their leads usually focus on angles not mentioned or emphasized in the A.M. paper or by the electronic media. Stories in P.M. papers should, of course, contain essential statistical information, but they also should tell the readers something they do not already know from reading a morning newspaper, watching television, or listening to the radio.

Writing for A.M. Papers

Streamlined, informative summary leads can be written in seconds—and often have to be when the reporter is on deadline. For example, wire-service and A.M. newspaper reporters who covered an Arizona State–Stanford basketball game could have written this summary lead:

> Lynn Collins scored 18 points to lead Arizona State past Stanford 75-57 Thursday night at the ASU Activity Center in a Pacific 10 Conference basketball game.

That lead contained all the essentials:

Who: Arizona State University's basketball team
What: beat Stanford
When: Thursday night
Where: ASU's Activity Center
Why/How: Lynn Collins scored 18 points to lead the team

Years ago, virtually all A.M. leads for the ASU-Stanford game would have been similar to the example above. But differences between A.M. and P.M. leads are not as pronounced as they once were. Gradually, during the past decade, A.M. approaches have become softer and more analytical, even when written under deadline pressure.

For example, *Arizona Republic* sportswriter Kent Somers led his game story with these paragraphs:

> Bill Frieder is barred from a few casinos for his ability to play blackjack, but that doesn't mean the Arizona State basketball coach has given up gambling.
>
> With only three weeks left in the regular season and a possible NCAA berth at stake, Frieder shuffled his lineup Thursday night and the result was a 75-57 victory over Stanford in front of 7,298 at the ASU Activity Center.
>
> The victory guaranteed the Sun Devils (15-8, 6-7 Pac-10) of a winning record in the regular season.
>
> "We talked about this being an important week and this was a big, big win for us," Frieder said. "This was a must game."

Somers' story continued with details of the lineup changes, more direct quotations from Frieder and some of his players, game highlights, and scoring and rebounding leaders.

Writing for P.M. Papers

Dale Hajek, for his story in the afternoon *Phoenix Gazette*, chose a different angle. Hajek put the game in historical perspective with this lead block:

> Bill Frieder knows how disappointed Arizona State basketball fans have been the last few years.
>
> That's why he took so much pride in his team's 75-57 victory Thursday night over Stanford.
>
> "It's very satisfying," the coach said after ASU clinched its first winning season since the 1983 team finished 19-14. "If you go back one year and nine months ago, there wouldn't be a lot of people who would agree we would be where we are right now."
>
> "I like my kids. I've told you that all year."
>
> With one of its major goals in the bag, ASU (15-8, 6-7 Pac-10) is setting its sights on bigger and better things—like finishing in the upper half of the conference and earning an NCAA tournament berth.

Hajek used a transition paragraph to move into a discussion of remaining games on the Sun Devil schedule before concluding his story with more coach and player direct quotes, narration of turning points in the game, and summaries of statistical leaders.

Normally, game stories for P.M. newspapers should provide readers with feature angles and descriptive writing that are not always possible in morning-after stories. However, the lines of demarcation between A.M. and P.M. writing styles have become blurred.

Writing Effective Leads

The most difficult task when writing a sports story is to structure the most appropriate, effective lead. Story flow often will fall into place naturally if the article begins with a suitable lead.

Leads can focus on a single element (Riverdale downed Hill City in high school football Friday night 21-20), on two elements (Tailback Dan Jones scored three touchdowns as Riverdale downed Hill City in high school football Friday night 21-20), or on multiple elements (Tailback Dan Jones scored three touchdowns and linebacker Mike Walters made fourteen unassisted tackles as Riverdale downed Hill City in high school football Friday night 21-20 to capture the Twin Valley Conference championship).

There is no magic formula for writing good leads. Reporters need to consider the merits of each story before deciding on the type of lead. Always remember, however, to make the lead accurate, readable, grammatical, and understandable. You also want to entice the reader to stay with the story to its conclusion.

Most leads fall into basic categories: summary; narrative; descriptive; contrast; background; staccato; direct address; question; quotation; and literary.

Summary Leads

Summary leads provide readers with the most important basic information in the story. Summary leads often answer the traditional five Ws and H: who, what, where, when, why, and how. Sometimes all of the five Ws and H are answered in the lead paragraph, which should not run more than thirty-five words. And sometimes these basic questions are answered in the first two or three paragraphs.

In this Associated Press lead paragraph, all of the important questions were answered:

> DETROIT—Travis Fryman's RBI single in the 13th inning scored Alan Trammell, giving the Detroit Tigers an 8-7 victory over the Milwaukee Brewers on Wednesday.

Narrative Leads

Narrative leads often are appropriate on feature stories. Unlike straightforward summary leads that provide readers with the most important information in the first paragraph of the story, the narrative lead paints a scene, takes the readers by the hand and ushers them into the heart of the story.

Joe Cowley, in a *Daily Kent Stater* story that captured a first-place award in the William R. Hearst Foundation's sports writing competition, lured readers into a story about playground basketball in New York City:

> The rusting wire fences and crumbling graffiti walls mark its entrance. The faded lines of paint on the dark asphalt draw its inner boundary.
> In its purest form, the game of basketball belongs to the city.
> There is no set number of players, one-on-one or five-on-five.
> The bouncing of the ball and the individual who carries out moves never seen before again sets the precedent of tales and legends that fall from the mouths of children, never to be recorded or seen in the outside world. A fantastic vision in their mind it remains.
> Just 10 feet from the ground to a metal rim.
> In that 10 feet, little boys dream, while older men think back and wish for something better.

> Because in the city many have dreams—dreams that fall hard.
> In the city they just don't play basketball—they live it.
> Four huge, rusted green fences surround it. Rims with no nets hang from its rusting backboards.
> Welcome to Manhattan, N.Y.—welcome to the Green Cages.
> Directly behind Manhattan's King Tower Projects, the Green Cages basketball courts have gained the reputation as one of the most competitive parks in the area.

After painting a scene of the physical surroundings, Cowley used a transition paragraph to move directly into vivid quotations from a variety of playground greats and to provide description of smooth individual moves:

> Just ask Syracuse guard Adrian Autry.

With that single-sentence paragraph, Cowley ushered the readers into the heart of the story.

Descriptive Leads

Descriptive leads, which normally run longer than other types, immediately thrust readers into the action. Bruce Buschel, in a lengthy profile on Boston Red Sox pitcher Roger Clemens, began his story in *The New York Times Magazine* with this paragraph:

> When Roger Clemens toes the mound, you can't take your eyes off him. Standing erect, he exhales deeply as his empty right hand falls politely to his side. Like a chubby-cheeked choirboy lifting an open hymnal, he raises the black Wilson mitt on his left hand to a resting place in front of his solemn game face. After a gentle rock backward, he reaches into his glove, as if to remove a bookmark, grasps the ball and, with a grimace and a grunt, commences the same windup that he had rehearsed before a full-length mirror after every Little League game.

This lead paragraph by *Sports Illustrated*'s William Oscar Johnson was equally captivating:

> The bar was lifted to its new height, and 5,000 spectators began to stamp their feet in the Anoeta Sports Palace in San Sebastian, Spain. Sergei Bubka, the husky Ukrainian, raised his pole and began to trot down the runway, slowly at first, then faster. The 5,000 began to yell. He reached the pit, planted the pole, lifted himself and seemed coiled

near the end of the perilously bent shaft. As the pole straightened, he rose upward as if he were riding the tidal wave of sound, and then flew across the bar and fell to the cushions below.

The single-sentence second paragraph provided the transition to the thrust of the story:

A pole vaulter had cleared 20 feet for the first time.

Contrast or Comparison Leads

Contrast or comparison leads are effective in stories that establish a relationship between "close-to-home and far-from-home" news angles or for "that-is-how-it-was" and "this-is-how-it-is" stories.

Here are the first three paragraphs of a story by Sam Smith in the *Chicago Tribune*:

Almost three years ago, the Atlanta Hawks were looking for a center whom they hoped would make the big shots and big plays for them.

So they signed Moses Malone after deciding that Bill Cartwright, whom the Knicks were offering, was no more than a second-string center who had about two years left in him.

But Friday, with Malone watching from the bench, where he was for most of the night while playing seven minutes, Cartwright hit the big shot for the Bulls, a 10-foot baseline jumper with three seconds left that enabled them to defeat the Hawks 99-96.

Here is the lead block of paragraphs from a story by Lee Shappell in *The Arizona Republic*:

CHICAGO—Matt Doherty was selected in the sixth round of the 1984 NBA draft by Cleveland, didn't make it, and currently is assistant basketball coach at Davidson (N.C.) College.

Jimmy Black was drafted in the third round in 1982 by New Jersey, didn't make it, and currently is acting head coach at South Carolina. He might soon be joining new Notre Dame Coach John MacLeod's staff as an assistant.

Doherty and Black were starters on North Carolina's 1982 NCAA championship team who can't let go of their ties to the game.

The other three starters—James Worthy, Sam Perkins and Michael Jordan—have stayed involved with basketball, too.

In the opening game of the NBA finals today, Worthy and Perkins, of the Los Angeles Lakers, try to become only the fifth pair of players ever to play on a collegiate team and an NBA championship team.

Background Leads

The primary thrust of news stories—particularly morning newspaper game stories—almost always belongs in the lead paragraph. Occasionally, however, when the background to a significant news story is nearly as noteworthy as the new development itself, a background lead is justified.

To put a Northwestern University football victory in proper perspective, Gary Pomerantz, of *The Washington Post*, began his story with this lead paragraph:

> EVANSTON, Ill.—They had lost an NCAA-record 34 straight games. They were 1,106 days removed from their last victory. Each loss, the players said, put another monkey on their back. Northwestern's football team was living on the Planet of the Apes.

Then, in the second paragraph, Pomerantz, by effectively utilizing a simile, dropped the news:

> But Saturday, all of that ended for these Wildcats, often called the "Mildcats." With freshman quarterback Sandy Schwab passing like Northwestern legend Otto Graham, and with senior tailback Ricky Edwards scoring touchdowns like Graham, Northwestern defeated Northern Illinois, 31-6, before 22,078 at home.
>
> And so ended the Streak of the Meek. Northwestern's last victory came against Wyoming on Sept. 15, 1979. When the Wildcats lost, 61-14 to Michigan State last year, they broke the NCAA record of 28 straight losses held by Kansas State and Virginia.

Omaha (Neb.) *World-Herald* sportswriter Lee Barfknecht emphasized the uniqueness of a trio of field goals this way:

> SOUTH BEND, Ind.—Before Saturday night, Notre Dame's Mike Johnston had kicked two field goals in his life.
>
> Both came when he was in high school. The longest was 33 yards.
>
> But Johnston's three three-pointers—from 35, 37 and 41 yards away—helped a brutish Notre Dame defense survive two lightning-bolt touchdowns by Michigan as the Irish beat the Wolverines 23-17.

Staccato Leads

Staccato leads—with information coming in short, rapid-fire bursts—can be particularly effective on sports stories. It would be legitimate, for example, to lead a story this way:

State University opened fall football camp today with 33 lettermen reporting.

But it would be more effective to begin this way:

Bodies ache. Adrenalin flows. Mouths thirst. Breathing is hard. Sweat is dripping. Players count the days. Fourteen to go.
State University opened fall football camp today with 33 lettermen reporting.

Here is a staccato lead by Leonard Laye of Knight-Ridder Newspapers that was published in the *Chicago Tribune*:

CHARLOTTE, N.C.—Eighty two games. Playoffs. Personalities. The rising heat of competition. The tinsel-tinged distractions.
Lord knows, Mike Dunleavy bought more than enough for any new coach when he took the controls of the Los Angeles Lakers.

Direct Address Leads

Editors often caution reporters against using direct address in news or even feature stories. Sometimes, however, direct address—putting the word "you" in the lead—can pull a reader into a story.

Bill Christine of the *Los Angeles Times*, who undoubtedly reasoned that only those sports fans who had been marooned on a Pacific island during the previous 24 hours would not already have heard that Oakland's Rickey Henderson had set a major league record for stolen bases, appropriately and tantalizingly started his story:

MILWAUKEE—Their names are Ted Simmons, Doc Medich, Robin Yount, and Wayne Gross. Remember them. By recalling the four in a few years, you'll be able to win some beers in almost any bar in the country.
When Rickey Henderson became the most prolific thief in baseball history by stealing second base in the third inning Friday night, (a) Ted Simmons was the catcher, (b) Doc Medich was the pitcher, (c) Robin Yount was the shortstop who thought he had tagged him out, and (d) Wayne Gross was at the plate.

Question Leads

Editors usually caution reporters against using question leads. It is too easy to use them as a crutch—posing a question rather than answering it in the lead paragraph. Still, particularly on sidebar stories, question leads can be the most effective way to move into a story.

After Nebraska set four NCAA records—including 883 yards of total offense—in crushing outmanned New Mexico State 68-0, this question lead on a sidebar story seemed perfectly logical:

> LINCOLN—Is there really anything to be gained when a team whip-saws its opponent 68-0?

Omaha World-Herald sportswriter Dave Sittler continued:

> "Heck yes, there better be," Nebraska defensive captain Steve Damkroger said Saturday after his Blackshirt unit helped hand a 68-0 whitewashing on New Mexico State.
> "Everytime you play somebody different you better learn something," Damkroger said. "And today we learned that we better figure out how to stop the draw, or teams will be running that against us the rest of the year."

Quotation Leads

As was the case with question leads, many editors do not approve of the use of quotation leads. Some quotation leads, however, are appropriate. They should be used, however, only when circumstances are such that they will capsulize the thrust of the story.

When underdog Arizona rallied for 10 points in the fourth quarter at Notre Dame for possibly the biggest victory in the history of the school, the UPI lead read:

> "It was just a matter of believing in ourselves," said Arizona Coach Larry Smith after his Wildcats shocked ninth-ranked Notre Dame, 16-13, on the final play of the game.
> Freshman Max Zendejas kicked a 48-yard field goal against the wind as the gun sounded to cap a 10-point fourth-quarter rally and gave Arizona, 2-2-1, its victory and hand the Fighting Irish their first setback in five games.

In a story about the amazing physical attributes of Raghib Ismail, Dave Anderson of *The New York Times* began with these three paragraphs:

> Notre Dame coach Lou Holtz likes to joke, "I didn't realize how fast Rocket was until I saw him playing tennis by himself."
> But for all the speed and success of Raghib Ismail as the Irish's tailback, slotback, wide receiver, kickoff returner and punt returner, his

coach is surprised not so much by what Rocket does in a game as by what he does in practice.

"He's done a standing flip with full equipment," Holtz said.

Literary Leads

Occasionally, circumstances in sports will parallel a literary title or reference. Such was the case when Mal Florence wrote this lead in the *Los Angeles Times*:

> The USC running back situation now reads like the plot from Agatha Christie's mystery novel, "Ten Little Indians," also titled "And Then There Were None."
>
> One by one, Trojan tailbacks and fullbacks have become inactive because of injuries this season, the latest being tailback Todd Spencer and fullback John Kamana. Both sprained their left knees in USC's 41-21 win over Stanford Saturday.

Obviously, any allusions to literature should be understandable and logical. Sports reporters should not puzzle readers with references.

Exercises

1. Examine the sports sections of at least six daily newspapers for a one-week period. Discuss what appears to be the coverage philosophy of each. Which newspapers, for example, place the most emphasis on high school sports? Which are more likely to publish enterprise stories that deal with major issues in sports?

2. Contrast the sports coverage philosophy of a metropolitan daily with a mid-size or small-circulation daily in your area.

3. Examine the sports section of your campus daily. Evaluate its quality in terms of depth and breadth of coverge and writing style.

4. Clip stories about the same game from a morning newspaper and from an afternoon newspaper. Discuss similarities and differences.

5. Clip from area newspapers examples of the types of leads discussed in this chapter. Would some stories have been more effective with a different lead? If so, rewrite them.

6. Discuss the best leads that you clipped. What qualities do they share?

7. Clip leads from *Sports Illustrated*. Compare them to the best leads from daily newspapers. What are the differences and the similarities?

Lee Barfknecht of the *Omaha* (Neb.) *World-Herald* is a master at providing extensive, incisive pregame coverage of the Nebraska Cornhuskers.

(Photo by Rich Janda)

CHAPTER THREE

Precontest Coverage

Effective, complete, well-reasoned pregame stories are predicated on one principle: preparation. Sports reporters must do their homework. When doing a pregame story for a college contest, the first step often is scanning materials sent by the sports information departments of both schools. Additional information can be found by examining newspaper clippings, record books, or other available materials. Statistics for high school teams often will be available only from the coach or by exploring newspaper clips. Unique angles can be uncovered by culling every available statistic.

Preparation for an effective pregame story does not end with an examination of statistics and past records. Coaches and players of competing teams can be interviewed along with coaches and players of common opponents. If the research and interviewing are carried out diligently, the precontest football story, after an appropriate lead, logically could contain the following:

- Time, place, and day of game.
- Possible impact of the contest on conference, state, or national standings.
- General information such as scores in recent games, particularly common opponents, and the series record.
- Names and statistics of top rushers for both teams.
- Names and statistics of top passers for both teams.
- Names and statistics of top receivers for both teams.
- Names and statistics of top defensive players for both teams.
- Key injuries for both teams.
- Quotations from coaches, players, etc.

- Complete season records to date.
- Starters by position, weight, and year in school.
- Top reserves who might see action.
- Details of radio or television coverage.
- Weather outlook.
- Crowd and tickets.
- Betting lines (if college contest).

Many of these factors could be examined when writing precontest stories for sports other than football. But each sport usually brings with it an additional set of questions to be answered.

Examining Pregame Releases

The sports information office at the University of Nebraska provided extensive background for writers preparing to cover an important Nebraska-Colorado football game. Like most pregame mailings from NCAA schools, the release contained more information about the upcoming contest than any writer would use. Still, diligent sportswriters read releases carefully before crafting their stories.

Here are some excerpts from the NU release that are representative of the information often contained in pregame mailings:

CORNHUSKER FOOTBALL CAPSULES
GAME 9   NEBRASKA (4-0-0/8-0-0) vs. COLORADO BUFFALOES
(4-0-0/7-1-1)

Date: Nov. 3   Memorial Stadium (73,650), Lincoln, Neb.
Kickoff: 3:07 p.m. (CST)   Radio: Nebraska Football Network
TV: ESPN

THIS WEEK: It's showdown time again in the Big Eight, and for the second straight year, it's Nebraska vs. Colorado, not the Huskers vs. Oklahoma. The Cornhuskers and the defending champion Golden Buffaloes go into the game tied for first place in the conference race at 4-0-0. The winner will be one win away from clinching at least a tie for the title, and will be virtually assured of the Orange Bowl berth which goes with the title. If Colorado wins Saturday and goes on to an undisputed title, CU would be the first team other than Nebraska and Oklahoma to win two-straight crowns since Missouri won Big Six titles in 1941 and 1942. The game will be televised nationally on cable by ESPN, with Sean McDonough and former Kansas and Pittsburgh Coach Mike Gottfried calling the game. With last week's 45-13 win at Iowa State, Nebraska is one victory away from its 22nd-consecutive nine-win season, a continuing NCAA record. Saturday's game is long-since a sellout, the 175th in a row at Nebraska's Memorial Stadium, another continuing NCAA mark. It will be the 66th-straight game in the Associated Press top 10 and the 115th in a row in the AP top 20 for the Huskers, who were fourth last week. Colorado was 10th last week and could move up after its 32-23 win over Oklahoma. NU has lost its last three games vs. top-10 teams since a 7-3 win at ninth-ranked OU in 1988. It's also the final 1990 home game for Nebraska, which has won 19-straight in Memorial Stadium since a 17-7 loss to Oklahoma in 1987. Schedules and scores for the Huskers and Buffs:

Nebraska	*Colorado*
13 Baylor 0	31 Tennessee 31 (at Anaheim)
60 Northern Illinois 14	21 Stanford 17
56 Minnesota 0	22 at Illinois 23
31 Oregon State 7	29 at Texas 22
45 at Kansas State 8	20 Washington 14
69 Missouri 21	33 at Missouri 31
31 Oklahoma State 3	28 Iowa State 12
45 at Iowa State 13	41 at Kansas 10
11/3—COLORADO	32 Oklahoma 23
11/10—at Kansas	11/3—AT NEBRASKA
11/23—Oklahoma	11/10—Oklahoma State
	11/17—Kansas State

THE SERIES: It's the 49th meeting in a series which began with a 23-10 Nebraska win at Boulder, Nov. 17, 1898. The Huskers lead, 34-13-1, although Colorado won 27-21 last year at Boulder to virtually clinch the Big Eight title. Nebraska has a 29-12-1 series edge in conference games since CU joined the then-Big Six Conference in 1948. The Huskers are 18-5 vs. the Buffs in Lincoln, including 15-5 at Memorial Stadium, where NU won the most-recent game, 7-0, in 1988. Nebraska has won 10-straight in the series since a 21-16 loss in 1967. CU was 10-8-1 in the first 19 games (1898-1961), Nebraska is 25-3 since.

THE COACHES: The Huskers' TOM OSBORNE (Hastings, 1959) is 176-38-2 in his 18th year as a head coach, all at Nebraska, and ranks as the winningest active coach in the NCAA's Division I-A with an .819 winning percentage. His 176 wins and 216 games coached are Nebraska and Big Eight records, while the 176 wins tie him with Ralph Jordan of Auburn (1951-75) and Frank Kush of Arizona State (1958-79) for ninth among all-time NCAA Division I coaches in victories at one school. The Buffaloes' BILL McCARTNEY (Missouri, 1969) is 53-46-2 in his ninth year as a head coach, all at Colorado. Osborne is 15-2 vs. Colorado (8-0 in Lincoln), 6-2 vs. McCartney (3-0 in Lincoln).

INJURIES: Freshman IB DEREK BROWN separated his right shoulder in the Iowa State game and will not play vs. Colorado. His status for the rest of the season will be re-evaluated later this week. FB OMAR SOTO, who missed the trip to Iowa State with a knee strain, is probable. TE WILLIAM WASHINGTON, who has missed the last three games with a sprained ankle, will play. Washington made the trip to Ames and was available, if necessary, but did not see action. TE CHRIS GARRETT, who broke his ankle vs. Oregon State, Sept. 29, is out for the rest of the regular season.

OFFENSIVE PLAYER-OF-THE-WEEK: For the second-straight game and the fourth time in eight games this year, junior IB LEODIS FLOWERS, who rushed for a career-high 208 yards, helped by a career-long 70-yard TD run, as he posted his sixth-straight 100-yard rushing game. That equals the third-longest 100-yard string in Nebraska history (Mike Rozier's in 1982), behind Rozier's 11-straight in 1983 and Bobby Reynolds' eight-straight in 1950. Flowers also scored three TD's for the first time in his career, and has scored at least one TD in six-straight games. He averaged 8.3 yards on his 25 carries to up his season per-carry average to 7.0. (He went into the ISU game averaging 6.7 per carry, third-best among the NCAA's top 21 rushers). Flowers increased his career rushing total to 1,579 yards as he passed four players, including San Francisco 49ers FB Tom Rathman, to climb to 18th on the NU career rushing chart. The three TD's also increased his career scoring total to 102 points as he moved from a tie for 36th up to a tie for 28th. He has 884 rushing yards in seven appearances this season and thus needs 116 in the last three games to record the 15th 1,000-yard season in Nebraska history (the 11th in the last 12 years). Flowers on his 70-yard TD: "I wasn't going to be caught. I was just thinking, 'Where is the end zone?' The field seems so long on those plays."

DEFENSIVE PLAYER-OF-THE-WEEK: For the second time this season, it's senior DT JOE SIMS, who had a career-high nine tackles, including five solo stops, two tackles for 8 yards in losses, a 4-yard sack, a pass breakup and three QB hurries. Said NU defensive coordinator and line coach CHARLIE McBRIDE, "I thought Joe Sims probably played the best game he's played since he's been here. He kind of shut down the whole inside. He and Pat Engelbert did a great job." Iowa State Coach JIM WALDEN on the Sims-led NU defensive line, "They're in your face and it's hard to throw over that. Did you see the size of that front? No offense to anyone, but you have to be realistic. My secondary looks good behind that front." Said SIMS, "We've heard about how the defense helps the offense, but today was the reverse. They helped us. We had to limit our pass rush because (ISU QB Chris) Pedersen is dangerous running and had been killing teams— even Oklahoma. So we couldn't go in there all-out until later in the game when we got the lead. We finally got in the backfield and started creating some havoc."

LAST GAME FOR SENIORS: Saturday's game will be the final home game for 33 Cornhusker seniors, all of whom are listed on the back page of this release.

SIMS ON COLORADO: "This is not a payback. We owe them one, but it's just a great game and one we're looking forward to. I think we can line up with them. We need a win over them to get the respect we don't get now. Saturday, if we pull out a win, then we'll get the respect we deserve."

KENNY WALKER UPDATE: The senior DT and Outland Trophy candidate from Crane, Texas, had seven tackles vs. Iowa State, including four unassisted stops, three of which were behind the line for 16 yards lost, including a 5-yard sack. He also had two QB hurries to increase his team-leading total to 16. Walker helped the Blackshirts record season highs in both tackles for loss (14 for 70 yards) and sacks (eight for 47). The sack was Walker's ninth of the season as he took over sole possession of sixth on the NU chart and pulled within six of the record 15 set by JIM SKOW in 1985. His three tackles for loss upped that season total to 17 (for 96 yards) as he moved into a tie for sixth on that chart with TONY FELICI (1981) and All-American BRODERICK THOMAS (1988). He needs eight more behind-the-line tackles to tie Skow's 1985 record of 25.

MICKEY JOSEPH UPDATE: The junior QB from Marrero, La., rushed for a career-high 123 yards on eight carries and had the longest run of his career, a 70-yard sprint to the ISU 18. It was the eighth-best rushing performance ever for a Husker QB, and the 70-yard run was the second-longest ever for a Nebraska signal-caller. He also completed four of four passes for 67 yards and a pair of TD's to freshman TE Johnny Mitchell. Said Joseph of his 70-yard run, "Leodis Flower gets a 70-yard run and outruns their safety to the end zone. I got loose on an option (also for 70 yards), but I got caught from behind. I had to take a lot of flak from the fellas on that one. But everybody is going to be concentrating on Colorado, and I don't think anybody will remember I got caught from behind." TOM OSBORNE said of Joseph, "Mickey scrambled well and ran the option well, but we'll probably get criticized for not throwing more. The touchdown at the end of the first half was not the deciding play, but it was a big play. In the second half, we executed the option better. I thought Mickey Joseph had a really fine day."

JOSEPH ON COLORADO: "I guess we've been eager to get to this point. We didn't step over anybody. We didn't look ahead. We took each step, and now we can get ready for the really big one. We played them last year for the Big Eight championship, and they came up with it. You have that down deep inside, and you're waiting on the game. That doesn't mean the rest of our games weren't big games. But this is the big one. They're one of the powerhouses in the Big Eight. Two big powerhouses are about to bump heads." Mickey's younger brother, VANCE JOSEPH, is a freshman QB at Colorado, and is listed third on the Buff's depth chart behind juniors Darian Hagan and Charles Johnson.

IOWA STATE COACH JIM WALDEN ON NU: "Don't give me that

'they ain't played anybody' crap. They're good. By the time they play somebody who is supposed to be 'somebody,' they'll be good. There's probably somebody coming real quick—next week will be somebody.''

NU COACH TOM OSBORNE ON IOWA STATE: "Once we got the defense settled down—after the long touchdown and some broken draw plays—we went to the dime 90 percent of the time, and we played well. The wind helped us a bit. This was a running-game day—a Big Eight day that you see at least three times in seven games in the Big Eight.''

OSBORNE ON COLORADO: "Colorado is supposed to have the most talent in the league, the toughest schedule—no question a tougher schedule than we've played. We'll have to get after them. It'll be a great ball game.''

CHARLIE McBRIDE ON THE BUFFS: "This is the worst situation we could be in as far as playing dime all week (to get ready for ISU) and not even playing the run defense that we're going to have to play (against Colorado). Now we're going to have to go back to the drawing board. (Eric) Bieniemy is a great inside runner. He hides behind those big guys, and you've got to go search him out. And that kid (Michael) Pritchard, who you'd better keep three or four eyes on because that guy, he gets two big plays a game.'' McBride is a 1962 Colorado graduate and was an All-Big Eight end and punter for the Buffs.

LB PAT TYRANCE ON COLORADO: "We don't really like to dwell upon the past and what happened last year. We're really focused on what we want to accomplish this season as far as goals—the Big Eight championship and really being in the national title hunt. That's our focus, not necessarily beating Colorado because of them beating us last year out in Boulder. Maybe if we defeat Colorado, it will get us a little respect. If not, then we'll have to wait until Oklahoma. If not then, we'll wait until the bowl game.''

HUSKERS IN NCAA STATS: IB LEODIS FLOWERS is ninth in rushing (126.3) and his 7.0 per-carry average is tied for first, among national leaders, with Mississippi's Randy Baldwin; TYRONE HUGHES is third in kickoff returns (31.2), 18th in punt returns (13.30); TYRONE BYRD is 11th in interceptions (0.45). As a team, Nebraska is first in rushing offense (387.5) and scoring defense (8.3); second in scoring offense (43.8), total defense (222.9) and kickoff returns (29.5); fifth in total offense (486.4) and pass defense efficiency (82.5 rating); seventh in punt returns (14.3); eighth in rushing defense (98.6).

NEBRASKA NOTEBOOK: Nebraska's offensive line has given up just two sacks in eight games, while the defense has racked up 38 . . . NU's 101-year record is 643-281-39 (.688); Nebraska ranks fifth in NCAA Division I-A in victories (one ahead of Penn State), ninth in winning percentage; the Huskers' all-time home record in 386-119-20 (.754), including 261-96-13 (.723) in Memorial Stadium . . . the Huskers have won 59-straight Big Eight games against teams other than Oklahoma and Colorado since a 35-31 loss to Missouri at home in 1978 . . . Ne-

braska has scored in a Big Eight-record 205-straight games since a 27-0
loss at Oklahoma in 1973.

Here are some excerpts from the Colorado release, which are equally
informative, streamlined and fast-paced:

QUICKLY . . . The defending Big Eight champion Colorado Buffaloes
(7-1-1, 4-0 Big Eight) travel to Lincoln for a Big Eight showdown with
the Nebraska Cornhuskers (8-0-0, 4-0 league) in a game in which the
winner will have the inside track to the league title and the Orange Bowl
bid that goes along with it . . . The game will be nationally televised on
ESPN, with kickoff at approximately 2:07 p.m. mountain time. Sean
McDonough (play-by-play), Mike Gottfried (color commentary) and
Kevin Guthrie (sidelines) will call the action, which will mark CU's
sixth appearance on national television this fall . . . These two teams
own two of the top three records in college football since the start of
1989 season: CU is 18-2-1, NU is 18-2 (Notre Dame's 17-2 is wedged
in between; CU's 18-1-1 regular season mark is the best since '89) . . . The
Buffaloes have won 12 straight Big Eight Conference games (dating
back to the '88 finale), adding to a new school best (the old Big
Seven/Eight mark was nine; a win Saturday ties the school mark of 13
as a member of any conference) . . . A sellout crowd of 73,650-plus will
attend the contest.
MORE RECORDS FOR ERIC . . . Senior tailback Eric Bieniemy, a
definite candidate for the Heisman Trophy, continues his assault on the
CU record book. He has now tied Charlie Davis (1971) and himself
(1988) for the most games in a season rushing for 100-plus yards
(seven). And he is staring at CU's season rushing mark, which is also
held by Davis (1,386 yards in 1971). Bieniemy has 1,228 yards on the
season, his 153.5 figure leading the nation. Colorado has had two
players lead the nation in rushing, but both before most of the parents
on this year's team were born: Kayo Lam in 1934 and Byron White in
1937. He needs just 159 yards to set a new season standard in CU
annals. How torrid has Bieniemy been? He's rushed for 100-plus yards
in seven of CU's eight games (with a low of 127; his only sub-100
"night" was against Texas, when he had 99). In the last five games,
he's galloped for 853 yards (170.6 per game). Eric's practically wiped
out Davis' name from the CU record book, except in one record that no
one has ever really threatened: Davis' 342 rushing yards against Oklahoma State in 1971.
ROCKET BOOSTER . . . Notre Dame may have the "Rocket," but
Colorado has its "Booster," as Mike Pritchard has numbers that are
comparable to Raghib Ismail's. Through games of last Saturday, Pritchard
had 1,050 all purpose yards, with Ismail in at 1,075. Both players rush,
catch and return kicks.
OFFENSIVE NOTE . . . Colorado is now enjoying some familiar suc-

cess on first down, after a rocky start earlier in the season. For the year, the Buffs are averaging 6.4 yards per first down play, with the best performance against Oklahoma. The Buffs ran 32 first down plays for 325 yards, or 10.2 per play. The Buffs have gained five or more yards on 105 of 222 first down plays.

DEFENSIVE NOTE . . . The Buffaloes have limited the opponent to zero or negative yardage on 223 of 616 plays this season, an amazing percentage of 36.2. If you eliminate the opponents' first drives of each game, the number increases to 38.4 percent (208 of 542). Colorado's opponents have scored first in eight of the nine games this season, but the Buffs have trailed at halftime in only three games (Stanford, 14-0; Washington, 7-3; and Oklahoma, 14-12). Colorado has won all three of those contests.

IN-THE-POLLS . . . Colorado was No. 8 in the United States International poll and No. 10 in the Associated Press polling prior to last Saturday's 32-23 win over Oklahoma (there likely will be little movement this week). The Buffs have been on a roller coaster ride all season, actually falling three times in the polls after victories. Colorado has been ranked in the Associated Press poll for 26 straight weeks (the low rank was No. 20 after losing to Illinois earlier this season). According to the weekly schedule rankings in USA Today, the Buffs have consistently been in the top five when ranking the nation's toughest schedules. The nine teams that Colorado have played so far this fall are 37-27-4 on the season. The Buffs are pursuing their all-time streak of consecutive weeks ranked in the AP, as the mark of 32 was set between 1971 and 1973.

QUOTE-OF-THE-WEEK . . . A couple this week. First, from all-Big Eight defensive tackle candidate Garry Howe, on the importance of the Oklahoma win: "This is a great win for us. But it's just one step toward our goal of being back in the Orange Bowl. Beating Oklahoma was the key to our season, as it dictated what this week really means. Now we just have to focus on Nebraska." And from All-Big Eight candidate (CB & PR) Dave McCloughan: "This has been tough the last couple of years. Playing these teams in a row is tough, really tough."

NEBRASKA WEEK INTERVIEW POLICY . . . Interviews with Colorado players this week will be curtailed by one-half day. Interviews with players will be allowed daily before 2:15 p.m. and after practice. The final time for interviews, in-person or telephone, will be after practice on Wednesday. Five players who have had more than their fair share of interviews will be available one day only: ERIC BIENIEMY (Monday); DARIAN HAGAN and ALFRED WILLIAMS (Tuesday at the Big Five Huddle or by phone); MIKE PRITCHARD (Tuesday) and KANAVIS McGHEE (Wednesday). Other players, including JOE GARTEN and MARK VANDER POEL, will be available on request.

Producing Fresh, Complete Previews

Lee Barfknecht, a sportswriter for the *Omaha* (Neb.) *World-Herald*, handles the University of Nebraska beat. His responsibilities include coverage of all twenty-one varsity sports at that Big Eight institution. Barfknecht, winner of several Associated Press state sports writing awards and recipient of Nebraska sportswriter of the year honors, naturally reviews releases from sports information offices before each game. But he also strives to ferret fresh angles and new information for his pregame stories through on-the-scene coverage.

Barfknecht and other *World-Herald* staffers produced an impressive array of pregame stories before the Nebraska-Colorado football game. In fact, to broaden the newspaper's preview coverage, Barfknecht traveled to Boulder, Colorado, the Saturday before to cover the Colorado-Oklahoma game; then, he stayed through the Wednesday before the Colorado-NU game.

Anatomy of Pregame Coverage

Saturday, Oct. 27. Barfknecht covered the OU-CU game, writing a 25-inch game story and a 10-inch game notes package. For the game story, he took the angle of Colorado peaking at the right time for a game that could win the Buffaloes the Big Eight title and get them in position to win a national championship.

Sunday, Oct. 28. For Monday's A.M. editions, Barfknecht wrote a "mood piece" column, focusing on CU player attitudes and the writings of the Denver newspapers, which were harshly critical of Nebraskans the year before. Colorado players and coaches were off-limits to the press. Meanwhile, *World-Herald* writers in Lincoln monitored NU Coach Tom Osborne's television show, interviewed him afterward, and wrote stories from that.

For Monday's afternoon editions, Barfknecht wrote an Orange Bowl story and a story from CU coach Bill McCartney's late-Sunday night television show. Barfknecht was careful to get interesting quotes high in the first portion of that story:

> BOULDER, Colo.—On his weekly television show Sunday night, Colorado Coach Bill McCartney noted that Nebraska has one of its best defenses ever, one of its best kicking games ever and an offense that leads the nation in rushing.
>
> That led co-host Dave Logan, a former CU All-American, to ask if McCartney will show up for Saturday's 3 P.M. showdown in Lincoln.

"I'll go," McCartney said, laughing. "But I don't know if I can get 60 guys to go along."

The odds of filling the team plane are better now. Saturday's victory over Oklahoma made sure of that, McCartney said.

"Our confidence has been growing, and yesterday helped some more," he said. "To go off of this game and go to Lincoln, that is just what we need.

"You worry about playing two heavyweights like this back to back. But if you can come out healthy, then it's probably well-advised to do it this way. And we have come out of this thing fairly healthy. I think it is to our advantage now."

McCartney said a strong week of practice is a must if the 7-1-1 Buffaloes want to beat 8-0 Nebraska.

"Nebraska has similarity to Oklahoma," he said. "But they have a lot of their own peculiarities that we have to attend to."

The story went on to report McCartney's assessment of Nebraska's victory over Iowa State and the performance of star NU players. Accompanying the story was a chart that provided statistical comparisons of Nebraska and Colorado, complete with their NCAA rankings.

Monday, Oct. 29. McCartney had his weekly press luncheon. In an interview after his press conference, he talked about the growing rivalry between Nebraska and Colorado and the hate mail he had received from NU fans. Barfknecht used that angle for his Tuesday morning story along with a practice report. In Lincoln, other *World-Herald* reporters covered the weekly Extra Point Club luncheon and practice.

Barfknecht's story showed that pregame pieces don't have to focus on statistics. Illustrating the human dimensions of the NU-CU rivalry, Barfknecht emphasized the growing hostility of the Nebraska fans. Here are his first seven paragraphs:

BOULDER, Colo.—When Colorado Coach Bill McCartney goes through his mail, he finds a lot of letters with return addresses from Nebraska.

And most of the messages inside aren't of the "Hi, how's it going?" variety.

"I don't think they like us. I don't think they like me, either," McCartney said Monday in an interview after his weekly press conference.

"There just aren't a lot of love letters coming in from Nebraska these days."

His comments came in reference to the rivalry being built between his 7-1-1 Buffaloes, ranked seventh and ninth nationally, and 8-0 Nebraska, rated second and third. Those two teams meet in Lincoln

Saturday in essence for the Big Eight title and a trip to the Orange Bowl.

McCartney and Nebraskans have a lot to say about a lot of things.

"I just sense a lot more hostility than a couple of years ago," he said. "I don't even want to get into it." But then McCartney did anyway.

The story went on to note that McCartney created the CU-NU rivalry when he hand-picked the Huskers as CU's rival nine years earlier. The story also quoted CU players, who shared their coach's enthusiasm for the Nebraska game.

For Tuesday's afternoon edition, the *World-Herald* published companion pieces from Boulder and Lincoln on special-teams play, which decided the game the year before. One Colorado special-teams player was from Omaha, thus making for a good local angle.

Tuesday, Oct. 30. In Lincoln, Osborne held his weekly press conference. In Colorado, Barfknecht attended a press gathering where CU players were available. For Wednesday morning editions, Barfknecht wrote a feature on CU tailback Eric Bieniemy and a notes package with a lead on Colorado backup quarterback Vance Joseph, whose brother Mickey was the starting quarterback at Nebraska.

The top to Barfknecht's Bieniemy story was packed with vivid quotations:

> BOULDER, Colo.—If you own a VCR, punch the buttons to make it click on for Saturday's 3 P.M. game between Colorado and Nebraska.
>
> CU tailback Eric Bieniemy says you won't regret it.
>
> "It's going to be one to remember 20 to 30 years down the line," he said. "I think Nebraska will play at a higher level than anything I've ever been part of.
>
> "Last year, they felt they were robbed. So they feel this is pay back time."
>
> But Bieniemy, the nation's leading rusher, has some accounts of his own to settle with the Huskers.

Barfknecht went on to detail injuries that plagued the Colorado running back during the previous two CU-NU games and to highlight Bieniemy's glittering statistics going into the Saturday contest. For Wednesday's afternoon editions, Barfknecht wrote on Colorado reaction to Nebraska's soft schedule, a season-long topic of arguments.

Wednesday, Oct. 31. Barfknecht grabbed a few more player interviews before heading back to Omaha. For Thursday's A.M. editions, the *World-*

Herald merely published routine practice reports to allow the first round of the state high school playoffs to take center stage. For Thursday's P.M. editions, Barfknecht wrote a story on Colorado's passing game, featuring quarterback Darian Hagan.

Thursday, Nov. 1. For Friday's A.M. editions, it was requested that Barfknecht write a prediction column. Sports Editor Mike Kelly also wrote one. The columns were displayed as a point/counterpoint across the top of the front sports page. "From the reaction we got," Barfknecht said, "the columns apparently were the talk of the town from coffee shops to radio shows." Later in the day, Barfknecht drove to Lincoln, covered Nebraska's practice, and wrote a story about Colorado's defense. That story began:

> LINCOLN—Like head-on collisions?
> Then buckle your seat belts for Saturday when Nebraska's offense tries to run the ball at Colorado's defense in a 3 P.M. game between Top 10 teams at Memorial Stadium.
> The Huskers, six-time national rushing champions in the 1980s, are first again at 387.5 yards a game. The Buffaloes are 18th at stopping the run, averaging 111.6 yards. Oklahoma's 174 yards last week was the most CU has allowed in a game this season.

Friday, Nov. 2. Barfknecht and staff writer Doug Thomas wrote companion game advances for the Saturday morning edition. Barfknecht wrote 15 inches from the Colorado camp; Thomas wrote 15 inches from the Nebraska side. The groundwork had been laid. During a one-week period, Barfknecht had mined pregame information extensively.

"After writing sixteen bylined stories and columns in seven days on one game, I was more than ready for that game to be played," Barfknecht said. "That's still not a personal record, though. In the seven days before the 1987 game between No. 1 Nebraska and No. 2 Oklahoma, I wrote twenty-one stories and columns." Most precontest coverage is limited to one or two stories. However, the extensive coverage Barfknecht and other *World-Herald* writers provided their readers during the week before the Nebraska-Colorado football game serves as a model. Precontest coverage is a staple of good sports pages. Reporters need to work hard to gather all relevant information and to craft angles that will lure readers into the stories.

Focusing on Individuals

Precontest stories for football and basketball certainly are given the most extensive coverage in most newspapers. Still, precontest accounts often are provided for significant encounters in other sports. More often than not, an outstanding individual will be the focus.

Track and field clearly is one sport where pre-event story emphasis can be on an individual. The annual Sun Angel Classic in Tempe, Arizona, generally attracts some of the world's top track and field performers. Readers naturally are interested in finding out who to watch. Sports reporter Lee Shappell of *The Arizona Republic,* in his pre-Sun Angel Classic story, singled out a jumper.

> For Arizona State's Deon Mayfield, a triple jumper who really is a *triple* jumper, tonight's competition in the Sun Angel Classic will be fierce.
>
> Mayfield has broken his school and Sun Angel Stadium records in the triple jump in each of the last two weeks. His most recent leap is 54 feet, 10¼ inches.
>
> But Mayfield, a sophomore from Altadena, Calif., has received more attention for his three-jump performances in the last two weeks. They are thought to be the best in the history of the sport.
>
> Two weeks ago in a dual meet with Tennessee, Mayfield triple-jumped 54-2½, long-jumped 25-2½ and high-jumped 7-0¾.
>
> In last week's dual meet with Houston, Mayfield, who had been sick with the flu all week, posted 54-10¼, 24-10 and 7-2¼. The triple- and high-jump marks were his lifetime bests.
>
> In the 6 P.M. meet today, Mayfield will concentrate on the triple jump, his best event.

The article went on to detail Mayfield's primary competition in the triple jump and to quote ASU's jumping coach. Summaries of other world-class athletes and their times and distances were provided.

Precompetition focus on an individual also is common in coverage of swimming. Definite lead material is when a freshman has a shot at an NCAA title. Melanie Hauser of the *Austin* (Texas) *American-Statesman* recognized this in one of her pre-NCAA championship stories:

> The program for this year's NCAA Swimming and Diving Championships mentions that—come Thursday morning—Texas freshman Rick Carey could quite possibly be afflicted with the malady known as "high-pressure palsy."
>
> The problem, as the writer explains it, is caused by the pressures associated with one's first collegiate championship and is characterized by "shaky" starts, nervous glances toward competitors and abnormally long stretches of time spent between the walls of the pool.
>
> In the past, the problem—indigenous to the NCAAs—has afflicted such standouts as UCLA's Steve Barnicoat, Miami's Jessee Vassallo

and Southern Cal's Chris Cavanaugh. Others, such as Texas' Clay Britt, Southern Methodist's Steve Lindquist and former USC star John Naber have been immune, winning NCAA titles their freshman years.

Carey seems destined to join the latter group when the three-day meet opens Thursday at the Walter Schroeder Aquatic Center (in Milwaukee). The question doesn't seem to be if he'll live up to his billing as the nation's best 200-yard backstroker, but rather how far he'll lower his American record.

Hauser's story quickly moved to quotations from coaches and competitors. She also provided times and records that Carey already had established. She discussed his strengths and weaknesses and used several direct quotations from him.

Focusing on Teams

Non-major-sport precontest coverage, of course, is not limited to leads that spotlight individuals. Even in nonrevenue sports, some teams are so dominant most readers relate to them and their accomplishments. In these situations, leads that emphasize team records are appropriate.

Mark Neuzil, assistant sports editor of the *Ames* (Iowa) *Daily Tribune,* did not have to look hard for his lead when Iowa State met Iowa in a college dual wrestling match:

> Once again, Iowa State and Iowa meet on the mat for the No. 1 ranking in the college wrestling world.
>
> When the season was young, it wasn't to be that way. Oklahoma, with a lineup that includes 10 All-Americans, was ranked first, ahead of the Hawkeyes and Cyclones.
>
> But Iowa State breezed past both teams to the Midlands championships and the Sooners proved to be their own worst enemy again by falling to Ohio State, 21-19, Sunday.
>
> That leaves ISU and Iowa in familiar positions. The winner of Saturday's 7:30 P.M. meet in Iowa's Fieldhouse will undoubtedly be crowned No. 1.

The story went on to quote the coaches and to provide a weight-by-weight analysis of wrestlers and records.

In the Iowa State–Iowa prematch story, with nationally prominent performers, the lead certainly could have focused on an individual. But, with so many stars and with two such highly ranked squads, it was natural to spotlight the teams and the overall significance of the match.

Prestories of dual track meets are not often given extensive play. Still, when two teams of national caliber collide, sports reporters react accordingly. Two of the perennial leaders in college track and field are Houston and Arizona State. Both teams generally are loaded with individual talent, but when a dual promises to be extremely close this angle can be explored in the lead of the premeet story.

Max Seibel of *The Phoenix Gazette* led his premeet account of a Houston–Arizona State dual with:

> Arizona State coaches Len Miller and Roger Kerr fear the worst as they await Saturday's track and field action at Sun Angel Stadium.
>
> "I have figured it out," said Miller, coach of the men's team that hosts University of Houston in a dual meet. "And I have Houston winning the meet, 79–77."
>
> "I've doped it out three or four times," says Kerr, whose women's team hosts Houston, Oklahoma and New Mexico in a quadrangular meet. "And every time, I have Houston winning by from 10 to 25 points."
>
> All of which means action should be fast and classy, because the two host teams are noted for their strength.

The story concluded with an overview of the women's competition that featured world-class competitors in the sprints, hurdles, high jump, and 4 × 100 relay.

Again, as was the case with the predual wrestling match coverage, the prominence of the teams and the probability of an outstanding meet were featured before moving to an account of star individuals.

Some precontest stories, particularly when a league or national championship meet is being held, can focus on the team favorite. These pre-event stories often contain direct quotations from coaches who have articulated opinions about the outcome.

Lee Barfknecht, the *Omaha World-Herald* reporter, began his story about a Big Eight gymnastics meet this way:

> The Nebraska gymnastics team leaves little doubt that its main goal is a fourth straight National Collegiate Athletic Association championship.
>
> Interviews with gymnasts and coaches are liberally sprinkled with references to the "nationals."
>
> But that doesn't mean the Cornhuskers will just go through the motions at the Big Eight championships tonight and Saturday at the Bob Devaney Sports Center.
>
> "These guys aren't going to say, 'This is just another meet we're going to plow through,'" said NU Coach Francis Allen.

"We've got guys who are trying to qualify for nationals. The better score you get, the better seed you get for nationals."

The Huskers, slowed by injuries in December and January, have romped to the top of the national rankings recently by dumping Big Eight foes Iowa State and Oklahoma twice in triangulars and pounding UCLA twice.

"In my past 20 years of coaching, I've never seen a team as strong as the present team at Nebraska," said Iowa State Coach Ed Gagnier.

"They are the toughest, best college team we've ever seen," Oklahoma Coach Paul Ziert said.

With such praise from its only Big Eight competition, will Nebraska's attempt to regain the league crown from Oklahoma be a contest? "I would say no," Allen said. "I think we'll score about 280. Iowa State's maximum is about 277 and Oklahoma is about 270."

But Allen said the meet will provide drama in other areas.

One will be the scrap for second place between the Sooners and Cyclones, with the winner probably clinching an at-large berth in the NCAA championships in Lincoln April 1–3.

"I think Iowa State and Oklahoma will have a real dog-fight," Allen said. "I would say it's do-or-die for Oklahoma if they want to qualify for nationals."

The premeet story continued with background on top individuals, injury reports, and more quotes from Coach Allen.

Precontest coverage can take various twists: It can focus on individuals; it can focus on teams; it can focus on strengths; it can focus on weaknesses; it can contrast participants; it can put a contest in historical perspective; or it can put a contest in national perspective.

Regardless of the sport or the thrust of the approach taken in the lead paragraphs, all precontest coverage requires good preparation, intelligent analysis, and sound writing.

Exercises

1. Clip pregame stories from area newspapers. Discuss their strengths and weaknesses. Does the pregame coverage published in daily newspapers in your area compare to the work of *Omaha World-Herald* sportswriter Lee Barfknecht that is featured in this chapter?

2. Write a pregame story based on excerpts from the Nebraska and Colorado sports information offices' press releases in this chapter or from a press release issued by the sports information office at your school.

3. Write a high school pregame story based on information you gather from clippings and interviews with players and coaches.

Coverage of Revenue-Producing Sports

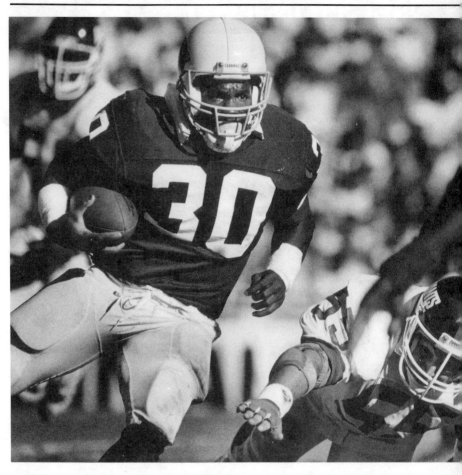

Football games receive extensive coverage in most of the nation's newspapers.

(Photo by Irwin R. Daugherty)

CHAPTER FOUR

Football

No intercollegiate or interscholastic sport, with the possible exception of basketball, receives more attention on the nation's sports pages than does football. Readers are accustomed to opening their weekend newspapers and seeing thousands of words—and numbers—that explain, interpret, or simply report football action.

Effective football coverage requires pregame preparation and the ability to: follow game action with an eye toward turning points and trends; interpret game statistics; gather meaningful quotations from coaches and players after the game; write an appropriate, logical lead; and structure a story by adroitly weaving analysis, statistics, and quotations.

The Preparation

Adequate preparation for football coverage extends beyond being in the stadium in time for the kickoff. The good sports reporter will carefully review relevant statistics for both teams, will be aware of key matchups in the lines, will know if an injury has forced one of the teams to use an untested defensive halfback, will know the weaknesses each team is trying to hide or exploit, will know if the teams had good or poor practices before the game, will know which running backs have been playing particularly well the last few games, and will know if the game is one the coaches have been pointing toward.

Naturally, these variables will change from contest to contest. But it is the job of the sports reporter to be fully aware of the strengths and weaknesses of each team before the game.

Charting/Watching Games

Reporters soon develop their own personal shorthand as they watch game action. At college contests, complete statistics generally are made available within 45 minutes after the game. Reporters do not have to be so concerned about keeping a complete running statistical account of college games—though many reporters feel more comfortable doing so. At high school games, however, reporters usually must "chart" the game themselves. High schools might provide a team statistical summary after the contest (sometimes), but seldom is a running log of each offensive play distributed.

Reporters soon develop a knack for watching action on the field and recording it as it happens on paper. A pocket-size notebook often is most convenient for the general assignment reporter, but sports reporters who intend to "chart" football games probably are most comfortable with legal-size paper. It becomes annoying to have to flip pages a lot while keeping running statistics.

Obviously, each reporter develops a record-keeping system with which he is most comfortable. A running log of football action—hand-written with the game in progress—could look like this:

1st Quarter

Hill City wins toss; elects to receive. Stockton kicks off into end zone. Ball downed.

Down	Yard Line	Play	Gain	Loss	Score	Time
1/10	20	Jones off tackle	3			
2/7	23	Blatchford right sweep	6			
3/1	29	Jones dive up middle	2			
1/10	31	Smith, pass from Alexander	9			
2/1	40	Jones, fumble (after hit by Reeves)		3		
1/10	37	Patterson, pass from Heiler (TOUCHDOWN)	37		6-0	9:57
		PAT—Johnson kick			7-0 (Stockton)	

—Stockton kicks off into end zone. Ball downed.

1/10	20	Blatchford left sweep	5			

There is, of course, nothing sacrosanct about this method of recording football action. Note, however, how efficient and comprehensive the running account is. When the reporter sits down to write a description of the action recorded above, it would read something like this:

> Stockton scored first on a 37-yard touchdown pass from Jay Heiler to John Patterson with 9:57 remaining in the first quarter.
> The touchdown—on Stockton's first play from scrimmage—came after Hill City running back Scott Jones fumbled after a vicious hit by linebacker Randy Reeves.
> Bill Johnson's kick put Stockton ahead 7–0.
> Hill City had moved the ball before the fumble. It effectively had mixed line plunges by Jones, end sweeps by Bill Blatchford and passes by quarterback Lee Alexander.

Naturally, most plays that occur during a game never make their way into print. But a running log enables a reporter to quickly scan for key series, downs, and scoring drives.

Reporters can enrich game coverage by adding description to statistics. This was done in the first paragraph of the example above. Nothing in the statistical log indicates that the tackle by Randy Reeves on Scott Jones was "vicious." But, the reporter, his memory jarred by the statistical log as he writes the story, can vividly describe the hit.

Chronological statistical accounts of game action are invaluable to reporters. Writers should, however, avoid falling into the trap of writing the game story purely from a chronological perspective. Lazy or inexperienced reporters find it easy to structure a logical lead and then proceed to a chronological summary of scoring.

Generally, a straight chronological approach should be avoided. Reporters must learn to decipher the running statistical account with an eye toward trends and turning points. These significant factors should be mentioned high in the story.

For example, Stockton beat Hill City 31–28 on a field goal by Bill Johnson as time expired in the game described above. The lead, obviously, would read something like this:

> A 44-yard goal by Bill Johnson with no time remaining lifted Stockton to a 31–28 non-conference high school football victory over Hill City Friday night.

Inexperienced reporters, after reporting that the game was won 31–28 on a last-second field goal, might turn in the second paragraph to a chronological game approach. The second paragraph *incorrectly* would read something like this:

> Stockton had grabbed the first lead in the game with 9:57 remaining in the first quarter on a 37-yard touchdown pass from Jay Heiler to John Patterson.

The third paragraph incorrectly would continue:

> Stockton also scored the second touchdown of the game with 11:24 left in the second quarter when . . .

Experienced sports reporters will not fall into the chronological reporting trap in a game story such as this. Logically, the reporter would check the running statistical summary to see what led to the game winning field goal. He or she would find this:

Down	Yard Line	Play	Gain	Loss	Score	Time
1/10	35	Cade, right sweep	32			1:32
1/10	33	Miller, left tackle	4			
2/6	29	Cade, left sweep	4			
3/2	25	Reid, pass from Heiler	12			:52
1/10	13	Miller, right tackle		1		:42
2/11	14	Heiler, tackled while back to pass		15		:32
3/26	29	Jones, dive up middle	2			:19
4/24	27	Time out— Stockton				:04
4/24	27	Johnson, FIELD GOAL FROM 34-YARD LINE				

The second and subsequent paragraphs could read:

> Stockton's victory chances appeared slim when, with 32 seconds left, quarterback Jay Heiler was thrown for a 15-yard loss, on a second-and-11 play from the Hill City 14-yard line, as he attempted to pass.
> Fullback Sam Jones then struggled for 2 yards on a third-and-26 play to the 27-yard line.
> Stockton let the time dwindle to four seconds before calling time out.
> Johnson, who was a perfect four-for-four on extra point attempts,

was called to try a field goal. The 44-yard attempt was the longest of Johnson's career.

Kicking soccer style from the left hash mark, Johnson drilled the ball through the goal posts with several yards to spare as the gun sounded.

From here, the game story would continue with a mixture of description, analysis, scoring details, and quotations.

Significant Statistics

Football statistics, like information on police blotters or in court records, can be confusing to the novice. But it does not take long to become familiar with football's most important statistical categories. A myriad of statistics can be culled from football games, but the Associated Press, in its agate packages, provides the score by quarters, individual scoring summary, attendance, first downs, rushing yards, passing yards, return yards, passes, punts, fumbles, fumbles lost, penalties, penalty yardage, and individual leaders in rushing, passing, and receiving. The AP statistical package is shown in figure 4.1.

Figure 4.1
LSU 24, FLORIDA 13

LSU	10	14	0	0-24
Florida	3	2	0	8-13

Fla — FG Gainey 28
LSU — Hilliard 11 run (Betanzos kick)
LSU — FG Betanzos 21
LSU — Hilliard 41 pass from Risher (Betanzos kick)
Fla — Safety, Risher tackled in end zone
LSU — Hilliard 3 pass from Risher (Betanzos kick)
Fla — Mularkey 5 pass from Peace
(Mularkey pass from Peace)
A — 73,152

	LSU	Fla
First downs	14	12
Rushes-yards	49-206	31-106
Passing yards	148	182
Return yards	32	86
Passes	9-14-2	23-41-2
Punts	7-40.3	6-47.6
Fumbles-lost	4-1	1-1
Penalties-yards	9-61	10-80
Time of possession	30:54	29:06

Individual Statistics

Rushing—Louisiana St.: Hilliard 26-127, Montz 8-46, James 7-22. Florida: Hampton 11-47, J. Jones 10-53, Peace 4-8.

Continued next page

Passing—Louisiana St.: Risher 9-14-2-148, Hilliard 0-1-0-0. Florida: Peace 18-29-2-149, Hewko 5-12-0-33.

Receiving—Louisiana St.: Hilliard 4-80, Scott 2-22, Martin 1-42. Florida: Dixon 6-57, Mularkey 4-37, S. Jackson 3-34.

Source: The Associated Press.

The statistics listed in the AP package are, of course, the most basic documentation of a football game. Other statistics that routinely are made available to the press after college football games—or that can be kept by reporters covering high school games—also can be important in writing game stories.

The NCAA form for final team statistics that is distributed after most college football games is shown in figure 4.2. The NCAA final individual statistics are shown in figure 4.3.

Figure 4.2

NCAA Team Statistics Form

	Utah (Visitors)	Arizona St. (Home)
First Downs	10	17
Rushing	11	8
Passing	4	7
Penalty	1	2
Rushing Attempts	53	42
Yards Rushing	164	124
Tackles-Yards Lost Rushing	7-28	8-44
Net Yards Rushing	136	80
Net Yards Passing	113	150
Passes Attempted	19	29
Passes Completed	10	14
Had Intercepted	3	1
Total Offensive Plays	72	71
Total Net Yards	249	230
Average Gain Per Play	3.4	3.2
Return Yards	3	90
Fumbles: Number—Lost	3-3	1-1
Penalties: Number—Yards	7-57	6-71
Interceptions: Number—		
Yards	1-0	3-76
Number of Punts—Yards	5-189	5-217
Average Per Punt	37.8	43.4
Punt Returns: Number—Yards	1-3	3-14
Kickoff Returns: Number—		
Yards	3-62	3-59
Possession Time	32:39	27:21

Source: National Collegiate Athletic Association.

Figure 4.3
NCAA FINAL INDIVIDUAL STATISTICS FORM

Utah (Visitors)

Rushing	Att.	Gain	Lost	Net	TD	Long
Monroe	19	57	—	57		7
Johnson	12	58	—	58	1	13
Sampson	4	6	1	5		4
Tarver	3	9	2	7		6
Graham	2	6	—	6		3
Vierra	9	8	18	-10		7
Cate	2	7	7	0		7
Lewis	2	13	—	13		7
Totals	53	164	28	136	1	

Passing	Att-Comp-Int	Yards	TD	Long	Sacks
Vierra	12-10-3	113		37	3
Cate	1- 0-0	—			1
Totals	19-10-3	113			4

Arizona State (Home)

Rushing	Att.	Gain	Lost	Net	TD	Long
Gittens	16	68	3	65		14
Clack	4	16	—	16	1	5
Wright	9	22	8	14		7
Cade	4	11	2	9		5
Lombardi	1	1	—	1		1
Hons	8	6	31	-25		
Totals	42	124	44	80	2	

Passing	Att-Comp-Int	Yards	TD	Long	Sacks
Hons	29-14-1	150		21	4
Totals	29-14-1	150			4

Continued next page

Figure 4.3 (Continued)

Utah (Visitors)

Pass Receiving	No.	Yards	TD	Long
Parker	2	43		37
Cox	4	49		21
Graham	3	13		7
Tarver	1	8		8
Totals	10	113		

Punting	No.	Yds.	Avg.	Long
Sanderson	5	189	37.8	45
Totals	5	189	37.8	

Field Goals	Att.	Made	Long
Fabringer	1	1	22
Totals	1	1	

All Returns	Punts			Kickoffs			Intercepted		
	No.	Yds.	LP	No.	Yds.	LP	No.	Yds.	LP
Monroe	-			3	62	27	-		
Wilson	1	3	3						
Kirkpatrick							1	0	0
Totals	1	3		3	62		1	0	

Arizona State (Home)

Pass Receiving	No.	Yards	TD	Long
Weatherspoon	3	44		21
Wetzel	2	19		10
Wright	3	18		7
Allen	3	48		18
Gittens	1	8		8
Cade	2	13		7
Totals	14	150		

Punting	No.	Yds.	Avg.	Long
Black	5	217	43.4	52
Totals	5	217	43.4	

Field Goals	Att.	Made	Long
Zendejas	5	3	45
Totals	5	3	

All Returns	Punts			Kickoffs			Intercepted		
	No.	Yds.	LP	No.	Yds.	LP	No.	Yds.	LP
Cade	-								
Gittens	3	14	6	3	59	23	2	40	36
Moyer							1	36	
Williams									
Totals	3	14		3	59		3	76	

Much of the information in the final team and individual statistics shown above makes its way into print when a football game is covered comprehensively. Still, there is even more information made available to the press that can be of value in writing game stories. This is provided in a chart that summarizes possession time and key plays.

A summary of key plays and all third down and non-kicking fourth downs can help a reporter isolate turning points. Summaries are provided by quarter. Listed are the down, yards to go, the play that was attempted, the result of the play (gain, loss, pass incompletion, penalty, etc.), and whether or not the key play attempt resulted in a first down. Possession time for the entire game and key plays for the first half of the Arizona State–Utah football game are listed in figure 4.4.

It might be significant when writing the game story for the Arizona State–Utah contest, for example, to point out that ASU could convert only three of nine first-half third down plays to first downs. Examining the statistics even more closely, it can be found that, when faced with third down and more than 5 yards to go, the Sun Devils passed on all five occasions. Never were they successful. The only third-down conversions were on short yardage situations—though ASU did pass on two of the occasions, and both went for good yardage (9 and 20 yards) and for first downs.

The diligent reporter will examine these statistics. Sometimes, they will be significant enough to merit inclusion in the game story—sometimes they will not.

Defensive statistics also are provided. Defensive leaders certainly should be mentioned in the game story. Some small colleges and high schools keep summaries only of tackles—assisted and unassisted. Most of the NCAA schools, however, provide complete defensive statistics: pass rushes; pass interceptions; fumble recoveries; tackles for losses; unassisted tackles; assisted tackles; pass deflections; and blocked kicks. Listed in chart form, it is easy to determine if a defender has had a particularly good all-around game.

If the reporter notices that a defensive back was credited with two fumble recoveries, four unassisted tackles, three assisted tackles, a pass interception, and two pass rushes, it should be reported. That, by anyone's standards, is a great night's work.

Most universities also provide reporters with a drive chart. This NCAA chart shows each offensive possession of both teams. Figure 4.5 is a list of Arizona State's offensive possessions against Utah. The numbers on the chart can be deciphered easily. At a glance, the reporter realizes that ASU could muster only two drives the entire game of more than 50 yards. Neither resulted in a score. In the second quarter, ASU put together a quick 54-yard drive. The chart indicates that, with 43 seconds left in the first half, ASU

Figure 4.4
Possession Time and Key Plays

	Arizona State		Utah	
First Quarter	7:05		7:55	
Second Quarter	6:04		8:56	
First Half Total		13:09		16:51
Third Quarter	6:01		8:59	
Fourth Quarter	8:11		6:49	
Second Half Total		14:12		15:48
Game Total		27:21		32:39

Key Plays and All Third Down and Non-Kicking Fourth Downs

Arizona State						Utah					
Qtr	Down	To Go	Play	Gain	1st	Qtr	Down	To Go	Play	Gain	1st
1	3	8	Hons pass inc.	-	No	1	3	1	Graham around right	3	Yes
1	3	10	Hons pass defl.	-	No	1	3	3	Monroe over right tackle	4	Yes
1	3	12	Hons pass inc.	-	No	1	3	15	Monroe around left	7	No
1	3	5	Hons pass inc.	-	No	1	3	8	Monroe (fumble) (pitch)	-2	No
						1	3	5	Monroe-draw play	1	No
			0-4						2-5		
2	3	1	Clack around left	5	Yes	2	3	1	Monroe over tackle	3	Yes
2	3	5	Penalty-motion	-		2	3	5	Vierra pass to Cox	4	No
2	3	11	Hons pass inc.	-	No	2	4	1	Vierra-QB keeper	7	Yes
2	3	4	Gittens-run	3	No	2	3	7	Monroe on option	2	No
2	3	2	Hons pass Wetzel	9	Yes	2	3	2	Graham on pitchout	3	Yes
2	3	2	Hons pass w/ Spoon	20	Yes	2	3	1	Johnson over middle	1	Yes
			3-5						4-6		
			Half: 3-9						Half: 6-11		

Source: National Collegiate Athletic Association.

Figure 4.5
Arizona State's Offensive Possessions Against Utah

Team	Qtr.	Drive Started — Yd. Line	Time	How Obtained	Drive Ended — Yd. Line	Time	How Lost	Drive Consumed — Yards	Plays	Time	Time
Arizona St.	1	25	15:00	Kickoff	37	13:00	Punt	12	6	2:00	
		20	8:06	Punt	20	7:12	Punt	-	4	:54	2:54
		47	7:12	Fumble Rec.	-	6:03	FG	47	5	1:09	4:03
		22	4:46	Fumble Rec.	-	3:55	FG	22	4	:51	4:54
		38	2:11	Punt		-	Qtr.			2:11	7:05
	2		15:00	Qtr.	25	14:01	Missed FG	37	10	:59	
		40	13:44	Pass Int.	49	11:36	Punt	9	4	2:08	3:07
		20	5:11	Kickoff	29	2:57	Pass Int.	9	5	2:14	5:21
		20	:43	Kickoff	26	-	Missed FG	54	7	:43	6:04
	3	12	13:11	Pass Int.	-	12:23	TD	12	3	:48	
		6	6:49	Punt	23	1:36	Fumble	71	13	5:13	6:01
	4	31	14:45	Punt	48	11:19	Punt	17	9	3:26	
		44	9:09	Punt	46	7:15	Punt	-2	4	1:54	5:20
		2	7:08	Fumble Rec.	-	5:32	TD	2	3	1:36	6:56
		1	3:20	Pass Int.	-	2:05	FG	1	4	1:15	8:11

Arizona State	First Quarter	Second Quarter	Third Quarter	Fourth Quarter	Totals — First Half	Second Half	Final
Time of Possession	7:05	6:04	6:01	8:51	13:09	14:12	27:21
Third-Down Conversions	0-4	3-5	2-3	2-5	3-9	4-8	7-17
Average Field Position	30	23	9	32	27	31	29

Source: National Collegiate Athletic Association.

started from its own 20-yard line after a kickoff by Utah. In seven plays the Sun Devils drove to the Utah 26-yard line. As time expired, ASU missed a field goal attempt.

The other 50-yard-plus drive came in the third quarter. ASU took possession of the football on its own 6-yard line with 6:49 remaining after Utah had punted. The 71-yard drive ended on the Utah 23-yard line after a fumble with 1:36 remaining. There were 13 plays in the series that consumed 5:13. The chart also indicates that Utah controlled the ball in the third quarter. ASU's two drives used up only 6:01.

The drive chart shows that ASU scored its final 10 points during the last five and one-half minutes of the game. The Sun Devils used three plays to go 2 yards for a touchdown with 5:32 remaining after recovering a fumble on the Utah 2-yard line.

The final ASU score came on a field goal with 2:05 remaining. ASU intercepted a pass and was stopped on the Utah 1-yard line with 3:20 remaining. After three plays, ASU could not put the ball in the end zone. On fourth down, the Sun Devils kicked a field goal. There were 2:05 remaining in the game.

The scoring summary possibly is the most basic chart reporters need to evaluate after a game. It contains the score by quarters, the running score, quarter and time of score, player who scored, play that led to the score, yards covered, time elapsed in drive, and yards and plays in the drive. The summary from the Arizona State–Utah game is shown in figure 4.6.

Again, football statistics are not difficult to interpret if the reporter merely will take a few minutes to scan them with an eye toward trends and turning points.

The key statistical charts, then, when covering a football game are:

■ Final team statistics (first downs, total offense, etc.).
■ Final individual statistics (breakdown of rushing, passing, receiving, punting, field-goal kicking, returns).
■ Quarter-by-quarter running chronology.
■ Possession time and key plays.
■ Defensive statistics (tackles, fumble recoveries, etc.).
■ Drive charts.
■ Scoring summaries.

Naturally, there is more to covering a football game than being able to gather and decipher statistics. Statistics provide the skeleton of game coverage. Quotations from coaches and players provide the soul.

Figure 4.6
Scoring Summary of the Arizona State–Utah Game

Score by Quarters

	1st	2nd	3rd	4th	Total
Arizona State	6	0	7	10	23
Utah	0	10	0	0	10

Running Score

ASU	Utah	Qtr	Time	Player	Play	Yards	Extra Points	Time	(Yds-Play) Drive
3	0	1	6:03	Zendejas	Field goal	45		1:09	47-5
6	0	1	3:55	Zendejas	Field goal	35		0:51	23-4
6	3	2	5:11	Fahringer	Field goal	22		6:25	88-15
6	10	2	0:43	Johnson	Rushing	1		2:14	35-7
13	10	3	12:23	Wright	Rushing	1	Fahringer = Yes	:48	12-3
20	10	4	5:32	Hons	Rushing	1	Zendejas = Yes	1:36	2-3
23	10	4	2:05	Zendejas	Field goal	18	Zendejas = Yes	1:15	1-4

Source: National Collegiate Athletic Association.

Interviews and Quotations

Reporters must scurry after the game to get quotations that will explain or shed new light on what happened on the field. It also is good to get quotations from players and coaches before the game. Statements made before the contest—particularly those that focus on a game plan—often provide impetus for postgame questions. Was the team able to do what it planned to do?

Postgame quotations are necessary for good game coverage. Reporters need to seek out interviews and to gather quotations shortly after the gun sounds. At high school games, reporters might be able to get a few words with coaches immediately. Some coaches, however, refuse to be interviewed until they have had an opportunity to meet with players in the locker room. Some high school coaches place their players off limits to the press. The important thing, particularly since the procedure for getting postgame interviews after high school games can vary so much, is to find out the ground rules for postgame interviews before the contest.

Circumstances for interviews after college contests are more uniform. Locker rooms generally are closed for a few minutes to the press. After the coaches have a chance to talk with players, the doors are opened to the media. Most head coaches, of course, will hold press conferences to give all reporters a chance to ask questions. Enterprising reporters, however, also will seek out quotations from assistant coaches and players.

Naturally, the first step toward getting good postgame quotations is to find out the procedures for getting the interviews. Once the reporter has done this, he should:

- *Be prepared to ask intelligent questions.* If a team fumbled the ball on its own 5-yard line with 35 seconds remaining, thus paving the way for a game-winning touchdown by the opponent, do not waste time with a question such as: "Coach, what do you think was the turning point of the game?" To begin with, the answer is obvious. Secondly, coaches have been known to throw temper tantrums in response to less ridiculous questions.
- *Be aware of the temperament of the coach.* This is not to say that reporters should throw only "softball" questions at short-fused coaches, but smart reporters will be wise enough to pose the soft questions first and save the adversary questions for later in the interview. An early adversary question—assuming the reporter knows he has time to ask additional ones—could end an interview abruptly. Of course, if on deadline, the reporter must ask his most pointed, relevant questions first.
- *Have questions prepared—but be flexible.* Reporters should jot down

questions before the interview. However, if an answer by the person being interviewed or if a question by another reporter leads logically to another topic, the reporter should not hesitate to ask questions on that topic.

■ *Be observant.* The sights and sounds in a postgame locker room can be almost as significant as the comments gathered during the interviews. Notice what the room looks like. Are players laughing? Are they crying? Are they stunned?

■ *Check with the trainer.* While in the locker room, check the status of injured players with the trainer.

■ *Remember to talk with assistant coaches and nonstar players.* Some of the best postgame interviews are conducted with assistant coaches and players who saw action but who were not necessarily the stars. While most reporters gravitate to the head coach and stars, they should not overlook other game participants who might have significant observations.

■ *Phrase questions carefully.* There are two basic types of questions that can be asked during an interview: open-ended and closed-ended. An open-ended question allows the source some leeway. For example, a coach could be asked: "How do you evaluate the play of your offensive line?" The question gives the coach room to maneuver and an opportunity to give a lengthy response. A closed-ended question, however, is phrased in such a way that the response will be limited to possibly a single word. For example: "Did the offensive line play well?" The answer to that question likely will be "yes" or "no."

Once a reporter conducts postgame interviews, he or she must select quotations for the story. Reporters should try to stay away from cliches. Some coaches and players, of course, seem incapable of responding to questions with anything but cliches. But, if questions are worded properly, some worthwhile direct quotations should be gleaned from the locker room.

A quotation such as the following that was in an AP story adds little to a game account: "Football is a simple game. You come down to your basic tackling and blocking. LSU blocked better than we did today, tackled better than we did today and they deserved to win."

What else is new?

Quotations should be used that interpret more specifically what obviously happened on the field. After South Carolina upset nationally ranked North Carolina, the AP quoted the winning coach: "My (offensive) coaches' plan was just to go ahead with the pitch sweep and the pass. We don't go very well up the middle, but we do very well with the end."

Direct quotations such as this are, of course, more specific than: "We just went out and did what worked well for us." Readers need to be told precisely what did work well.

Once the reporter had conducted his interview, and is deciding which statements to weave into his story, he should:

- *Use direct quotations only on the most vivid, germane comments*. Do not waste direct quotations on commonplace statements such as: "We really took it to them." Took what to whom? Save direct quotations for statements such as: "We knew the right side of their defense was weak so we ran nearly three-fourths of our line plunges that way." That is, obviously, a more graphic way of saying, "We really took it to them."
- *Use paraphrases of statements that are significant, but which are not vividly worded*. If the coach says, "We had planned all week to pass the ball more than we usually do," do not quote him directly. Make it: Coach Jones said his game plan called for more passing than usual.
- *Intersperse direct quotations and indirect statements*. Stories simply read more fluidly when direct quotations, indirect statements, game analysis, and statistical documentation are skillfully woven together.
- *Make use of good quotations even if they do not fit the main game story*. If an extensive interview is conducted with a coach or player, several significant quotations could be gathered. If there is not room for all of them in the main game story, reporters should consider blending them into a sidebar.

Game Coverage

Pregame football coverage requires diligence and organizational skills. Chapter 3, which outlines the precontest strategies of *Omaha* (Neb.) *World-Herald* sportswriter Lee Barfknecht, illustrates the hard work that effective pregame coverage requires. Game day coverage is no walk in the park for a sportswriter who faces deadline pressure.

Games are fun for fans in the stands; sportswriters enjoy them, too, but they don't have the luxury of showing up at kickoff, filing out of the stadium immediately after the game, and heading out for a satisfying meal. Whether a sportswriter is covering a high-school game on a Friday night or a college clash on a Saturday afternoon, concentration and long hours are required.

Barfknecht had been looking forward all week to the Nebraska-Colorado game. In the next section, he presents a first-person account of his game coverage.

A Day on the Job with Lee Barfknecht

10:00 A.M. "With a 3:07 P.M. CST kickoff, I got a rare chance to stay home long enough Saturday morning to watch the ESPN and CNN college football preview shows. One of my assignments is to monitor national press coverage of Nebraska football. Still, I wanted to get to the stadium at least three hours before kickoff. One reason was the weather the morning of the game was 35 degrees, steady rain and a north wind of 20 mph, so I needed to monitor field conditions and be aware of any changes in pregame routines. Also, representatives from seven bowls and about twenty national newspapers were scheduled to attend. Arriving early would give me time to obtain background information on the bowl situation and on how teams in other parts of the country were performing.

11:00 A.M. "I left Omaha and drove 60 miles in the usual heavy pregame traffic to Lincoln. The Interstate 80 traffic often is bumper-to-bumper and moves at 50-60 mph.

12:10 P.M. "Arrived at the press box and ate lunch with reporters from *The National*, the *Kansas City Star,* and the *Rocky Mountain News,* and an Orange Bowl representative. We discussed the Top 25 polls (I am an AP voter) and how unpredictable the season had been.

12:15 P.M. "Noted that Nebraska's groundskeeper brought his tractor and blade onto the field to squeegee water off the artificial turf.

1:00 to 2:00 P.M. "The press box filled rapidly. I interviewed representatives from the Orange, Sugar, and Citrus Bowls before the game, trying to determine how Nebraska might fit into their plans, win or lose against Colorado.

1:30 P.M. "Noted the squeegee tractor was making its second tour of the field. And it was still raining.

2:00 P.M. "Our reporting team for the game gathered. It's a four-man crew—sports editor Mike Kelly (column), myself (game story and bowl situation sidebar), Doug Thomas (Nebraska locker room sidebars), and Steve Sinclair (Colorado locker room sidebars). All of us also contribute to a Game Notes package.

3:00 P.M. "People finally settle into their seats to await kickoff. Late afternoon games make for a brutal day for me. The copy deadline for our first edition is 6:00 P.M., meaning I have to write 'running' during timeouts from the first quarter on. Because TV games run long, we have been granted fifteen extra minutes on our 'bulldog' (first) edition.

4:33 P.M. "First half ends with Nebraska leading 6-0. Two radio stations want me to do halftime interviews, but I turn them down because I am writing to meet our tight first deadline. Also, I note that the tractor squeegees the field one more time.

4:55 P.M. "Second half begins. I wrote 11.4 inches of running on the first half. As the game progresses, I will add to that in hopes of getting 20 inches for the bulldog.

5:27 P.M. "Third quarter ends with Nebraska leading 12-0. I insert that quarter's action into my game story and begin formulating ideas for a lead about the Huskers moving into strong contention for the national championship because it was just announced that No. 1 Virginia had lost to Georgia Tech.

5:41 P.M. "Colorado tailback Eric Bieniemy has scored two touchdowns, throwing the game into doubt and elevating the blood pressure of all writers with tight deadlines.

5:50 P.M. "Bieniemy scores again after a Nebraska fake punt fails. It appears Colorado will win, so I begin writing a lead about Bieniemy, who fumbled five times in the first three quarters, becoming the hero at the end.

6:00 P.M. "Bieniemy scores his fourth TD of the quarter, and I try to round out my story, leaving blanks for the final score.

6:07 P.M. "Game ends. Colorado wins 27-12. I fill in the blanks and do what polishing I can in three minutes.

6:10 P.M. "Dial our computer and transmit 22.1 inches for our first edition. It arrives in Omaha at 6:12, beating the deadline by three minutes.

6:13 P.M. "Grab my coat and race for the Nebraska interview room. The elevator reserved for reporters has long gone, and they are now clogged with fans from the booster-club section. So I run down the 80 rows of steps, across the field, under the south end zone, outside the main gate, and back in through the football office doors to reach the interview room. As a precaution against missing Coach Osborne's postgame remarks, I sent a backup tape recorder down with another reporter. But I got there just seconds into his opening statement. With all the chairs taken, I walked through the crowd and sat on the floor next to the table where Osborne was sitting. Don't be bashful.

6:25 P.M. ''Nebraska players begin to file in for interviews. Some come up from the closed locker room after showers. Others are still in their gear. Some don't come at all. You hope the absentees aren't the ones you want to talk to.

6:45 P.M. ''After talking to four players and two assistant coaches, I head back to the press box. Fortunately, I bump into a Citrus Bowl official to get more comments for my bowl story.''

Facing Deadlines

Once back in the press box, Barfknecht went through his notes, transcribed some taped interviews, and decided how to revise his first game story. His next copy deadline was 8:45, but he set a self-imposed limit of 8:30 because he still had to do his bowl sidebar and contribute to the game notes.

Before starting to write, Barfknecht learned that *World-Herald* research and that of the NU sports information office showed that Colorado's 27 points were the most ever scored against Nebraska in the final quarter of any game in its 101-year history. So, Barfknecht decided to incorporate that fact, Bieniemy's bizarre day, and Nebraska's scrambled national championship hopes into his revised game story. At 7:15, assistant sports editor Bob Tucker called from Omaha to ask each *World-Herald* writer for a list of stories they were writing. Tucker and day sports desk chief Brian Lahm made up the newspaper's Husker Desk on game day.

At 8:35, Barfknecht filed his final game story, then began work on his bowl sidebar. Copy deadline for the *World-Herald*'s Platte edition, which follows the Platte River and I-80 through central Nebraska, was 8:35. Some sidebars had been written, some had not. Copy deadline for the Iowa edition, which reaches 30,000 readers in western Iowa, was 9:45. Copy deadline for the Lincoln edition was 10:45. By that time, the *World-Herald* team had assembled: (1) Kelly's column and a short Colorado defense sidebar; (2) Barfknecht's game story; (3) sidebars by Thomas on NU's defensive line, quarterback Mickey Joseph, NU's fake punt and NU's secondary; and (4) Sinclair's sidebar on CU Coach Bill McCartney, quarterback Darian Hagan, CU players saying that they are the new power in the Big Eight and the CU defense. In addition, the reporting team combined for a 12-inch notes package, which Barfknecht led with the tractor squeegeeing the field.

At 11:00, after final proofreading, the *World-Herald* staffers called Omaha for an all-clear and made the hour drive home.

Organizing the Game Story

There is no magic formula for organizing a football game story. Many games lend themselves to a summary lead in which the most important elements— who, what, when, where, why, and how—are jammed into a rapid-fire, staccato first paragraph, followed by direct quotations, followed by scoring plays, and concluded with leftover tidbits.

Here, for example, is the lead paragraph from an Associated Press story:

> NEW ORLEANS—Tony Thompson ran for 151 yards and two touchdowns, the last with 31 seconds left Tuesday night, to rally 10th-ranked Tennessee to a 23-22 victory over Virginia in the Sugar Bowl.

When a game is singled out for extensive coverage by a daily newspaper or a wire service, the reporter needs to work hard to put together the most comprehensive, readable account possible. As discussed earlier in this chapter, pregame preparation is essential. Information that might be relevant when putting together the game story should be stockpiled. The reporter should have the information at hand and not have to search frantically for it at the end of the game. Statistics should be kept, gathered, and deciphered. Postgame interviews should be conducted. When the groundwork has been laid, it is time to write the story.

An appropriate lead must be written (various types are discussed in chapter 2). In his lead block of paragraphs, Barfknecht emphasized the national championship implications of the Nebraska-Colorado game, quotes from NU Coach Osborne, and the role of running back Bieniemy:

> LINCOLN—What is believed to be the biggest fourth-quarter scoring explosion against Nebraska in its 101 years of football apparently has blown the Huskers out of this season's national championship chase.
>
> Colorado tailback Eric Bieniemy, who through three quarters Saturday fumbled five times and lost three, ran for four touchdowns in the final period—from 1, 2, 3, and 5 yards out—to rally the No. 7 and No. 9 Buffs to a 27-12 victory over No. 2 and 3 Nebraska before 76,464 fans at Memorial Stadium.
>
> The Huskers had allowed just one rushing touchdown through eight games and six TDs overall before CU's 27-point outburst in the final 14:43. Those also were the first points Colorado had scored in Lincoln in five years.
>
> "At the end, I thought we'd be the stronger team," NU Coach Tom Osborne said. "But they got their running game going, and we didn't get it untracked.
>
> "Once they got ahead, they made a couple of big plays and big catches and that was the difference."
>
> The victory virtually assures Colorado, 8-1-1 overall and 5-0 in the

Big Eight, of an Orange Bowl trip and a second straight league title, making it the first school other than Nebraska or Oklahoma to accomplish that since Missouri in 1940-41.

The Buffs finish with home games against Oklahoma State and Kansas State.

For the Huskers, the loss dropped them to 8-1 and 4-1, and left them wondering what might have been.

Note that Barfknecht relied extensively on background to put the significance of the game in perspective.

After his lead block, Barfknecht effectively used a transition paragraph to move into a narrative of game action, with direct quotes and analysis interspersed. His transition paragraph:

Despite heavy clouds, rain and 38-degree temperatures, things looked bright for Nebraska after three quarters—Miami bright.

Barfknecht closed his seventy-one-paragraph story with relevant team statistics (NU's yardage total of 232 was its lowest in four years) and direct quotes from Coach Osborne.

Complete Game Coverage

Writing *the* story for a football game is a major undertaking. Newspaper coverage of high school contests and even most college football games usually is limited to one story. Daily newspapers that cover nationally prominent college teams, however, go well beyond publishing a single, comprehensive game story. These newspapers usually devote 25 inches or more to the main game story, but they also publish sidebars, statistical summaries, and photos that consume hundreds more inches.

The *Omaha World-Herald*'s coverage of University of Nebraska football is impressively comprehensive. The *World-Herald* typically will devote up to five full pages (about 600 column inches in its six-column per page format) to day-after coverage.

When the Cornhuskers defeated rival Oklahoma 28–24 to earn a trip to the Orange Bowl, Steve Sinclair wrote a 45-inch game story. But the coverage did not stop there. The *World-Herald* also provided its readers with an 18-inch column by sports editor Michael Kelly, plus sidebars such as:

- Steve Pivorar's story of Oklahoma's perceptions of the traps and misdirection plays run by the Cornhuskers;
- Lee Barfknecht's story of the "Bounceroosky"—a bounce pass trick play that set up a Nebraska score;

- Dave Sittler's story of a Nebraska defensive end who made a key interception;
- Pivorar's story about Sooner quarterback Kelly Phelps, who refused to question Oklahoma's late-game strategy to abandon its running attack for the passing lanes;
- Sittler's story about Nebraska defensive players' thoughts when Oklahoma was driving late in the game;
- Barfknecht's story about Nebraska offensive players' perceptions of the game;
- Tom Allan's story from the Oklahoma locker room; and
- Sittler's story that focused on Nebraska's defensive coordinator.

The *World-Herald* also carried game-story leads written by reporters from other newspapers who covered the contest (under the headline "What Others Said") and, in a question-answer format under the headline "The Answer Box," explored some tidbits that did not make their way into the main game story or the sidebars.

"The Answer Box" is a regular feature. It enables staffers to get interesting pieces of information to readers without slowing down the narration of the game story. Questions posed after the Oklahoma game, for example, included: "Why did Nebraska try an onside kick in the first quarter?" and "Why did Nebraska end up with twelve men on the field one time?"

In addition to thousands of words, the *World-Herald* carried a full-color photo on page one, a full-color photo on the lead page of the sports section, scattered black and white photos throughout the sports section, and a complete picture page of highlights.

Sideline Coverage

Tom Allan, roving reporter for the *World-Herald*, covered the sideline for more than thirty seasons of Nebraska football. His stories were an essential part of the *World-Herald*'s football game coverage. Allan started covering the sidelines in the early 1950s voluntarily because he thought there should be more coverage than the game story. He quickly found that by simply turning his back to the main focus of action on the field, he could find some excellent stories. Allan cites stories about:

- A county attorney who exerted his external sophomore spirit by working as a peanut vendor on game days.
- A Nebraska fan who, at the Nebraska–Louisiana State Orange Bowl game in 1971, lugged in a huge carnival teddy bear. Appropriately attired in Nebraska colors, the man sat the bear in the seat beside him.

A policeman quickly was on the scene. "You can't do that," the policeman said. "Hell I can't," replied the fan. "Here's its ticket."

Allan admits he is somewhat of a maverick. "Writers are supposed to sit in the press box," he said. "Photographers are supposed to brave the elements atop photo decks or prowl the sidelines. But as a combination man, I like to do my writing and picture taking on the sidelines." It is work but, according to Allan, it can be fun.

One of his favorite stories is the time Glenn Boles, an old army friend, was head linesman at a Nebraska football game. After Boles had called a 5-yard penalty against Nebraska for off-sides, Allan warned the official he was vulnerable "because of his asininity." "The very next play the Huskers pulled a student body left sweep," Allan said. "A chain gang member dropped his marker. Boles, back-tracking fast, tripped over it and was engulfed by hurling bodies. When we dug him from the bottom, fearing the worst, Boles lay there dazed. He looked at me and asked, 'How'n hell did you know?' "

A few plays later, during a timeout, Allan took the opportunity to tell Boles how much the photographers appreciated the fact his legs were so bowed they could still get pictures between them. Boles turned to the Husker bench and snapped, "Get him off my back or I'll give you a penalty." Allan relishes telling the rest of the story. Longtime Husker trainer Paul Schneider, not knowing of the Boles-Allan friendship, frantically screamed at the official, "He's not with us. He's not with us. He works for the *Des Moines Register!*" Boles laughed so hard he fell to his knees.

Sideline features enliven a sports section. Game coverage is, of course, a must. But feature sidebars add zip to the total coverage package. They often can focus on elements the fans in the stands do not see.

Exercises

1. Clip a featured college football game story from *Sports Illustrated.* Clip a major story on the same game from a daily newspaper. Discuss the similarities and differences.

2. Write a ten-paragraph football game story based only on statistics supplied to you by the sports information office from an area college.

3. Cover a football game. Write an A.M. and P.M. version. Compare your stories to those published in area newspapers.

4. Discuss in class problems you encountered in getting postgame interviews. Discuss also your successes.

5. Write a sidebar to your game story.

6. Compare your game coverage shorthand to others in your class.

Sportswriters often sit courtside to report action at exciting NCAA basketball games.

(Photo by Irwin R. Daugherty)

CHAPTER FIVE

Basketball

If you turn to the sports section of a daily newspaper in winter and look at the datelines, you'll see that, across the country, basketball coverage dominates.

AMES, Iowa—Calbert Cheaney scored 18 of his 29 points in the second half and teamed with Eric Anderson to lead a decisive 19-4 run that carried No. 6 Indiana past Iowa State 87-76 Friday night.

NEW YORK—St. John's finished its Big East regular season with a 68-58 victory over Georgetown Monday night.

JOHNSON CITY, Tenn.—Keith "Mister" Jennings had 19 points and seven assists as East Tennessee State (25-4) downed Virginia Military 88-76 Saturday.

STILLWATER, Okla.—Byron Houston scored 31 points for Oklahoma State as the Cowboys beat Colorado 79-67 Saturday to move into a tie for first in the Big Eight.

SYRACUSE, N.Y.—Billy Owens scored 33 points as Syracuse clinched at least a share of the Big East regular season title with an 89-68 victory over Pittsburgh Saturday.

ROCK HILL, N.C.—Freshman Jarvis Lang scored 23 points and blocked four shots as North Carolina-Charlotte used a punishing second-half press to score 66 points in making up a 12-point deficit to down West Virginia 110-103 Saturday.

These summary leads only begin to tell the story of what happened in these games. Daily newspaper reporters filed accounts from these and hundreds of other college and high school contests played on one weekend. There probably is no busier time for sports staffs than basketball season.

Charting/Watching Games

Reporters who cover basketball games soon develop their own methods for recording significant plays and turning points. Most reporters adopt note-taking systems similar to those used by sports information staffs at colleges and universities.

Naturally, the best game stories are written by reporters who watch the game, sift through statistics, review their notes, talk with coaches and players, and then put together a complete account.

Reporters should pry information from all available sources. Before these compete accounts can be written, however, reporters must be able to decipher game statistics. When covering college basketball, reporters should review official game statistics compiled by the sports information staff. Those who cover high school or junior high school games, where journalists must keep their own running score and statistics, also should review their summaries before writing a game story.

To illustrate how a contest can be reconstructed by examining play-by-play summary charts (on which scores, time, and description of plays are listed), an Arizona State–UCLA basketball game will be examined. When ASU plays host to UCLA, the ingredients for a powerful game story are present. One year, for example, both teams entered the game rated among the nation's Top 10; both had played in the NCAA tournament the year before, with UCLA advancing to the finals; and ASU had defeated the Bruins twice the previous season—a situation for which UCLA wanted to atone.

Because ASU captured the game 78-74 in three overtimes, the reporter should start with the statistics for the third extra period. Leads usually focus on an individual star, a turning point, or winning shot; seldom is a story put together chronologically. Key plays of the third overtime are described in figure 5.1.

The score was tied at 71 going into the third overtime. The numbers on the left represent the time remaining (overtime periods in college are 5 minutes each; each regulation half is 20 minutes). There is description of the action, the score for ASU, the score for UCLA, and the point spread. The first basket of the last overtime was scored by Paul Williams with 4:49 left; he hit a 10-foot jump shot while driving the left baseline that put ASU ahead 73-71. At the 3:27 mark, Johnny Nash hit the first of a one-plus-one free throw (he missed the second) to give ASU a 74-71 advantage. With 2:08

remaining, UCLA's Cliff Pruitt made one free throw (X) but missed the second (0); the successful shot brought UCLA within 2 points, 74-72.

With 1:05 left in the overtime, Williams hit a layup from the left side on a pass from Alton Lister to put the Sun Devils in command, 76-72. After Walt Stone picked up a personal foul (pf) with 11 seconds remaining, UCLA's Michael Holton hit both free throws to cut the ASU lead to 76-74. Then, with 8 seconds remaining in the period, Sun Devil guard Byron Scott made two free throws after being fouled by Rod Foster (who picked up his fifth and final foul) to ice the game 78-74. With 3 seconds left, ASU's Tom Kuyper had a one-plus-one free throw, but he missed. The final score: 78-74.

The sports reporter should then look over the second overtime statistics, shown in figure 5.2. The second overtime started with the score tied at 63. UCLA led 69-67 before Scott hit a 20-foot jump shot to tie the game with 1:17 remaining. UCLA's Kenny Fields made two free throws with 33 seconds left to lift the Bruins into the lead, 71-69. Nash, though, hit an 8-foot jump shot from the right side with 3 seconds left to tie the score. The game went into the third overtime.

Next statistical stop: the first overtime. The plays are described in figure 5.3. The first overtime started with the score tied at 57. The Sun Devils scored first on a follow shot by Lister with 3:58 left. Later, with ASU leading 63-61, Ralph Jackson was given credit for a six-foot shot in the lane after a goal tending call on ASU's Sam Williams. With 56 seconds left, the score was tied at 63. There was no more scoring in the period.

How did the game get into overtime? Closing plays of regulation time are shown in figure 5.4. The chart shows that Jackson hit a 21-foot jump shot from the top of the key to tie the score at 57 with 53 seconds left. That ended regulation period scoring. The reporter should then look at the remainder of the game's scoring descriptions.

In this game, Arizona State sprinted to a 39-28 halftime lead; the Bruins outscored the Sun Devils 29-18 in the second half to send the game into overtime. First half statistics show Arizona State took a 20-19 lead on a 10-foot jump shot by Sam Williams with 8:36 remaining. The Bruins never led again in regulation, but they methodically chipped away throughout the second half, tying the game on Jackson's jump shot.

The reporter then should turn to the final box score, shown in figure 5.5. The abbreviations at the top of the box are standard: field goals made; field goals attempted; free throws made; free throws attempted; rebounds; personal fouls; total points; assists; turnovers; blocked shots; steals; minutes played. Team totals appear at the bottom of the box under the names of individuals. Field goal shooting was very close: UCLA hit 30 of 63 for 48 percent; Arizona State hit 31 of 69 for 45 percent. The Bruins hit 14-24 from the free throw line (58 percent); ASU converted 16-25 (64 percent).

Figure 5.1
Key Plays of the Third Overtime, ASU-UCLA

TIME	ARIZONA STATE vs UCLA Second Half	ASU	UCLA	SPREAD
	DESCRIPTION			
5:00	Third overtime center jump Lister and Fields ASU controls			
4:49	P Williams 10 ft jump shot bs 1 off drive	73		A 2
3:27	pf Daye (3p;7t) Nash shoots 1 @ 1 X 0	74		A 3
3:27	Pruitt for Daye			
3:02	pf Scott (3p;bonus) Sanders shoots 1 @ 1 0			
2:33	Jump ball Nash and Pruitt UCLA controls			
2:08	pf Lever (4p;bonus) Pruitt shoots X 0			
	Stone for Lever		72	A 2
1:47	pf Pruitt (2p;bonus) Nash shoots 1 @ 1 0			
1:47	Daye for Pruitt Foster for Holton			
1:37	Jump ball Scott and Fields ASU controls			
1:37	Time out UCLA			
1:26	pf Jackson (3p;bonus) Scott shoots 1 @ 1 0			
1:05	P Williams lay in 1 s from Lister	76		A 4
0:47	pf Lister (5p;bonus) Sanders shoots 1 @ 1 0			
0:47	Kuyper for Lister			
0:47	Time out ASU			
0:21	pf Sanders (3p;bonus) Stone shoots 1 @ 1 ft lane violation			
0:18	Time out UCLA		74	A 2
0:11	pf Stone (2p;bonus) Holton shoots two X X			
0:11	Pruitt for Holton			
0:11	Time out ASU			
0:08	pf Foster (5p;bonus) Scott shoots 1 @ 1 X X	78		A' 4
0:08	Holton for Foster			
0:03	pf Sanders (4p;bonus) Kuyper shoots 1 @ 1 0			
0:00	FINALS ASU 78 UCLA 74			

Figure 5.2
Second Overtime Statistics

ARIZONA STATE	vs	U C L A	Second Half			
TIME	DESCRIPTION			ASU	UCLA	SPREAD
5:00	Center jump S Williams and Fields					
	UCLA controls					
4:55	Daye jump shot from Sanders				65	LA 2
4:33	pf S Williams (5p;bonus) Holton shoots 1 @ 1				66	LA 3
	X 0					
4:33	P Williams for S Williams					
4:10	Lister 8 ft jump shot ang r from Nash			65		LA 1
3:40	pf Scott (2p;bonus) Jackson shot 1 @ 1 X X				68	LA 3
3:25	pf Sanders (2p;5t) non shooting					
2:57	Scott lay in off steal by Lever from Lever			67		
2:32	pf Lister (4p;bonus) Holton shoots two X 0				69	LA 1
1:41	Jump ball Jackson and Lever ASU controls off					LA 2
	out of bounds					
1:28	pf Jackson (2p;6t) non shooting					
1:17	Scott 20 ft jump shot at the key			69		
1:07	Time out UCLA					
1:07	Foster for Holton					
0:33	pf Lever (8p;bonus) Fields shoots two X X				71	LA 2
0:16	pf P Williams (2p;bonus) Jackson shoots					
	1 @ 1 0					
0:03	Nash 8 ft jump shot ang r from Lever				71	
0:00	SECOND OVERTIME ASU 71 UCLA 71					

Figure 5.3
Plays

ARIZONA STATE   vs   U C L A   Second Half

TIME	DESCRIPTION	ASU	UCLA	SPREAD
5:00	Center jump s Williams and Sanders ASU controls			
4:18	Jump ball Lister and Fields ASU controls			
3:58	Lister follow shot	59		A 2
3:05	Foster 18 ft jump shot bs 1 off drive		59	A 2
2:34	Lister 4 ft jump shot bs 1 from Nash	61		A 2
1:40	Sanders follow shot		61	
1:19	Nash 16 ft jump shot in key from Lister	63		
1:15	Official time out			
1:15	P Williams for Lister			
0:56	6 ft shot in lane by Jackson goal tending S Williams		63	
0:56	Lister for P Williams Holton for Foster			
0:11	Time out ASU			
0:11	Time out ASU			
0:00	END OF FIRST OVERTIME ASU 63 UCLA 63			

Closing Plays

TIME	DESCRIPTION	ASU	UCLA	SPREAD
7:12	Sanders for Pruitt	50		A 9
6:38	S Williams 16 ft jump shot l of key from Scott		43	A 7
6:17	Fields lay in l s off loose ball		45	A 5
5:46	Nash bad pass			
5:38	Daye 13 ft jump shot in lane off break	52		A 7
5:24	Scott bad pass			
5:00	S Williams 16 ft jump shot in key from Nash		47	A 5
4:25	Daye lay in l s from Sanders			
4:25	Time out UCLA			
4:25	Pruitt for Fields Foster for Holton			
4:11	10 sec back court violation ASU			
3:43	Foster 20 ft jump shot ang l from Jackson		49	A 3
3:27	Lister lay in r s off lob from Scott	54		A 5
3:00	Jackson 18 ft jump shot in key		51	A 3
2:39	Lever 10 ft jump shot bs r	56		A 5
2:17	pf Lister (3p;bonus) Sanders shoots 1 @ 1 X X		53	A 3
2:17	Fields for Sanders			
1:59	Time out ASU			
1:59	Sanders for Pruitt			
1:37	S Williams bad pass			
1:33	Daye lay in		55	A 1
1:16	pf Fields (2p;4t) Lever shoots two X 0	57		A 2
0:53	Jackson 21 ft jump shot top of key		57	
0:41	Time out ASU			
0:08	Foster for Holton			
0:05	Time out UCLA			
0:00	OVERTIME SCORE ASU 57 UCLA 57			

Figure 5.5
Official NCAA Basketball Box Score

OFFICIAL NCAA BASKETBALL BOX SCORE   Date_____   Site ASU ACTIVITY CENTER

VISITORS (Last Name, First)

No.	U C L A		FG	FGA	FT	FTA	REB	PF	TP	A	TO	BLK	S	MIN
11	Sanders, Mike	f	8	16	3	7	8	4	19	2	3		1	53
30	Daye, Darren	f	7	10	1	2	3	3	15	3	2		3	43
54	Fields, Kenny	c	4	6	2	2	6	2	10	1	4		2	47
10	Foster, Rod	g	7	15	0	0	1	5	14	5	2		1	33
14	Holton, Michael	g	1	3	4	6	5	0	6	2			2	32
3	Jackson, Ralph		2	7	3	5	2	3	7	6	6		1	46
24	Agrillaga, Randy			DNP										
31	Knight, Curtin			DNP										
34	Pruitt, Cliff		1	4	1	2	1	2	3	1	1		1	17
35	Easton, Mark		0	1	0	0		2	0					3
44	Sears, Dean			DNP										
45	Anderson, Tony		0	1	0	0		1	0					2
	TEAM REBOUNDS (Included in Totals)						8							
	TOTALS		30	63	14	24	34	22	74	20	18	0		11

FG %: 1st Half 13-30 = 43   2nd Half 17-33 = 515   Game 30-63 = 476

FT %: 1st Half 2-4 = 500   2nd Half 12-20 = 600   Game 14-24 = 583

Deadball Rebounds 3

HOME

No.	A S U		FG	FGA	FT	FTA	REB	PF	TP	A	TO	BLK	S	MIN
14	Nash, Johnny	f	6	14	1	3	11	0	13	9	2	1	3	55
30	Williams, Sam	f	5	10	3	4	12	5	13	3	3	2	1	40
53	Lister, Alton	c	10	13	2	2	12	5	22	6	6	1		52
11	Scott, Byron	g	4	16	7	11	8	3	15	2	4	1	2	51
12	Lever, Lafayette	g	4	11	1	2	4	5	9	3	4		5	49
10	Bressant, Pierre													
13	Pollard, Jim													
32	Williams, Paul		2	3	2	2	2	2	6		3			16
33	Kuyper, Tom		0	0	0	1		0	0					1
34	Thomas, Bruce													
31	Stone, Walt		0	2	0	0		2	0		2			10
52	Everett, Warren													
50	Boyer, Walt													
54	Warring, Ron													
	TEAM REBOUNDS (Included in Totals)						2							
	TOTALS		31	69	16	25	51	22	78	20	24	5	11	

FG %: 1st Half 14-29 = .483   2nd Half 17-40 = .425   Game 31-69 = .449
FT %: 1st Half 11-14 = .786   2nd Half 5-11 = .454   Game 16-25 = .640

OFFICIALS: Charlie Ra... Terry White, Ron Labetich

Technical Fouls:

Attendance 14,384

Deadball Rebounds 1

SCORE BY PERIODS	1st H.	2nd H	OT	OT	FINAL
UCLA	28	29	6	8	74
ASU	39	18	6	8	78

Arizona State, though, had a significant 51-34 rebounding advantage. Four UCLA players scored 10 or more points; Mike Sanders led with 19; four Sun Devils also were in double figures. Center Lister had a big night: 10 of 13 field goals and 2 of 2 free throws for 22 points. He added 12 rebounds and 6 assists.

Obviously, the reporter should get player and coach quotations before writing a complete story. Relying solely on the statistics, however, a 200-word story something like this could be written quickly:

> TEMPE, Ariz.—Paul Williams scored two baskets in the third overtime to lift Arizona State University to a 78-74 victory over UCLA in a Pacific 10 Conference clash here Friday.
>
> The Bruins overcame a 39-28 halftime deficit to tie the score at 57 on a 21-foot jump shot by Ralph Jackson with 53 seconds left in regulation play.
>
> Though they had led for most of the game, the Sun Devils appeared doomed in the second overtime until Johnny Nash dropped in an 8-foot jump shot from the right side with three seconds left to propel the game into the third extra period.
>
> It was not until ASU guard Byron Scott made two pressure-packed free throws with eight seconds remaining in the third overtime that the partisan ASU crowd of 14,384 breathed a sigh of relief. Scott's free throws gave the Devils their final four-point spread.
>
> Though field goal shooting was close (UCLA hit 48 percent; Arizona State hit 45 percent), the Devils enjoyed a comfortable 51-34 rebounding advantage.
>
> Seven-foot Alton Lister paced the Sun Devils. He scored 22 points, snatched 12 rebounds and dished out 6 assists.
>
> Nash, who played all 55 minutes, and Sam Williams gave support. Both forwards scored 13 points; Williams tied Lister for rebounding honors with a dozen and Nash contributed 11. Scott was the fourth Devil in double digits; he scored 15.
>
> Mike Sanders paced UCLA with 19 points and 8 rebounds.

The story logically then would flow into player and coach quotations, team records, effects on conference and national rankings, next games, and so forth.

Significant Statistics

Always check individual and team statistics before a game. This is particularly important when covering teams for the first time. If a player has a good night in relation to his season average, it can be a factor in the game's outcome. If, for example, Walt Stone enters a game averaging 9.2 points and 4.6 rebounds but scores 22 points and grabs 11 rebounds, it is worth reporting. Similarly, if Byron Scott enters the game averaging 21.2 points and scores 23, it might be worth noting that he scored close to his average. Such comparisons can extend beyond scoring and rebounding averages. If Chris Beasley enters a game shooting 42.6 percent from the field and hits 8 of 10 attempts, his hot shooting should be mentioned in the game story. These individual statistical tidbits give added meaning to a game story.

Team statistics also should be compared to season averages if relevant. For example, if one team enters a game shooting 47 percent from the field, but hits only 35 percent of its shots while losing, this likely was a factor. The cold shooting could be due to a strong defense by the opponent or it could be attributed to a team's inability to hit open shots.

Most teams keep charts showing where on the floor shots were taken. The number of the player is listed; if the shot is successful, the number is circled. There are exceptions, but generally the team that hits the most shots in the lane (in the "paint" as television commentators are fond of saying) often will win. This is another statistical category that can be examined to help explain the outcome of a game.

The shot chart for the first half of the Arizona State–UCLA basketball game showed that both teams scored eight baskets inside the lane. Of the eight baskets scored by ASU, six came on layups. Of UCLA's eight, two were layups. The first-half shot chart figure 5.6 showed that ASU's No. 53 (Alton Lister) scored three layups and two shots just outside the lane. This might be worth noting in the game story.

There are not as many statistics to interpret after a basketball game as there are after a football game. Still, a reporter needs to review them carefully before putting together a game story.

The key statistical charts, then, when covering a basketball game are:

- *Official box score.* This provides the score by periods, the final score, the officials, technical fouls, and the attendance. It also provides the following team statistics: field goal percentages by half and for the game; free throw percentages by half and for the game; field goal attempts; field goals made; free throw attempts; free throws made; fouls; assists; turnovers; blocks; and steals. It provides the following individual statistics: field goal attempts; field goals made; free throw attempts; free throws made; rebounds; personal fouls; points; assists; turnovers; blocks; steals; and minutes played.
- *Running score.* This chart chronologically describes action. Description of plays includes: who controls the center jumps; who makes field goals and from where on the floor; turnovers; personal fouls; violations; free throws; time outs; and assists. The precise time the play occurred is noted, along with the score.

Figure 5.6
First-Half Shot Chart

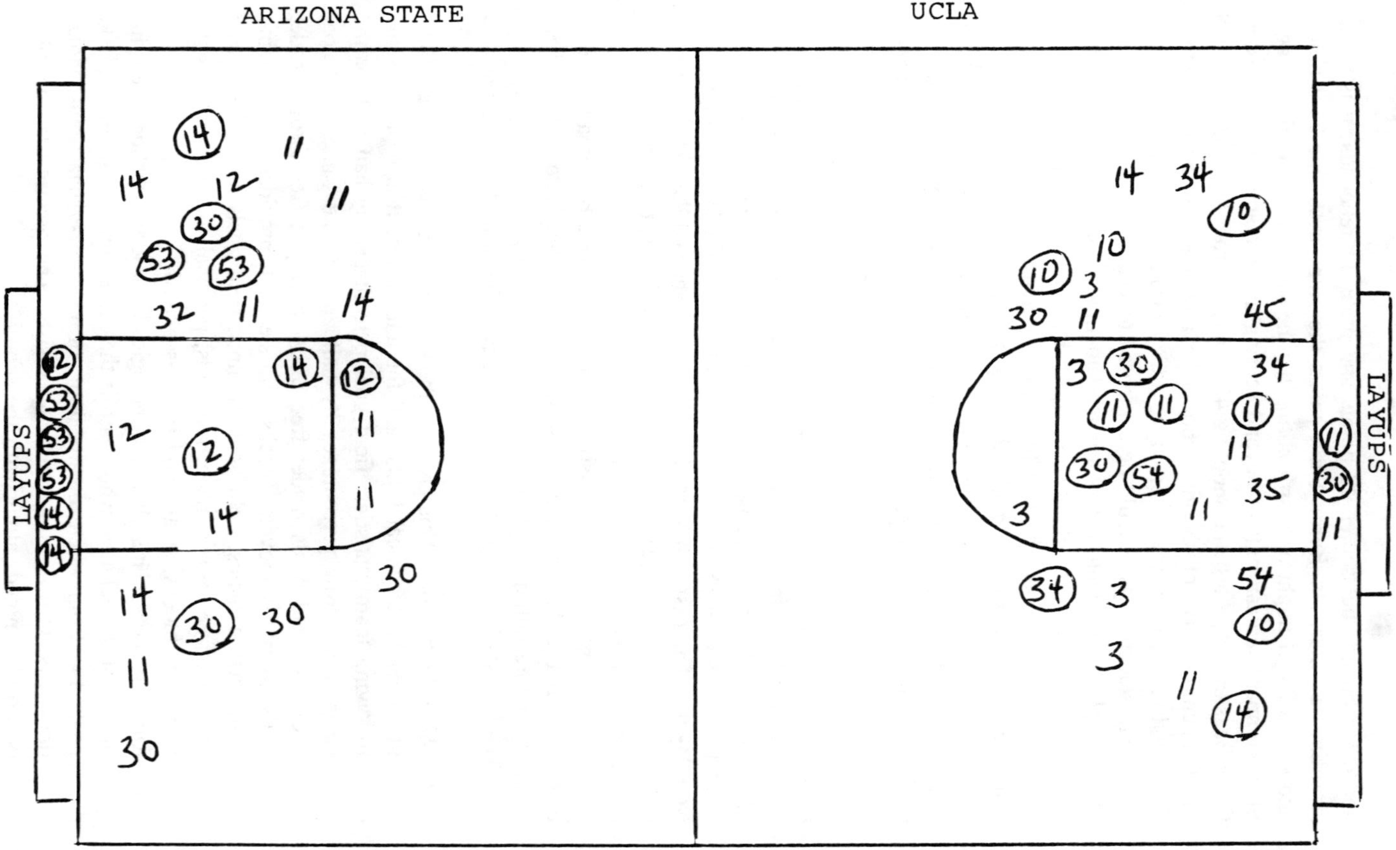

▪ *Shot chart.* A shot chart is kept for each period. This chart, as noted earlier, shows the places on the floor from which shots were attempted. It also shows if they were successful. At the bottom of the chart there often is a chronology of turnovers. The chart describes the turnover (fumbled pass, lane violation, and so forth); records the time the turnover was committed; and lists the number of the player who made it. A quick glance at the chart tells not only who made crucial turnovers but it also shows which team made the most.

Preparing for Game Coverage

Bruce Pascoe, a sportswriter for the *Las Vegas Review-Journal,* covers what is traditionally one of the country's finest college basketball teams: the UNLV Rebels. Although it was the Saturday before a UNLV–New Mexico State Monday night clash, Pascoe already was thinking about the game. Because New Mexico State was playing at San Jose State and UNLV was at home to play California, Irvine, that Saturday, the reporter had not been able to do much advance work. However, before heading to UNLV's game, he called New Mexico State sports information director, Steve Shutt, to ask when the Aggies would be returning to Las Cruces on Sunday. Shutt said the team's flight into El Paso, Texas, was due at 2:00 P.M., with arrival in Las Cruces scheduled for 3:30 and practice at 4:00. The Rebels would be arriving in Las Cruces just before their 7:00 P.M. practice.

Shutt said the best time to get ahold of NMSU players and Coach Neil McCarthy was after their practice. Because Pascoe would get into Las Cruces at 1:30 P.M., though, he decided to go to the workout early. He needed to gather information for an advance and a sidebar for Monday's editions.

"Because New Mexico State doesn't have too many interesting players, I don't think the sidebar should be an individual feature," Pascoe said. "Instead, I hope to just talk to several players and get a feeling for whether they think this is their last chance to beat UNLV. They may meet again at the Big West Tournament in Long Beach California, but UNLV shouldn't have trouble with a neutral site like that.

"I got quotes from two Rebel players after the Irvine game talking about how tough it is to play at New Mexico State. Experience has proven it's hard to catch these guys the day before a road game, and since my deadline is 8:00 P.M. tomorrow (Sunday), I don't want to take any chances. However, I figure I can catch (Coach Jerry) Tarkanian before the Las Cruces practice tomorrow."

Sunday, Feb. 23. Pascoe arrived in Las Cruces and drove around "mostly just out of curiosity." Pascoe said he wanted "to see if there were any signs that the town was into the game." There weren't. Even though Shutt had told Pascoe that NMSU's practice probably would be closed, the reporter went to the arena twenty minutes before to see for himself.

"I found another guy with a notepad on the sidelines," Pascoe said. "I asked if he was a writer. He turned out to be Phil Casaus from the *Albuquerque Journal,* which was good, because I figured he would know what was up. He said he didn't know if we would be kicked out, so we looked for Aggie Coach McCarthy. McCarthy wasn't in his office, and he eventually showed up late."

Casaus yelled to McCarthy across the court to see if practice was open. The coach couldn't hear and eventually walked over to the reporters. He said the Aggies would be going only forty-five minutes or so and that it was no problem for the journalists to stick around. However, he started complaining about how busy he would be after practice; he had a radio interview from New York and had to take a recruit out for dinner. Pascoe asked him if he would be available for a few minutes after practice; he said no.

"Fortunately, however, he came over to Phil and me later during practice, muttering how poorly the Aggies were playing and how their minds had been on the Rebels during their previous four games," Pascoe said. "So I threw in a couple more questions, realizing this might be my only interview opportunity. He talked about how they didn't space out during games, but that they had trouble with mental preparation beforehand."

Unexpectedly, McCarthy tossed out a nugget that Pascoe would be able to use in a "notes" column. "McCarthy complained out of nowhere about the fact that Dick Vitale would be covering the game for ESPN," Pascoe said. "McCarthy talked about how Vitale had called him up out of the blue and started babbling about how he had been assigned to cover the game at the last minute because it was so big. He also mentioned how this game had picked up national significance because it was seen as the Rebels' last roadblock before the NCAA tournament. So, right here, I figured I had a lead note item on Vitale, albeit a weak one, and a good general quote about the game from McCarthy."

While he was waiting for practice to end, Pascoe asked Casaus and some Las Cruces television reporters about the crowd atmosphere at the Pan American Center, the homecourt of the Aggies. "I had heard that the crowd liked to throw jalapenos at the games, and apparently they had in the past, but the reporters said that wasn't quite true. But they did attest to the incredible noise in the arena."

After practice, Pascoe decided to seek out some Aggie players. "The players were great," he said. "I got two starters, William Benjamin and Michael New. Even though I had plenty from New and Benjamin, the sports information people came up with a quote sheet. This is really unheard of for a regular-season game like this, but these guys are pretty efficient. I never depend on quote sheets, though, because the quotes are usually lousy. But, I did pluck a quote from Randy Brown off it, the one guy I had wanted to talk to but missed. So that was helpful.''

While he was waiting for the sports information office to finish the quote sheets, Pascoe finished off his game chart (basic information to accompany the pregame story: opponent and record; time and location of game; seating capacity of arena; details about television and radio coverage; New Mexico State lineup; UNLV lineup; and tidbits, such as series record, score of last meeting and so forth). ''I had done most of the game chart on the plane, but I couldn't do updated statistics until now. So I sent that in [to the newsroom].''

It was now 6:00 P.M. UNLV would practice at 7:00, so Pascoe decided to run back to the hotel to see if he could catch Coach Tarkanian. ''Usually, his quotes are much better in places like hotel lobbies and airports, when he has plenty of free time, than immediately before or after a practice,'' Pascoe said. ''Sure enough, he was in the lounge with a couple of UNLV fans. Since he seemed to be having a good time, I was wary of interrupting his fun with questions. I really like to respect peoples' personal time, unlike a lot of reporters. So I asked Joe Hawk, UNLV's SID, if he thought I could interrupt Tark. Hawk said Tark actually might like to see me, especially if he didn't like the fans.''

So, Pascoe approached the coach, who said he would be happy to answer a few questions. They talked for about ten minutes, while the fans listened.

''I asked mostly standard questions about how tough this game would be, whether it was their final hurdle (as expected, he said no), and, for my notes, I asked about Vitale. I thought maybe he would say something about Vitale in a negative, joking tone, especially since Vitale incorrectly predicted Arkansas would beat UNLV two weeks ago. But Tark doesn't seem to mind Vitale's massive ego and he only smiled about him saying, 'he's crazy.' Then again, nobody really bothers Tark much. He's a very tolerant person.''

It was almost 6:45 now—and the bus to practice was ready to leave. Pascoe went back to the hotel, finished off the notes and headed to practice. At that point, he had two stories left to do: the main advance and a sidebar. He had about two and one-half hours before deadline.

Not needing any more quotes, Pascoe went to practice anyway, ''just in case something happened—an injury, Tark yelling at someone, or anything like that.'' As is his custom, Pascoe sat in the stands and typed. He finished the advance just about the time practice ended at 8:00 P.M. The reporter then went to the SID's office to transmit his story. He stayed in the office to write the sidebar. He had only a few minutes to write the piece, transmitting it at 9:25 (8:25 Las Vegas time), just ahead of deadline. ''I would have liked to have been quicker,'' he said. ''But I felt like I did OK considering the volume of stuff I had sent and the lateness of getting everybody interviewed.''

After he finished his stories, Pascoe's most pressing problem was getting something to eat in Las Cruces, a town of 45,000. ''There was only one answer at ten o'clock: Denny's.''

The Pregame Stories

Pascoe's advance—a twenty-three-paragraph, fast-paced bundle of information, quotes, facts and anecdotes—was an easy read. The lead block of paragraphs effectively pulled *Review-Journal* readers inside:

> LAS CRUCES, N.M.—They might even throw jalapenos at you.
>
> OK, so maybe that's a little exaggeration, but those are the kind of stories told about the Pan American Center, site of today's 9 p.m. Big West Conference game between UNLV and New Mexico State.
>
> And, besides, isn't a different kind of test needed for these seemingly indestructible 25-0 Rebels?
>
> So far, the ''tests'' for his team have been a little weak.
>
> —There was Steve Smith, the rest of Michigan State's basketball team and 21,000 Spartan fans in Auburn Hills, Mich. That didn't work.
>
> —There were Pete Carril's caterpillars from Princeton. They held UNLV to just 69 points, but that didn't work.
>
> —There were those wacky surfer students at UC Santa Barbara, where, old timers might recall, the Rebels lost their last game. That didn't work.
>
> —There were pig calls and the second-best team in the country in Fayetteville, Ark. That didn't work.
>
> Can anybody, or anything, beat this team?
>
> Maybe a 15th-ranked team that has won 29 straight at home, the second-best in the Big West? Maybe that team boosted by an already high-flying crowd that will have plenty of pre-game fiesta time?
>
> Maybe flying jalapenos?
>
> Maybe not.
>
> ''I think their fans will definitely be into it,'' Rebel guard Greg Anthony said. ''But that's something our guys are used to. It's a big game, but we'll just try to take them (the crowd) out of the game, get our game going, play defense and try to create transition opportunities.''

Pascoe used the quote from Anthony as a transition to move into the second half of his story that featured quotes from other Rebel players along with quotes from Tarkanian and NMSU Coach McCarthy and one of his players. The groundwork Pascoe had laid—testing the jalapeno legend on New Mexico journalists, gathering coach and player quotes, and putting the game in perspective by recounting other "challenges" the Rebels had faced—was apparent in his advance.

The lesson is clear: good advances are predicated on hard work and a flair for isolating the unusual and significant. Pascoe also made good use of the quotes he had gathered from NMSU players and their coach—to say nothing of a little Southwestern lore he had picked up—in the fifteen paragraph sidebar that he wrote in minutes in the SID's office. Pascoe's first four paragraphs set the stage for the quotes that followed:

> LAS CRUCES, N.M.—Somehow, legend goes, Billy the Kid escaped here well before an execution order on him could be carried out. But the New Mexico State Aggies are hoping to get a tighter grip on the UNLV basketball team tonight.
>
> Forget the Rebels' 25-0 record. Their mental toughness. And the revenge factor from an 83-82 UNLV loss here last year.
>
> This 21-3 bunch of Aggies thinks it can win. Really.
>
> "We feel when we're playing here, we can beat anybody," Aggie guard William Benjamin said.

Pascoe's fifteen-paragraph "notes" column featured some leftover tidbits from Saturday night's UC Irvine game, including a narrative account of rap star M. C. Hammer taking "a parade-like walk down Gucci Row during the middle of the first half" and later giving a brief talk in the Rebel clubhouse. But, the lead item was built around the out-of-the-blue observation by NMSU Coach McCarthy about broadcaster Vitale being on hand for the Aggie-Rebel game.

Pascoe undoubtedly brought smiles to the lips of many of his readers with this lead block:

> LAS CRUCES, N.M.—Oh, no. He's back.
>
> Mr. Loudmouth, Dick Vitale, was assigned by ESPN to cover today's UNLV-New Mexico State game at the last minute. That's right, the man who incorrectly picked Arkansas to beat UNLV is back to watch the Rebels' last big test of the regular season.
>
> UNLV Coach Jerry Tarkanian, saying he never had any problem with Vitale's prognostication ability, just smiled about the thought of having Vitale around.
>
> "He's crazy," Tarkanian said.
>
> But New Mexico State Coach Neil McCarthy apparently wasn't quite sure what to make of it.
>
> "He calls me up the other day, 'Neil, how ya doing? This is Dick Vitale,' " McCarthy said. "I've never even talked to the guy before. He goes on and on, saying, 'Hey, they moved me to your game because it's so big.' "

> Despite Vitale's love for hyperbole, he was actually telling the truth. Vitale and Mike Patrick will team up for this one, replacing the usual Big West team of Quinn Buckner and Barry Tompkins.

Pascoe's pregame package was complete: a comprehensive main story, a readable piece on the views of New Mexico State toward the game and an entertaining, informative notes column.

Monday, Feb. 24. Pascoe had planned to attend the Rebels' shootaround (their light workout the day of a game) at noon, even though he usually did not. "The team normally just walks through what the other team will be doing," Pascoe said. "Also, media presence usually is frowned upon. But a week ago, against Long Beach, the Rebels had a poor shootaround and Tark really got on them for it. So I planned to watch this one to see if it might happen again.

"However, I was awakened at 9:30 A.M. and felt awful. I went back to sleep, and the next thing I knew, it was 1:25 P.M. Oops."

Later, Pascoe called SID Hawk to see if anything eventful had happened at the shootaround. He said nothing had, except that Vitale marched around at midcourt during the middle of practice. "I can't believe Tark lets him do that stuff," Pascoe said.

As always, Pascoe picked up every newspaper in sight to see what was being written about the game. He read the *Albuquerque Journal, El Paso Times,* and *Las Cruces Sun-News.* He found little new information in them, though he did notice a quote in the *Times* from UNLV's Larry Johnson about how tough the crowds are at New Mexico State. The Johnson quote interested Pascoe because, he said, the UNLV star and three other Rebel starters "won't talk to me."

Covering the Game

The ESPN-televised game was scheduled for a 10:00 P.M. tipoff (9:00 Las Vegas time), thus making for what Pascoe termed a "brutal deadline." The *Review-Journal*'s street (first) edition has a 9:30 P.M. deadline. The final (home) edition has a computer deadline of 11:15 and must be off the floor by 11:30. Because the Rebel-Aggie game would end at about 11:05 Las Vegas time, Pascoe would have to file his story immediately afterwards, then get a few quotes and take advantage of the opportunity to file again at 11:35 for the edition that goes to about 85,000 of the 100,000 homes.

Before the game, Pascoe reviewed notes from both teams' SIDs. He jotted down items that he would have to get in the game story (like NMSU's twenty-nine-game homecourt winning streak, the Big West regular season title—if UNLV won—and some other similar items).

At halftime—with UNLV on top 46-37—Pascoe wrote about 12 inches on first-half highlights. "The Rebels played pretty well, and I figured they probably would hang on and win," Pascoe said. "The crowd didn't seem to bother them, even though it bothered me. I wish I had earplugs. Anyhow, I started to think about how my lead would be if UNLV won."

During second-half timeouts, Pascoe continued to write. By the four-minute mark, with UNLV up by 12, it was pretty much over. Pascoe banged out a lead and had everything ready to go, except individual scoring totals, by the time the game was over. He ran up to the SID's office, got a couple of leading scorer totals from one of the sports information workers, inserted them, and sent the first story. It was 11:17.

"By now, Tark was done talking in the conference room, so I corralled him in the hallway, apologized for missing his speech, and asked him to comment on the game quickly," Pascoe said. "He gave me a generic response about how playing well in the hostile environment was great, and I took off, knowing I could go into further detail on the follow-up story tomorrow.

"The UNLV players were leaving, too. I grabbed the last significant player I saw, Greg Anthony, but that was a risk because he rarely talks to local media. However, he did, saying how the crowd wasn't a problem and how the game wasn't tougher than any other game.

"Then I went back to the conference room, where McCarthy was finishing up. I got a few quotes from him, then they brought in a player, William Benjamin, from whom I got a few more. I then left. It was about 11:25."

Pascoe spent the next twelve minutes rewriting the top of the story, plugging in quotes there and midway through it. He sent the story in at 11:36, when the desk editors at the *Review-Journal* told him it would reach all home editions because the press was down. "That was good, because this game was big enough that people probably would want to see quotes and more detail than just play-by-play," Pascoe said.

Pascoe then noticed that McCarthy was doing a telephone interview with a New York radio station. The reporter waited until McCarthy was off the telephone, then he asked him a few questions that he would use for a follow-up story.

Writing the Game Story

Playing off the "tough crowd" theme that had run throughout his advances, Pascoe began his game story with this lead block:

> LAS CRUCES, N.M.—Crowd? What crowd?
>
> UNLV's basketball team, while defeating New Mexico State 86-74 Monday night before 13,007 fans at the Pan American Center, certainly heard it: The decibel levels rivaled your basic heavy metal concert.
>
> And they might have seen it, with hand-held banners asking for the head of UNLV Coach Jerry Tarkanian and fluorescent papers waved at Rebel free-throw shooters.
>
> But did they notice it? Hardly.
>
> "The crowd doesn't bother us," Rebel guard Greg Anthony said with a crafty-looking smirk after the game. "The only thing it does is give them a boost."
>
> For that reason, this one was tough—UNLV's toughest of the season. Although UNLV led the game much longer than it did during a 114-86 victory over UC Irvine on Saturday in the Thomas & Mack, it never led by more than 18 points, the closest of any game this year.
>
> Even the Rebels' 112-105 victory at Arkansas on Feb. 10 featured a 23-point Rebel lead, and the Rebels' victory over New Mexico State at the Thomas & Mack Center on Feb. 16 (oddly, by the same score) featured a 29-point lead.
>
> "I thought the kids played really great," Tarkanian said. "To come into an environment this hostile and play this well is really great."

Of the remaining sixteen paragraphs in Pascoe's story, three contained direct quotations that he had gathered after the game. Most of the last half of the story provided play-by-play highlights and significant team and individual statistics.

Deadlines for morning newspapers are tight after night games, particularly late-starting encounters like the UNLV–Aggie clash. Reporters must not only construct pieces of their stories during stops in game action but also scurry to gather post-game quotes and to write their stories under pressure.

Tuesday, Feb. 26. At the airport, as UNLV and Pascoe were waiting to board the flight to Las Vegas, the reporter tried talking to Anthony, but he said he did not want to talk further. "So, when we got into Las Vegas, I got a couple of other players to talk at the baggage claim (they were off Tuesday and soon would scatter) for the follow-up, mostly asking about what it felt like to be on the verge of going undefeated," Pascoe said. "I then hustled over to the weekly Rebel luncheon, where Tark was discussing the game. I would use this for the follow-up, too, the last bit of information on the Aggie game I would get."

Exercises

1. Examine a complete package of basketball statistics supplied by the sports information office from an area college. Which are the most significant?

2. Write a ten-paragraph basketball game story based only on statistics supplied to you by the sports information office.

3. Clip stories about the same basketball game from three different newspapers. Which story is best? Why?

4. Cover a basketball game. Write an A.M. and P.M. version. Compare your stories to those published in area newspapers.

Coverage of Non-Revenue-Producing Sports

The excitement of college baseball is drawing
record crowds across the country.

(Photo by Irwin R. Daugherty)

CHAPTER SIX

Baseball

I n their coverage of high school and college athletics, daily newspapers devote the most space to football and basketball. Baseball rates a strong third, according to a random survey of the country's sports editors.

High school and American Legion baseball receive good fan support, particularly in those communities with strong programs. Perennial college baseball powers such as Miami, Arizona State, and Texas regularly play before crowds that make owners of many minor league franchises envious.

Arizona State, which has qualified for the College World Series (CWS) in Omaha fifteen times since 1964, has played before more than 13,800 fans in ten of its games there. But the Sun Devils do not have to play in a national tournament to draw big crowds; they attract nearly 8,000 to significant home games and they once played before 21,000 in an exhibition in Japan. Each year, nearly a quarter-million people watch Arizona State. Not surprisingly, the Sun Devils receive extensive coverage.

The University of Texas at Austin also receives considerable attention. The *Austin American-Statesman* and the *Daily Texan*, the student newspaper at the university, regularly staff Longhorn games. The *Dallas Morning News* also keeps readers abreast of the team.

Steve Campbell, while a college student, helped the *Daily Texan* cover Longhorn baseball and earned a summer internship at the *Dallas Morning News*. His background paid off: He was assigned to cover the College World Series and to key on the University of Texas. Not many college student interns receive that kind of opportunity. "I took a lot of background on the Texas team with me to Omaha," Campbell said. "I knew the team pretty well. So I worked hard to get a line on the other seven teams that qualified." Campbell scoured brochures of the other entries and reviewed Texas statistics. He had learned early in his career the importance of preparation.

The Texas writer takes pride in developing interesting, informative leads. Because many sports page readers already have heard the score of a game on radio or television, Campbell likes to use delayed leads. "I think newspapers might just as well run a wire story if they want only a summary lead," Campbell said. "Why should a newspaper spend money to send a reporter to a game if he is going to merely write a straight summary lead?"

Campbell has found that the more experience he gets covering baseball, the easier it is for him to write accurately, comprehensively, and quickly. "At the College World Series, I sometimes had less than 30 minutes after a game to file my stories," he said. "It was frantic. I would go through ten or fifteen tentative leads during the course of the game. I had to act fast once the game was over."

Campbell's sound statistical background and his knowledge of Texas and the other CWS entries helped him to write his stories on deadline. It takes skill to weave significant statistics into a narrative account without ruining the pace of the writing. "I think it is important for the writer to decide which statistics are most important," Campbell said. "Baseball is a game of numbers, but numbers turn a lot of readers off. I try to include only the most important statistics in my stories."

Indeed, reporters should tell what happened at a game—that is most important—while subtly working in the statistics that are most significant.

The Scoring

Baseball teams produce enough statistics to swallow sportswriters. Statistics "junkies" thrive on baseball. The statistical cornerstone for hitters is their batting average; the magic number for pitchers is their win-loss record.

In addition to batting averages, which are computed by dividing the number of hits by the number of official at bats, the following statistics are relevant to hitters:

- Batting averages against left-handed pitchers.
- Batting averages against right-handed pitchers.
- Runs scored.
- Runs batted in (RBI).
- Game-winning runs batted in.
- Doubles.
- Triples.
- Home runs.
- Total bases.
- Walks.
- Strikeouts.

- Stolen bases.
- Sacrifices.
- Sacrifice flies.

For fielders, put outs, assists, and errors are important statistics. The number of double plays turned is a significant team statistic. For pitchers, in addition to won-lost record, the following statistics are important:

- Games appeared in.
- Games started.
- Games completed.
- Games saved.
- Innings pitched.
- Hits surrendered.
- Earned runs surrendered.
- Earned run average (ERA).
- Walks given up.
- Strikeouts.
- Wild pitches.
- Hit batters.
- Runners allowed on base per inning.

Before writers cover a baseball game, they should review significant team and individual statistics. As emphasized in the chapters on football and basketball, sound preparation is the key to effective coverage.

When covering high school or American Legion contests, reporters should check with each team for copies of their season statistics. Newspaper clippings of previous games should be reviewed when possible. Sports information offices generally keep the media informed about college teams.

When Arizona State qualifies for the College World Series, the ASU sports information office routinely sends the following information to the media (in addition to complete statistics):

- An overview of the season (winning and losing streaks).
- ASU's record in the College World Series.
- National rankings.
- Overview of ASU's first-round opponent.
- ASU's record against other CWS entries.
- Number of players returning to ASU who were on previous CWS teams.
- Tentative Sun Devil lineup (one when facing left-handed pitchers; another when facing right-handed pitchers).
- Tentative starting pitchers.

Figure 6.1

Box Score of the Texas-Alabama CWS Championship Game

TEXAS	ab	r	h	bi	ALABAMA	ab	r	h	bi
Botes 2b	5	0	1	0	Elbin 3b	3	0	0	1
Brumley ss	5	1	3	0	McClendn dh	4	0	1	0
Killingswth dh	4	2	2	1	Magadan 1b	4	1	2	0
Tolentino 1b	5	1	2	1	Skates lf	4	0	0	0
Hearron c	3	0	0	0	Stallings cf	4	0	2	1
Labay rf	3	0	1	1	Velleggia c	4	0	0	0
Suttan lf	3	0	0	1	Lake 2b	4	0	0	0
Trent cf	3	0	0	0	Smithey rf	3	1	2	1
Burrows 3b	3	0	1	0	Shipley ss	3	1	0	0
TOTALS	**34**	**4**	**10**	**4**	**TOTALS**	**33**	**3**	**7**	**3**

Texas	000	002	200-4
Alabama	001	010	001-3

Game winning RBI–Killingsworth.
E–Hearron. LOB–Texas 9; Alabama 4, DP–Alabama 1.
2B–Burrows, Magadan. 3B–Killingsworth. HR–Smithey (5).
SB–Trent (14). S–Sutton. SF–Elbin.

	IP	H	R	ER	BB	SO
Texas						
Clemens W, 13-5	9	7	3	3	0	9
Alabama						
Browne L, 11-2	7²⁄₃	8	4	4	3	8
Brauchie	1¹⁄₃	2	0	0	0	0

HBP–Trent by Browne, Hearron by Browne. WP–Clemens 2.
T–2:20. A–14,957.

Newspapers generally publish baseball game stories with either a complete box score (see figure 6.1) or a bare linescore summary (see appendix). The complete box score of a Texas-Alabama game is shown in figure 6.1.

Writing Game Stories

When Campbell covered Texas in the College World Series the Longhorns opened against tournament newcomer James Madison in a late afternoon contest. Longhorn fans who had listened to the radio or had watched television would have known the score before they opened their morning papers. Thus, Campbell used an anecdotal lead to begin his story for the *Morning News:*

OMAHA, Neb.—Calvin Schiraldi has carried the nickname "The Nibbler" for three years, and it's killing hitters.

They wait for Schiraldi to get too cute, to try to pinpoint every pitch. They wait for the Texas pitcher to make mistakes and beat himself, as he sometimes used to do.

They wait. And wait. For nothing.

Schiraldi gave James Madison nothing to wait on in the first round of the College World Series Friday night, throwing a 5-hitter to help No. 1 Texas take a 12-0 victory at Rosenblatt Stadium before 9,000.

Campbell effectively used the Schiraldi anecdote to draw readers into the story. Then the writer jammed essential facts into the fourth paragraph: the winner; the score; where the game was played; the size of the crowd; and that Schiraldi allowed just five hits.

Before moving to play-by-play of key innings, Campbell gave his readers information on upcoming tournament games, direct quotations, and key statistical information. Campbell wrote:

The Longhorns (62-14) will play Oklahoma State (48-14) at 7:10 P.M. Monday. Oklahoma State defeated Stanford (40-16-1), 3-1, in Friday's second game.

"We came out tight and didn't swing the bat well early," Texas coach Cliff Gustafson said. "Schiraldi's pitching and our defense kept us in the game early. I thought Schiraldi was outstanding."

Of course, Schiraldi really didn't have to be. Mike Trent of Dallas Samuell (3-for-4) tied a CWS record by scoring four runs, and the Longhorns banged out 16 hits to break up what started out as a close game. The Dukes (37-12) still had a chance until Texas broke loose for eight runs in the eighth inning.

"I wouldn't say we outclassed them," said Schiraldi (13-2), who walked two and struck out five for his fifth shutout. "It's their first time here (in the CWS), and they were nervous. I was a little nervous early."

The Longhorns didn't do much with the bats early—except watch. In the first four innings, Dukes lefthander Justin Gannon (6-2) struck out six. Five were on called third strikes.

Note how Campbell effectively worked statistics into the game account. He mentioned Trent's record-tying performance, provided the season record for James Madison, noted the eight-run outburst by the Longhorns, gave Schiraldi's pitching record, and told that the James Madison pitcher fanned batters for half the outs in the first four innings.

Campbell used a staccato lead, combined with background information, when he reported the second-round Texas victory over Oklahoma State:

OMAHA, Neb.—Strange ending, strange game. No. 1 ranked Texas vs. No. 3 Oklahoma State, 11 innings. Five errors, many wasted opportunities.

It figures. When the Longhorns and the Cowboys met in the College World Series two years ago, the game lasted 13 innings and ended at 1:38 A.M. This one ended just after 11 P.M., but it was just as crazy.

The game-winning hit came from a guy with 58 at-bats and a .207 average coming into the game. He was in only because the one who plays ahead of him had been replaced by a pinch-hitter three innings earlier.

On a night like Monday, it came down to reserve third baseman Jamie Doughty's 2-out double to right-center to score Mike Trent of Samuell High School with the winning run in a 6-5 victory over Oklahoma State.

What is amazing is how the Longhorns (63-14) ever allowed the game to reach that point. Thanks to four errors, three of which led to two costly unearned runs, Texas wasted an 8⅔-inning, 12-strikeout performance by starting pitcher Roger Clemens. Kirk Killingsworth of Plano (12-3) finished up the last 2⅓ innings for the victory, but he didn't pitch nearly as well.

That's the kind of night it was. And because of it, the Longhorns advance to play the winner of the Michigan-Alabama game (Tuesday, 7:10 P.M.) Thursday at 7:10 P.M. in the winner's bracket of the series.

"We made some mistakes that could have really hurt us," Texas coach Cliff Gustafson said. "Roger did a tremendous job, and if he had had a little support, he would have come out much better."

The game account concluded with description of key plays and more direct quotations.

Campbell focused on pitcher Schiraldi again in his story of the third Texas game in the series. This was the crucial winner's bracket contest that matched the tournament's only two unbeaten teams. Campbell delayed telling readers the score until the second paragraph:

OMAHA, Neb.—The dark side for the Texas Longhorns: Calvin Schiraldi, the team's top starting pitcher, was fortunate to last five innings against Alabama Thursday night.

The bright side for the Longhorns: Schiraldi pitched the last 5⅓ innings and nailed down a 10-inning, 6-4 victory in a College World Series game halted by two rain delays that totaled 62 minutes.

Schiraldi was responsible for letting the game go into extra innings— both on the plus and minus side for Texas. He carried a 4-3 lead into the eighth inning, which disappeared when David Magadan hit a solo homer to left that tied the score. But when Magadan came up with two on and two out in the bottom of the ninth, Schiraldi came through with a strikeout—his 8th of 11 on the night.

"I was just rearing back and throwing as hard as I could," Schiraldi said. "The ball tailed away from him (Magadan) and jumped up. I've never thrown as hard as I did tonight."

After the lead block of paragraphs, Campbell provided statistical specifics and details of the top-of-the-10th scoring by Texas:

> An RBI double by Bill Bates and a run-scoring single by Mike Brumley in the top of the 10th gave Schiraldi his 14th victory in 16 decisions. The victory also assures Texas (64-14) of a spot in the final. The Longhorns will play Michigan at 8:10 P.M. Friday. Alabama (45-10) will play Arizona State at 5:10 P.M.

Campbell could have led just as easily with the 10th-inning scoring. Certainly, it would have been appropriate to emphasize that in the first paragraph. Campbell closed his story with more direct quotations and some statistical highlights. Again, the writer showed he had done his homework; he noted that Texas cleanup batter Jose Tolentino, who was struggling through a 1-for-10 CWS batting slump, notched his 72nd RBI, which tied the school record set in 1974.

In his coverage of the fourth Texas game of the series, Campbell again delayed the score; this time he presented it in the third paragraph. His staccato lead was crisp:

> OMAHA, Neb.—Mike Capel pitched. The Texas Longhorns got him enough runs. The two always go together. Never fails.
>
> Friday night at Rosenblatt Stadium, the Longhorns' hitting didn't have to be all that hot. Their offense amounted to a fifth-inning grand slam by shortstop Mike Brumley, and that was plenty.
>
> Capel did the rest, shutting down Michigan on four hits to give Texas a 4-2 victory before 13,031 in the College World Series.
>
> The Longhorns (65-14) can win their first national title since 1975 with a victory over Alabama (46-10) at 7:10 P.M. Saturday. An Alabama victory would force a second game 7:10 P.M. Sunday.
>
> The Crimson Tide earned its way into the final with a 6-0 victory over Arizona State earlier Friday.
>
> "I think our chances are better with two shots than with one," Texas coach Cliff Gustafson said. "I don't think that we'll have much trouble getting up for the game tomorrow. The fact that a national championship is on the line should be enough. I just hope we don't get too keyed up."

After giving readers the score of the Texas-Michigan game, Campbell devoted most of the first half of his story to the upcoming championship contest. It was not until the second half of his story that he returned to details of the Texas-Michigan encounter.

In the first three paragraphs of his account of the series' title game, Campbell gave readers the score and made reference to a pair of rallies. He then turned to an overview of the series, plugged in more specifics on the championship game, inserted some direct quotations, and closed with statistical highlights.

The beginning of Campbell's story:

> OMAHA, Neb.—The Texas Longhorns, who defeated Alabama, 4-3, Saturday night to win the College World Series, couldn't have done it the easy way. That would have been—well—too simple.
>
> And that wouldn't have been the Longhorns' style.
>
> This time, it took a pair of 2-run rallies to give Texas a come-from-behind victory over Alabama at Rosenblatt Stadium before 14,957.
>
> "Nothing to it," Longhorn coach Cliff Gustafson joked after winning his second national championship in 11 tries at the CWS. "We waltzed right through it."
>
> That Texas did—on paper. The victory gave the Longhorns (66-14) their fourth national title and made them the third team in the last 10 years to go through the CWS undefeated.
>
> But it was anything but a waltz. Two of the Longhorns' five victories in the series came in extra innings, and this one wasn't over until Longhorns starter Roger Clemens got out of a ninth-inning jam, in which Alabama (46-11) had the tying run on base.
>
> The Crimson Tide's David Magadan doubled and scored on Allan Stallings' single to cut the lead to 4-3, but Clemens retired Frank Velleggia and Fermin Lake to end the game. Clemens struck out nine and walked none for the Longhorns, who had a 2.25 ERA in the CWS.
>
> "Truthfully, the talent on this ballclub isn't as good as some of the talent we've had on other ballclubs," said Gustafson, whose 1975 team won the national championship. "That's what makes this one so sweet. This is a bigger thrill than the 1975 club, just because of the talent. The pitching has been the key to our ballclub all year."

Campbell, writing for a Texas newspaper, chose to emphasize the Longhorns' tradition and their knack for winning close ballgames despite not having the talent of previous squads. He waited until the end of his story to describe the winning rally in the top of the seventh. The fourth—and crucial—Texas run crossed the plate in that inning when one of the slowest Texas players, Jose Tolentino, beat out a bunt to score a runner from third base.

Steve Sinclair, sportswriter for the *Omaha World-Herald,* chose to lead with the Tolentino bunt. This shows that there often are several potential leads for a baseball story. The important thing is to fully develop the lead. Sinclair's lead paragraphs flowed nicely:

> Nobody at Rosenblatt Stadium knew what Jose Tolentino had on his mind but Jose Tolentino.
> Alabama's players were caught by surprise. Texas' players were caught by surprise. Texas coach Cliff Gustafson said he'd like to take some credit but he didn't have anything to do with it.
> "Jose did it on his own," Gustafson said. "I was just as surprised as they were."
> Tolentino's surprise was a drag bunt in the seventh inning. It knocked in what proved to be the decisive run in Texas' 4-3 victory over Alabama in the College World Series championship game Saturday night before a crowd of 14,957.
> The Series attendance of 115,700 set a record for a nine-session CWS.
> Texas went undefeated in the five tournament games to win its fourth national championship.

Clearly, statistics add specificity and detail to baseball game stories. But good writers never strangle readers with the statistics that pour from every game. Instead, they search for ways to carefully blend the statistics with anecdotes, key plays, and direct quotations.

Exercises

1. Discuss coverage given to college, high school, or American Legion baseball in area newspapers. Do some newspapers provide better coverage than others? What makes their coverage better?

2. Invite to class your school's baseball coach. How does the coach rate the quantity and quality of coverage given to baseball by area dailies? Does the coach have suggestions for improvement?

3. Write a ten-paragraph baseball game story based only on statistics supplied to you by the sports information office or from a box score clipped from an area daily.

4. Cover a baseball game. Be sure to write a complete account by using statistics and interviews with coaches and players.

Some college golf stars hone their games as
they prepare for the professional tour.

(Photo by T. J. Sokol)

CHAPTER SEVEN

Golf

More high schools and colleges are fielding golf teams than ever before. Competition in district, state, and national tournaments is becoming more spirited. Bruce Farris, who covers golf for the *Fresno* (Calif.) *Bee*, has noticed. Instead of concentrating on "major" sports, many students choose to play golf. "Some of them were good football players who happened to take up golf and then stayed with it," Farris said.

The nation's golf courses are luring more weekend players, too. These players also are newspaper readers who like to keep up with their favorite golfers—amateur and professional. During the past decade, many daily newspapers have responded to the increasing interest in golf by providing more extensive coverage of professional tournaments as well as men's and women's prep and college meets.

Golf is a challenging, but enjoyable, sport to cover. Farris likes to focus on individuals. "There is a story in each player," he said. "Whether the player is good or not, you can always find something interesting. But you must ask them. Did they have a brother or a father who played? How did they get started? You quickly discover that statistics don't make very interesting reading. Statistics are important in golf, but I like to concentrate on the players."

Farris, who regularly covers the NCAA championships, spends much of his time at golf tournaments "walking around talking to coaches, competitors, and fans." Farris said there are "some very fascinating individual stories just waiting to be told."

The *Fresno Bee* reporter works hard to develop individual angles. "Some golfers are reluctant to talk," he said. "But I don't give up on them. Other golfers are very outgoing and eager to talk." Farris cautions, though, that reporters should not try to talk to golfers while they are playing. The time for interviewing is before and after competition.

Preparation and attention to detail are keys to effective golf coverage. For example, the reporter should note:

- *The lay of the course.* Is it long (the number of yards)? Is it hilly? Is it flat? Are there a lot of trees? Are the fairways wide? Are the fairways narrow? Are there a lot of sand traps or "bunkers" as the professionals call them? Does the course favor long hitters? Does the course place a premium on precise approach shots? Are there a lot of water hazards?
- *The condition of the course.* Are the fairways lush and green? Are they wet? Has the rough been mowed? Are the greens fast?
- *The weather conditions.* Is it windy? Is it humid? Is it chilly? Is it raining? Is it sunny and calm?

All these factors will influence the quality of play. The reporter should also consider:

- *Scores on the front and back nines.* Did golfers shoot lower scores on the first 9 holes of an 18-hole course or on the second 9 holes? Were scores for most players consistent on the front and back nines?
- *Particularly difficult holes.* Were scores high on any single holes? For example, were scores consistently above par on the par-4, 423-yard eighth hole? Why?
- *Particularly easy holes.* Was there an unusually high percentage of birdies on the par-3, 132-yard 5th hole?
- *The play of the leaders.* Who was putting particularly well? Who was consistent? Who was erratic?
- *The "surprise" players.* Were there golfers who did not play as well as expected? Were there golfers who played better than expected?

The Scoring

Consideration of the above factors will add detail to coverage of a dual meet or tournament, but golf still is a sport of numbers—a game of pars, bogeys, double bogeys, birdies, eagles, and possibly even double eagles. Most high school and college meets are *medal* or *stroke* play. Individuals, and teams, with *lowest* scores win. Generally, five golfers constitute a team. Scores of the top four players are added to determine the team total for a given round of 18 holes. If it is a 36-, 54-, or 72-hole tournament, the team scores for each day are added for the final total.

Match play is not as common as medal play. In match play, golfers compete head-to-head to win holes. For example, if John Jones shoots par on the first hole but Jim Smith shoots bogey, Jones wins the hole. If Jones defeats Smith two-up, that means Jones won two more holes than Smith in 18-hole competition. If Jones defeats Smith one-up in 19, that means that the golfers were tied after 18, but Jones won the 19th (extra) hole. If Jones defeats Smith two and one, that means that Jones won with a 2-hole lead after the 17th hole. Since Smith had no chance of winning the match, the final hole was not played.

Excellent golfers shoot par or below par consistently. Par is established for each of the 18 holes. Par 4s are most common on most courses, with about an equal number of par 3s and par 5s. Par for most 18-hole courses is 71, 72, or 73.

In coverage of golf, *par* is the cornerstone reference: John Jones shot a 3-under-par 68 to capture the tournament crown, or John Jones, hindered by three out-of-bounds shots on the back nine, finished with a four-over-par 75. Other common terms: *birdie* (one stroke under par; for example, a 3 on a par-4 hole); *eagle* (two strokes under par; for example, a 2 on a par-4 hole); *bogey* (one stroke over par; for example, a 5 on a par-4 hole); and *double bogey* (two strokes over par; for example, a 6 on a par-4 hole).

Lists showing individual and team leaders normally accompany coverage of high school and college tournaments. The list of individuals shows scores for each 18-hole round (separated by hyphens) and a final total. The summary for the top ten individuals when the NCAA Division 1 golf championships were held in Fresno, California, follows:

x-Jim Carter, ASU	75-68-72-72—287
Scott Verplank, Okla. St.	72-69-74-72—287
Paul Thomas, Texas	73-68-74-72—287
Doug Harper, Fresno St.	69-71-74-73—287
Bill Tuten, Houston	73-71-70-74—288
Brad Faxon, Furman	74-68-69-77—288
Peter Persons, Georgia	72-71-73-72—288
Sam Randolph, USC	72-69-74-74—289
Mark Brooks, Texas	74-72-74-70—290
Andrew Magee, Okla.	73-72-74-71—290
x—won on first hole playoff	

The list of team scores also is published. The team standings:

Oklahoma State	1,161
Texas	1,168
Houston	1,170

Ohio State	1,173
Clemson	1,176
Georgia	1,179
UCLA	1,181
North Carolina	1,185
Oklahoma	1,185
Brigham Young	1,186
Texas A&M	1,186
Fresno State	1,189
Missouri	1,193
Wake Forest	1,193
Pacific	1,197

Writing Meet Stories

Farris provided extensive coverage of the NCAA tournament for the *Fresno Bee* when it was held in that California city. In addition to features, he wrote a main tournament story for each of the four days of competition. His statistics were supported with direct quotations and anecdotes. The *Bee* sportswriter did not have to scratch for a lead at the end of the first 18 holes of play: host Fresno State was the unexpected pacesetter. Farris began his story:

> What will happen today when Fresno State University's golf team wakes up to the fact that it leads the 86th annual NCAA Championships at San Joaquin Country Club is anyone's guess.
>
> For now, Coach Mike Watney's team can savor another vintage moment in this banner FSU sports year.
>
> Jay Delsing of UCLA and Greg Garde of Florida State University lead the individual standings with 4-under-par 68s, one better than FSU sophomore Doug Harper.
>
> FSU held a one-stroke lead over Pac-10 champion UCLA and was two ahead of North Carolina. FSU wasn't ranked in the top 20 of the 32 teams playing in the grueling 72-hole test this week.
>
> Action today will start again at 7:30 A.M., with Oklahoma State, Georgia and Texas first off the No. 1 tee.

With basic information tucked into the lead block of paragraphs, Farris used a transition sentence that focused on the weather to discuss the hot-shooting Fresno State team:

> Wednesday was much more pleasant than either Monday or Tuesday, when sticky, humid conditions prevailed during practice rounds. It was

especially nice for the Bulldogs, who grabbed the NCAA golf lead for the first time in the school's history. FSU will have all night and morning to savor it before teeing off in today's second round at 12:30 P.M.

Waiting is nothing new, since the Bulldogs had to wait nearly five hours before they were sure they actually led.

The Bulldogs went off in the morning wave and were finished before the last of the afternoon group teed off.

Junior Eric Peterson shot a steady, par-72, John Erickson bogeyed the last three holes but finished with a 1-over-73 and senior Jim Plotkin shot a 75. The fifth member, junior Jim Hamilton, shot a non-counting 78. The high score on each team is thrown out daily.

FSU was 3-under-par with three holes to play, but stumbled a bit.

Nevertheless, the Bulldogs find themselves seven ahead of pre-tournament favorite Oklahoma State and four ahead of defending champion Houston.

In the next block of paragraphs, Farris put the spotlight on quotations from the FSU coach and from individual star Harper:

"We played a good, solid round," Watney said. "We staggered a bit at the finish, but a lot of teams did that. I'm just pleased to have a good round at the start. I think the big thing was we stayed away from disaster. It will be interesting to see how we handle leading the NCAA."

Harper believed it was his best round of the year. He had three birdies and no bogeys.

Three hours before the final team finished, Harper was back at the movie theater where he works.

"I was in a hole in my drive on 18, and all I could do was punch it out on the fairway. I still got a par," said the 20-year-old sophomore, a native of Los Angeles.

Harper, the best putter on the Bulldog squad, sank birdie putts of 30 feet on No. 5, 20 feet on No. 7 and seven feet on No. 14. He lipped out a 12-footer on the 10th hole and an eight-footer on the 17th.

In the above paragraphs, Farris adroitly mixed the statistical details of Harper's putting with direct quotations and the reference to the golfer going to work at a theater. Farris followed his own advice: When covering golf, talk to the players—find out what makes them unique as individuals.

Farris closed his opening round story with direct quotations from other Fresno State players and from UCLA's Delsing, the individual leader.

During the second round of play, Oklahoma State soared into the team lead and Fresno State's Harper moved into the No. 1 individual's spot. Again, the lead block of paragraphs by Farris centered on team and individual leaders:

Oklahoma State's Cowboys went on a birdie binge Thursday to take over the top rung at the halfway mark of the 86th annual NCAA Golf Championships at San Joaquin Country Club.

Coach Mike Holder's pre-tournament favorites are 1-up on North Carolina's steady Tar Heels after a team 4-under-par 284 and a 580 total.

While first-round leader Fresno State dropped to fourth place in the team standings, Bulldog sophomore Doug Harper held onto the individual lead, also by one stroke with a 69-71—140.

There is a five-way logjam at 141 with Scott Verplank of Oklahoma State, Paul Thomas of Texas, Jay Delsing of UCLA, Jeff Wilson of University of Pacific and Sam Randolph of USC.

UCLA is four shots behind the Cowboys in third place with Fresno another two back at 586. Rounding out the top five is UOP, another Pacific Coast Athletic Association team, tied with Oklahoma at 588.

"The first day we were trying to keep from losing instead of trying to win," said Holder, whose team finished second to Houston in the 1982 NCAA. "I think the boys were frustrated and disappointed after the first day (the Cowboys trailed Fresno by seven), and I told them we would have to play more aggressively instead of trying to aim the ball for a spot on the fairway.

"We had to get rid of the negative thoughts and the other teams and just play golf one shot at a time. I was encouraged by what we did. The first round is the toughest, but the second day is very important, a pivotal round."

In the next block of paragraphs, Farris spelled out precisely how Oklahoma State grabbed the lead. He provided details on front-and back-nine scores and on the hot-putting Cowboys:

The Cowboys cruised along not creating much excitement on the first nine, making the turn at 5-over. However, on the back, the Cowboys shifted into high gear and shot 9-under-par.

Willie Wood, who had first-round 78 and was 3-over on the first nine Thursday, turned it around with a 33 second nine and a 71.

Wood had only 10 putts on the second nine, but even that took second to freshman teammate Verplank, who took 24 putts in a sparkling 3-under 69.

The final block of paragraphs focused on the Fresno State star, Harper. Farris wrote:

Harper, who will have to be excused from his usher's job at UA Cinema tonight, had some scary moments on the first nine (he teed off on 10) but steadied for a 1-under-35 on the front side.

"I've been playing real well for the past week, so I'm not really surprised, but I was a little nervous at the start today," Harper said. "I made a bogey on 10, almost made one on 12 and then I rolled in 12-foot putts on 15 and 16 for birdies."

Harper made a bogey from a bunker on 17.

His second nine was a rock-steady eight pars and a 12-foot birdie on the par-5, water-protected sixth.

Harper said, "I don't think playing San Joaquin is a big advantage for me because it plays differently with the tighter fairways and faster greens than when we practiced."

Harper worked a 5:30 to 11:30 P.M. shift at the theater Wednesday after shooting his 69 and was scheduled for the same tonight. However, the Bulldogs will be going off late, and he will have to make different arrangements.

For his coverage of the third round, Farris led with specifics on the team leader before moving to the race for the individual crown:

Oklahoma State coach Mike Holder figures playing defending champion Houston one round with a 5-shot spot is pretty good odds even if it's for the 86th annual NCAA Golf Championships.

On the other hand, Houston's venerable mentor Dave Williams is just happy to be that close going into the windup of the 72-hole event on the San Joaquin Country Club.

The Cougars shot the low round of the day Friday at 285 to gain five shots on the Cowboys, who lost a few to the wind on the final five holes.

Host Fresno State is seventh but only four shots behind third-place UCLA.

Brad Faxton of Furman, who went into the tournament as one of the favorites, took over the individual lead with a 3-under-par 69 and a two-round total of 5-under 211.

Fresno sophomore Doug Harper started the day with a 1-stroke lead, shot a 2-over-par 74 and dropped into a three-way tie for second at 214. Bill Tuten of Houston, who had a 70, and Trevor Dodds of Lamar University at Beaumont, Texas, who had the low round of the tournament with a 5-under-par 67, also are at 214.

In the next block of paragraphs, Farris focused on Oklahoma State, telling how the wind bothered the Cowboys during the final 5 holes. Farris quoted several of the individual leaders, including Fresno State's Harper, "who drew the biggest gallery of the tournament" and who "was probably more nervous than in the first two rounds."

Farris had multiple elements to work into the lead of his final tournament story: Oklahoma State won and Arizona State's Jim Carter won a playoff to capture the individual crown. In the first four paragraphs, Farris provided the essentials:

> Oklahoma State Coach Mike Holder has a way to go to catch Dave Williams of Houston, but he's working hard at it.
> Holder's Cowboys never looked back Saturday in winning their fifth NCAA Golf Championship at the San Joaquin Country Club. It also was the fourth in Holder's 10-year stay at Stillwater, putting him 10 behind Williams in total wins. The margin was seven strokes over fast-closing University of Texas, nine over third place Houston.
> The individual title was something else. Jim Carter of Arizona State survived a four-way, one-hole playoff with a par to become the first-ever Sun Devil NCAA champion.
> In the playoff, Carter defeated Fresno State's deadly putting sophomore Doug Harper, Paul Thomas of Texas and freshman sensation Scott Verplank of Oklahoma State. Each had finished at 1-under-par 287.

In the next block of paragraphs, Farris gave details of Oklahoma State individuals and direct quotations from their coach. Farris wrote:

> "For the coach and players the NCAA is a survival pit," said an elated Holder, who finished second to Houston a year ago. "I'm physically and emotionally drained. As a coach, you're on an emotional treadmill."
> What did he tell his players before the round?
> "I told them not to look right, left or back, just go out and shoot par," he said. "We were doing even a little better than that, but we threw away a few shots on the last four holes. But I think we played better than at any time this week."

Farris also gave hometown readers specifics on Harper's performance:

> FSU's Harper was the first of the individual leaders to finish, treating a gallery of some 500 to an exciting 1-over-par 73.
> "Exciting" because he hit the water three times (drives on No.1, No. 12 and No. 16) for bogeys. "Exciting" because he drained birdie putts of 40 feet on No. 2, 8 feet on No. 6, 25 feet on No. 7 and 50 feet on No. 17. And he narrowly missed a birdie at 18 that would have given him the title.

In the final paragraphs of the story, Farris described the playoff action vividly. This excerpt is illustrative of the detail Farris provided:

Harper hit a 9-iron but caught a flyer out of the Bermuda—a common occurrence for many players during the week. The ball hit a spectator and bounced down the hill in back of the green, into the rough.

Clearly, Farris has a knack for mixing detail with the human dimension.

Exercises

1. Discuss coverage given to college, high school, and amateur golf in area newspapers. Do some newspapers provide better coverage than others? What makes their coverage better?

2. Invite your school's golf coach and an area sportswriter known for good golf coverage to class. Do they have tips to improve coverage of golf?

3. Cover an area golf tournament. Write both A.M. and P.M. versions of the story. Compare the stories to those published in area newspapers.

Gymnastics meets are receiving more coverage in the country's newspapers.

(Photo by Irwin R. Daugherty)

CHAPTER EIGHT

Gymnastics

Gymnastics receives good coverage from daily newspapers in those areas where the sport is popular. Interest in gymnastics probably never has been greater on the international level. Still, many colleges, universities, and high schools have dropped it in recent years.

Steve Sinclair, a sportswriter for the *Omaha* (Neb.) *World-Herald*, interviewed Jerry Miles, who was director of the National Collegiate Athletic Association's men's gymnastics championships when the competition was held at the University of Nebraska in Lincoln. Miles told Sinclair that NCAA officials were concerned about the future of the sport. "It's a major, major concern because schools are dropping (it). Much of it goes back to economics," Miles said.

Often, when a college or university drops gymnastics it has nothing to do with the excellence of the program. Rather, it is in reaction to a strained budget. When colleges and universities drop programs, there is a domino effect down to high schools.

Despite the fact that gymnastics has been dropped from some college and high school programs, many newspapers, such as the *World-Herald*, provide extensive coverage of the sport. *World-Herald* reporters understand gymnastics and thus are able to cover it more effectively. *World-Herald* sports editor Michael Kelly said that his newspaper's coverage of gymnastics "definitely is influenced by Nebraska's dynasty" in university competition.

"Gymnastics is one of those minor sports that, I think, always has been kind of mysterious to sports fans," Kelly said. "One thing that used to bother me about gymnastics coverage was that our stories would say Nebraska won 281.5 to 280.5. Most readers would have no idea what that score meant—except that Nebraska had more points. The stories contained no frame of reference. The score meant that Nebraska accumulated 281.5

points out of a possible 300. One thing that we do—and I think it helps the reader—is give the final raw score and put it in perspective by saying Nebraska averaged 9.38 per routine out of a possible 10.''

Kelly said it is ''refreshing'' to cover gymnastics because it is a sport that often does not command major media attention. Therefore coaches and athletes are often eager to cooperate with the press.

The *World-Herald* sports editor said it is important for reporters to read as much as they can about gymnastics before covering it. ''Gymnastics is not difficult to understand after you go to two or three meets,'' Kelly said. ''Basically, the scoring system is one of deduction. Gymnastics has a very unforgiving scoring formula. Unlike in football, where a player can fumble the ball but get it back and score a touchdown, the gymnast pretty much has had it if he makes a mistake during a routine. I think it is a very exciting sport to watch and to report. One of the benefits from the standpoint of the fans is that each routine is over in maybe 45 seconds and you get the score right away.''

Kelly instructs his reporters to talk to coaches and athletes after a meet. ''I think it is important to work a lot of quotes into a story,'' Kelly said. ''Writers should take the mystery away from gymnastics. Gymnasts are athletes just like football and basketball players. They have the same pressures—maybe more because gymnastics is an individual sport. Once a competitor is on the high bar, he definitely is on his own. There is no one to help him. I try to emphasize that, too. Gymnasts always are rooting for each other.''

World-Herald sports reporters do not get bogged down with numbers early in their stories about gymnastics meets. ''There are a few readers who are real experts,'' said Kelly. ''They are going to read all the numbers and technical terms. But you need to write for the guy who is picking up the paper and saying, 'What is this all about?' We want the subscriber to read something he or she might not ordinarily read. If you can grab the reader at the beginning of the story with a good human angle, you can hook him into the story and make him read all the way to the end.''

The Scoring

A gymnast may be scored by two or four judges. When four judges are used, the high and low scores are disregarded and the middle scores are averaged. If two judges are used, the scores are averaged. Judges score a routine or exercise by totaling points from four areas for a maximum of 10.0.

Individual scoring is computed from the following:

- ▪ *Execution.* This is worth a maximum 4.4 points. Judges evaluate the gymnast's form—whether his or her legs are together and straight. Judges also evaluate a gymnast's rhythm, smoothness, and technical execution.
- ▪ *Combination.* This is worth a maximum of 1.6 points. Judges evaluate whether each movement in the exercise or routine contributes to the total exercise.
- ▪ *Difficulty.* This is worth a maximum of 3.4 points. Judges evaluate the level of difficulty of the routine. The more difficult, the higher the point total.
- ▪ *Risk, originality, and virtuosity (known as ROV).* Each is worth .2 for a maximum total of .6. Judges determine whether the gymnast displays ROV. Risk is shown by performing difficult movements in which the chance of a fall is heightened; originality is when the gymnast performs moves that are unique and unusual; virtuosity means the moves are performed at the highest level of excellence.

Men's competition in college includes six events: floor exercise; pommel horse; long horse vaulting; still rings; parallel bars; and horizontal bar. The top five individual scores for each team in an event is 50 points (maximum of 10.0 for each of the top five individuals). For example, if individual scores for team members in the floor exercise are 9.5, 9.5, 9.6, 9.3, and 9.7, the team total is 47.6. Maximum team score for six events is 300. Any university that can score more than 275 is very competitive.

The four women's events are side horse vaulting, balance beam, uneven parallel bars, and floor exercise. Maximum team total in women's competition is 200 points.

Writing Meet Stories

Few daily newspapers cover gymnastics as extensively as the *World-Herald*. After the Nebraska Cornhuskers captured a fourth consecutive national championship, the *World-Herald* carried a lead story jammed with statistics and direct quotations, a sidebar feature on an individual Husker champion, a feature on an unexpected Nebraska individual victory in the parallel bar competition, and a column by sports editor Kelly that contained analysis and observation.

Coverage of gymnastics comes alive when there is a blend of quotations and statistics. This is apparent when examining the main meet story written by Sinclair. His lead focused on two items of primary significance: the individual effort of All-American Jim Hartung and the record-tying fourth consecutive national crown won by Nebraska. Also mentioned high in the story was that Nebraska had broken its NCAA record team point total. Sinclair wrote:

> LINCOLN—The Jim Hartung era in Nebraska gymnastics ended as it began.
>
> The Cornhuskers' story in Hartung's four years has been: One, two, three, four times a champion.
>
> The Huskers wrapped up their record-tying fourth NCAA championship Saturday before a crowd of 8,715 at the Bob Devaney Sports Center. Once again the Cornhusker leader was Hartung.
>
> "I'd say if we had a dynasty, it just graduated," said Nebraska Coach Francis Allen. "Now we can start worrying about coaching theories. Our dynasty is graduated."
>
> Allen's reference was to Hartung and the role he has played in establishing Nebraska as the top team ever in college gymnastics.
>
> "He didn't do it by himself, but he was awfully influential," Allen said. "Because we got him, we got Phil Cahoy. Then we got Scott Johnson and Jim Mikus. It was just a snowball effect. He was the little center. He was the little snow granule we started with."
>
> Hartung, Cahoy, Mikus and Johnson were the power behind Nebraska's winning performance. It was a smash.
>
> The Cornhuskers broke their own NCAA record with a score of 286.45 The Huskers set the previous mark of 285.95 in last year's preliminaries.
>
> UCLA finished second in the three-team final. Despite a school-record 281.80 points, the Bruins trailed Nebraska by a margin of 4.65. Penn State was third at 275.65.

Sinclair then gave details of outstanding individual performances before providing more direct quotations from Allen and some comments from Hartung. The story closed with an overview of Nebraska's underclassmen who would be eligible to compete the following year.

The *World-Herald* also published a chart that showed the team scoring breakdown for each event:

Event	NU	UCLA	Penn State
Floor	48.00	46.90	45.60
Horse	47.90	46.15	45.15
Rings	47.30	47.20	45.75
Vault	48.00	47.65	47.40
Parallel Bars	47.20	47.10	47.05
Horizontal Bar	48.05	46.80	44.70
TOTAL	286.45	281.80	275.65

The chart clearly illustrated Nebraska's team superiority in each event—particularly the horizontal bar. It told the story more effectively than several paragraphs of text. Thus, more space was left for analysis and direct quotations in the main meet story.

Even to the uninitiated reporter who covers a gymnastics meet, the pressure that is placed on the competitors is evident. Primary meet stories often focus on team winners and statistics, but reporters also should seek angles to bring the coverage to life. *World-Herald* reporter Dave Sittler's sidebar on Cornhusker gymnast Steve Elliott captured much of the drama of the meet. Sittler effectively mixed direct quotations and mood-setting description. He began his story:

> Nebraska gymnast Steve Elliott, whose high-flying athletic abilities have placed him in some lofty places, found himself at an unexpected new level Saturday night.
>
> "I'm in heaven," Elliott said moments after he captured the second of his two individual titles on the final night of competition at the NCAA gymnastics championships.
>
> After living up to his role as favorite by winning the second floor exercise crown of his career, Elliott thrilled the partisan crowd of 10,851 fans at the Bob Devaney Sports Center by tying for the vault title.
>
> Iowa State gymnastics coach Ed Gagnier called Elliott "the most charismatic" performer in college gymnastics. Elliott also demonstrated that he can produce under pressure.
>
> In both events, the Cornhusker senior from Amarillo, Texas, was forced to pull all the stops after previous competitors posted impressive scores.
>
> Arizona State's Mark Spallina was the first to challenge Elliott, when the Sun Devil athlete hit a 9.8 in floor exercise.
>
> The last of 10 qualifiers to perform, Elliott brought the crowd to its feet when he hit a 9.85 to edge Spallina for the championship.
>
> "Spallina really put some pressure on me that I didn't need," said Elliott, who won the floor exercise crown as a sophomore. "I knew I had to go out and be a little flashy and stick my dismount."
>
> Elliott said when he did complete his dismount routine, he was confident he had overtaken Spallina.
>
> "When I did the punch front and brought my feet together and arm out to the side, it was a great feeling," Elliott said. "The crowd just seemed to swallow me up with their cheers."
>
> Elliott returned the favor by blowing kisses to the crowd and then racing off the mat to place a bear hug around teammate Scott Johnson.

Sittler went on, with equally vivid writing, to describe Elliott's surprise victory in the vaulting competition. The early paragraphs in the story, however, clearly illustrated how a reporter can capture the emotion and pressure of gymnastics competition by weaving facts, background, direct quotations, and observation.

In his early paragraphs, Sittler provided these elements: *facts*—Elliott captured two individual titles; *background*—Elliott won the floor exercise for the first time as a sophomore; *direct quotations*—the Iowa State coach called Elliott "the most charismatic" performer in college gymnastics and Elliott told how he had to be a "little flashy" to win and how the "crowd just seemed to swallow" him up with their cheers; and *observation*—Elliott was the last of ten qualifiers to perform and he blew kisses to the crowd before placing a bear hug around a teammate.

World-Herald subscribers who read this account were made to *see* what happened at the meet. Uninspired reporting would have stopped with a summary lead mentioning that Elliott captured two individual titles: one in the floor exercise with a score of 9.85 and one in the vault with a score of 9.9.

Sports editor Kelly supplemented the straight news and feature coverage with a column that described the emotions of the crowd and competitors. Kelly began his column with:

> Emotions surged electrically.
> The crowd buzzed in the Bob Devaney Sports Center, fired up about the expected assault on the NCAA gymnastics scoring record. In the locker room, the Nebraska Cornhuskers were getting psyched.
> "We were all just yelling and screaming," Husker sophomore Jim Mikus said.
> Penn State marched on to the floor first, and then UCLA, acknowledging the applause of the Nebraska crowd. When the Huskers entered the arena to compete for the national championship, the roar of the fans seemed as loud as any for the football or basketball teams.
> "The adrenalin just flowed through your body," Mikus said. "It made your hair stand up."
> After that, Nebraska definitely turned on the power.
> "Nebraska was awesome," said UCLA's Peter Vidmar, who won the NCAA all-around championship Friday night. "There was no way we could catch them."

The column went on to describe other "twists," "flips," "splits," and "lifts." Kelly's writing complemented the news coverage superbly.

Naturally, not every gymnastics competition will merit the comprehensive coverage the *World-Herald* supplied after the NCAA championship meet. Still, the writing style—the description, the use of direct quotations, the mood-setting background, and the factual insights—is worthy of emulation.

Gymnastics is a sport that can be brought to life in daily newspaper reporting. Once reporters become familiar with the scoring and basics of routines and exercises, they are ready to cover gymnastics with understanding.

Exercises

1. Discuss coverage given to college and high school gymnastics in area newspapers. Do some newspapers provide better coverage than others? What makes their coverage better?

2. Invite your school's gymnastics coach to class. How does the coach rate the quantity and quality of coverage given to gymnastics by area dailies? Does the coach have suggestions for improvement?

3. Write a pre-meet story that features a star gymnast. Contact the sports editor of an area daily to see if he or she is interested in publishing the story. Sports editors occasionally are interested in freelance stories about minor-sport athletes.

4. Cover a gymnastics meet. Write a meet story and compare it to stories published in area newspapers.

Good sportswriters—and photographers—often focus attention on star performers.

(Photo by T. J. Sokol)

CHAPTER NINE

Swimming

Most daily newspapers publish routine articles about local swimming meets and wire service stories about national-caliber competition. Seldom, however, does a newspaper sportswriter consider himself or herself to be an expert in coverage of swimming.

Melanie Hauser of the *Austin* (Texas) *American-Statesman* is an exception. She is among the few who specialize in swimming coverage. "When I joined the staff of the *American-Statesman* no one had a particular interest in swimming," she said. "I jumped at the chance to get the beat since I had been a swimmer in high school and always had been interested in the sport. I have been able to expand my beat to include international swimming as well as national."

Hauser, after nearly a decade of covering swimming, knows most of the nation's top competitors. The University of Texas at Austin perennially ranks among the country's best in both men's and women's intercollegiate competition. Thus, the swimming beat takes on special importance in Austin.

Hauser covers football, basketball, golf, and other sports. But she considers swimming to be her domain. "I keep up with swimming on a year-around basis," she said. She subscribes to national swimming publications to keep posted on the top age group and collegiate performers. She also stays in contact with coaches and swimmers around the nation. They keep her informed of which teams are swimming well at particular times of the year.

As is the case in other non-revenue sports, a grapevine of athletes, coaches, and reporters who have a particular interest in keeping up with latest developments and trends often develops.

"I always try to get to a meet an hour ahead of schedule so I can talk to the coaches,'' Hauser said. ''After I tap into the grapevine I am in a better position to find out about any injuries or problems that might have cropped up during the week, to determine which individuals are swimming particularly well and are peaking for the meet, and just to get a feel for what is and will be happening.''

Hauser keeps a running score of the meet. By scoring the meet event-by-event as it progresses, she can more easily spot trends and turning points.

''I like to focus on key events and series of events when I write my meet story,'' said Hauser. ''Most readers have no concept of what good times are, but they can relate to an explanation of how a team won a meet. For example, Texas once turned a dual around by outscoring its opponent 48–5 in five events in the middle of the meet. That is a statistic that people can relate to.''

In addition to carefully recording times and scoring as the meet progresses, Hauser develops her strategy for post-meet interviews. She waits until the meet is over before she interviews swimmers.

''I find that it is best not to try to interview athletes immediately after they finish a race,'' she said. ''They usually are already thinking about their next event. Reporters who cover football don't interview running backs between series of plays; I don't interview swimmers between events.''

Hauser emphasized the importance of ''talking to a lot of people'' at swimming meets. ''Don't be afraid to talk to the coaches for terminology explanations or for opinions about which swimmers are in top form,'' she said. ''The key to good coverage of swimming is to learn about the sport. Coaches realize that most sportswriters do not have a strong working knowledge of swimming. The coaches generally are more than willing to answer questions—particularly if that could lead to more informed, complete coverage of their sport.''

The Scoring

Scoring can vary from meet to meet. In dual meets, the top three places in individual events generally are scored 5–3–1. One team, however, cannot capture all the points. If one team sweeps the first three places, that team would get only 8 points. If the top swimmer on the other team finishes fourth, he or she would be awarded 1 point. Winners in dual meet relays get 7 points. The second-place team does not score.

Twelve places are scored in most major swimming meets. The winner is awarded 16 points in individual events. Places two through twelve are awarded the following points: 13, 12, 11, 10, 9, 7, 5, 4, 3, 2, and 1. Twelve places are also awarded for relays. Points for each place are doubled. For example, the winning team receives 32 points.

The top six finishers in an NCAA men's championship meet in the 100 freestyle were: 1, Tom Jager, UCLA, 43.06. 2, Christopher Cavanaugh, Southern California, 43.56. 3, Keith Armstrong, Southern Illinois, 43.63. 4, Per Johnson, Auburn, 43.68. 5, John Van Meter, Tennessee, 43.82. 6, Peng Slong Ang, Houston, 43.86.

Obviously, it was a very close race. The top six swimmers finished within eight-tenths of a second of each other. For team scoring, UCLA captured 16 points; Southern California gained 13 for second place; Southern Illinois earned 12 for third; Auburn received 11 for fourth; Tennessee was given 10 for fifth; and Houston notched 9 for sixth.

Newspapers generally will list individuals who swim on winning relays. For example, in the same NCAA meet, the results of the 400 freestyle relay were: 1, Florida (Geoff Gaberino, Donald Gibb, Albert Mestre, Mike Health), 2:54.06. 2, Southern Methodist, 2:54.54. 3, UCLA, 2:55.12. 4, Texas, 2:55.95. 5, Arizona State, 2:56.48. 6, Alabama, 2:57.51.

Florida earned 32 points, Southern Methodist received 26, UCLA garnered 24, Texas grabbed 22, Arizona State notched 20, and Alabama was given 18.

In addition to individual and relay winners, newspapers publish a list of the top teams and their scores. For example: 1, Florida, 238; 2, Southern Methodist, 227; 3, Texas, 225; 4, Stanford, 170; 5, Alabama, 157.5; 6, UCLA, 152; 7, Arizona State, 141.5; 8, California-Berkeley, 101.5; 9, Auburn, 78.5; 10, Ohio State, 57.

Writing Meet Stories

Hauser's coverage of dual and national meets clearly shows that swimming stories need not be limited to a short scoring summary and a direct quotation from the head coach.

The *American-Statesman* writer used an anecdotal lead to pull readers into her account of a Texas–Arizona State women's collegiate dual meet. She wrote:

> As the meet was drawing to a close, Arizona State broke into a final rendition of their newly adopted theme song—Pat Benatar's "Hit Me With Your Best Shot." And, as they had done so many times before, the Texas Longhorns fired away.
>
> Hitting the Sun Devils with all the best shots they could muster Sunday afternoon proved more than enough as the third-ranked Longhorn women came away with their second 79–70 dual meet victory in as many days at the Texas Swimming Center. But unlike Saturday's upset

win over No. 1 Stanford, the meet against No. 2 ASU didn't go down to the wire.

In the first two paragraphs, Hauser provided the essentials: Texas won the meet 79–70 Sunday at the Texas Swimming Center. But she also contrasted the victory to another big win over the nation's top-rated team the day before, and, because she was poolside at the meet, she was able to structure the anecdotal lead that helped capture the flavor of the competition.

Hauser, in the third, fourth, and fifth paragraphs, explained when Texas broke away and she provided some excellent direct quotations from the Texas coach. Hauser wrote:

> Taking control midway through the schedule of events, the Long-horns snapped a 35–35 tie and cruised to the win, locking the meet up with two events to go as senior Erin Beiter took an easy win in the three-meter diving. But, even though the meet wasn't as close as it appeared, Texas coach Paul Bergen started the day a little more worried than usual.
>
> "I was worried about how we'd feel after such a big victory against Stanford," said Bergen. "In a way, today proves that yesterday's win wasn't a fluke. We obviously weren't as emotionally charged up, but in some cases, we swam better than we did yesterday.
>
> "We took care of business. It's like a professional athlete. A basketball player, baseball player or football player isn't as charged up about every game they play as they would be for a championship, but they've got to go out and do it every time. I think in some cases, we proved a lot about what we're made of."

It was not until the sixth paragraph that Hauser turned to the top individual performances. In some meet stories, of course, the top individual performances might be featured in the lead. A reporter, however, must make a decision, on a meet-by-meet basis, about what is most deserving of top-of-the-story recognition. Quickly, Hauser capsulized the top individual performances. She wrote:

> For the record, Texas won 11 of the day's 17 events, with Jill Sterkel and Kim Linehan turning in another pair of sensational performances and upping their weekend totals to six individual wins each. Sterkel, who won Saturday's meet with an awesome final leg of the freestyle relay, won the 50- and the 100-yard freestyles and 50 butterfly, while Linehan came out on top in the 200 and 500 freestyles and 200 butterfly.
>
> Sophomore Carol Borgmann proved that she too was a force to be reckoned with, winning the 100 individual medley for the second

straight day with another solid time, while sophomore Kim Black bounced back from a disappointing performance against Stanford to win the 1,000 freestyle and finish second to Linehan in the 500.

Hauser elected not to slow the narration of the paragraphs that outlined top individual performances with times. Of course, she would have had they been record breakers. All times were listed in the agate-type results that followed the story.

After providing more details on individual performances, Hauser examined the impact of the loss on Arizona State. She wrote:

> Before the meet, Arizona State coach Bill Rose said he thought his young team was overrated at No. 2. If he had his way, he said, fifth would be a little more realistic. But the Sun Devils, who host Stanford in two weeks for another important showdown, can leave Austin feeling good.
>
> Although they won only six events, the Devils' depth—in particular freestylers Gail Amundrud, Darcee Douglas and Kathy Shipman—and enthusiasm should put them in the thick of things at March's AIAW championships in South Carolina.

Hauser's story contained clear evidence that she had done her homework. She was aware of the depth that the visiting team had; she had talked to both coaches before and after the meet. As a result, she was able to close her story with an analysis of both teams' chances of gaining a national championship.

Hauser's writing tone in her story of an NCAA men's collegiate championship matched the enthusiasm that the Texas team had generated in storming to a commanding meet lead on the eve of the finals. Hauser focused on a record-setting performance in her lead:

> For the most part, Clay Britt's race had been an amazing swim, just as the entire day had been for the Texas swimming team which appears to be tantalizingly close to the NCAA championship.
>
> After coming within a half-second of finding himself in the consolation heat Friday night, the Texas sophomore took advantage of an outside lane to lower his American record in the 100-yard backstroke by three-hundredths of a second to 49.08.
>
> Enter Texas coach Eddie Reese. "You know you're better than that," said Reese. Britt grinned back.
>
> With Reese, things should always be just a little better—a philosophy which explains why the Texas Longhorns are just a few short hours away from claiming their first NCAA title.
>
> Whether you want to call the day amazing, awesome, sensational or

just plain great, the 'Horns took full advantage of their strongest day to set a pair of American records and extend Thursday's two-point lead to 63 points going into today's final day of competition at the NCAA Swimming and Diving Championships at the Texas Swimming Center.

This marks the first time since Tennessee won the title in 1978 that a team has gone into the final day with a virtual lock on the title.

"It really looks like we're going to win. Even a sports writer could see that now," Reese said before turning serious.

Thanks to a 116-point explosion Friday, the Longhorns collected 181 points in two days, leaving Florida, UCLA, Auburn and the surprising Southern Methodist Mustangs to contend for second.

The Gators—thanks to an amazing final leg from David Larson on the 800-yard freestyle relay—are second with 118 points, followed by UCLA at 113, SMU at 108, Auburn at 93 and Southern Cal at 82.

Hauser's story continued with an overview of the outstanding individual performances.

Texas went on to win the national championship—as Hauser predicted. The Texas title came on the heels of a close second-place finish the year before. Hauser, again showing a significant knowledge of the sport, used a background lead on that NCAA championship story. It put in perspective the accomplishments of the Longhorns who made a run at the championship. She wrote:

> It began last fall with a group of swimmers who were sure to contend for the national title, but no one knew quite when. One swimming magazine picked them to finish sixth at the NCAA championship, another predicted fifth. Even coach Eddie Reese said they'd be no higher than fourth. Talk of Texas contending for a national championship, it seemed, was best left for next year.
>
> But Texas, a team that scored only 12 points to finish 21st at the [NCAA meet two years earlier], had a different idea. Taking full advantage of doors left open by favored Florida, the Longhorns gave defending champion California-Berkeley a run for it at Harvard's Blodgett Pool Saturday night before finishing second to Cal by a mere 14 points—234–220.
>
> Florida finished third at 200, followed by UCLA at 192, Auburn at 168, Southern Cal at 147 and SMU at 137 in one of the most tightly contested races in recent history.

Hauser then moved to direct quotations from Longhorn coaches and players before analyzing the top individual performances in the meet.

Stories by the *American-Statesman* reporter clearly show that swimming does not have to be a sport that is covered with the enthusiasm most newspapers show for printing local bowling scores. It is a sport whose drama can be captured by examining performances in crucial events, by doing extensive background on the teams and individuals, by working at understanding the sport, and by using vivid direct quotations.

Exercises

1. Discuss coverage given to college, high school, and summer youth swimming in area newspapers. Do some newspapers provide better coverage than others? What makes their coverage better?

2. Invite a local swimming coach to class. Ask the coach to discuss new rules or emerging issues. Does the coach have suggestions for feature stories or for ways meet coverage can be improved?

3. Write a pre-meet story that features a star swimmer.

4. Cover a swimming meet. Write a meet story and compare it to stories published in area newspapers.

It takes a knowledgeable sportswriter to cover tennis effectively.

(Photo by Henri Cohen)

CHAPTER TEN

Tennis

More than a decade ago, Penny Butler and some of her tennis-playing friends in Phoenix were lamenting the lack of coverage *The Arizona Republic* gave to their favorite sport. Butler wrote a letter to the *Republic*'s sports editor, asking him if she could write a column on tennis.

"The sports editor told me there were no opportunities for anyone to write such a column, that space in the sports section was tight," Butler said. "He told me he had people standing in line wanting to write columns. At the end of his letter, though, he said he would be glad to talk further with me."

Butler made an appointment; she took with her fifteen ideas for feature articles. She was hired. Her assignment: write two features a month.

Normally, when a daily newspaper sports editor assigns a reporter to cover tennis there is a hitch: the reporter is a writer who does not know the rudiments of tennis and would rather be covering football or basketball. Butler was confronted with another dilemma: she knew tennis well but she had no writing experience. As it turned out, her desire to report effectively, her knowledge of the sport, and her academic background (she was graduated from Vassar) more than compensated for her lack of journalism training. She learned reporting on the job. Butler, an avid tennis player and mother of four, took her husband's blessing and worked the two-features-a-month assignment into a half-time job covering the sport at all levels.

"I loved it when the National Football League players went on strike," she said. "All of a sudden, the newspaper had extra space for tennis. The editors were glad to see me walk in the door."

The Phoenix writer learned one lesson early. "You have to remember that all readers are not avid tennis fans," she said. "You must write to make the sport understandable. When I write a story, there are subtleties of strategy that I would like to include because they would be significant to a tennis player. But they would not be significant to the general public. There has to be a blend: Don't talk down to the tennis players who read your stories, but don't write over the heads of the average reader.''

Butler watches the play in a tennis match intently; she likes to write descriptively. She looks for:

- *Service breaks.* A match can turn on one service. "If a player is serving and she loses her serve, it is called a service break for the opponent," Butler said. "That gives the opponent an advantage. A lot of times, if the players are evenly matched, one service break will dictate the outcome of the match. That can be a detail worth reporting."
- *Double faults.* When serving, a player has two opportunities to hit the ball over the net into the service area for each point. The service changes hands at the end of each game—a minimum of four points. "If a player is unable to get his first serve in consistently, or if he double faults, that often is significant to the outcome of the match," Butler said. "In major tournaments, percentages are calculated for first serves that land in the service court. When covering a college or high school match, where such statistics are not kept, the best a reporter can do is generalize. The reporter can say that John Jones missed a high percentage of first serves. There often is a correlation between getting first serves in and the outcome of the match."
- *Baseline players.* A player who continually hits from the backcourt, who does not rush the net, is called a baseline player. The baseline player, who usually plays a steady game, is more comfortable with groundstrokes—backhands and forehands. "That kind of player, however, can be devastated by drop shots (which fall just over the net)," Butler said. "If the person stays rooted to the baseline, that person often has problems."
- *Topspin.* Players who are able to put a lot of topspin on the ball (they start with their racquets low and come over the ball so that, because of the trajectory of the hit, the ball bounces high when it lands) often are effective.
- *Serve and volley.* As a player serves the ball, she or he quickly follows the ball toward the net. The purpose is to cut off the return with a quick volley. "To serve and volley effectively requires speed and strength," Butler said. "This often is worth noting in match stories."
- *Effective lobs.* A lob is a high-arcing defensive shot. The aim is to hit the ball over the head of an opponent playing too close to the net. Ideally, the shot will land near the baseline and the opponent will be unable to return it. "Lobs are most effective against opponents who are playing the net aggressively," Butler said. "Of course, lobs can

backfire. If the lob is hit ineffectively, and falls short, the other player can use an overhead smash to put the ball away and win the point.''

Butler normally selects the top matches to watch (in college and high school, six singles matches are played simultaneously). ''I focus my attention on the match involving the number one players,'' she said. ''If the match is close, I usually will watch all of it. If it is lopsided, I will watch another match that is more competitive.''

When she covers college or high school matches, Butler always checks the records of the individuals and teams. ''I gather as much information as I can from newspaper clippings and by talking with coaches and players,'' she said. ''There usually is a lot of information available for college tennis. The Intercollegiate Tennis Coaches Association (ITCA), for example, publishes preseason rankings for teams and individuals in both men's and women's competition and periodically updates the rankings throughout the season.''

Butler also keeps a notebook filled with biographical information on the best players of all ages in the Phoenix area. ''Then, when I cover a tournament like the Phoenix Open, with 150 to 200 persons entered, I have background on most of the top local players. I just have to gather information on the out-of-state players.''

In addition to stockpiling information about competitors and teams before the competition and then carefully watching play, Butler always tries to get direct quotations from players in key matches. ''It is interesting to get their insight about what happened during the match,'' Butler said. ''I like to talk to losers as well as winners. Sometimes, though, it is difficult to talk to a loser right after a match. I usually wait until the person has calmed down.''

Butler said her stories are ''a combination of following the action point-by-point, getting some key quotations to give added insight, and reporting the results.''

The Scoring

In college and high school competition, there are six singles and three double matches. The No. 1 player for one team is matched against the No. 1 player for the opponent and so on through No. 6. Thus, in dual meets, the match between the No. 6 players counts as much as the match between the No. 1 players. A team is awarded one point for each singles or doubles victory.

A player must win two out of three sets to win the match. There are games within sets. In open and professional competition, a game continues until one player wins by at least 2 points. For example, the first time John Jones scores, he is ahead 15–love; when Sam Smith scores, it is 15–15. If the players continue to trade points, the score becomes: 30–15; 30–30; 40–30; and deuce (tied at 40). To win the game, one player must get 2 points in a row.

In college and high school competition, however, there is no deuce. The first player to score 4 points wins the game. Colleges and high schools score this way: 1–0; 1–1; 2–1; 2–2; 3–2; and 3–3. If the score is tied at 3 in college or high school, the next point wins the game.

A player wins a set if he or she captures six games before the opponent wins more than four (for example, 6–4, 6–3, 6–2, 6–1, or 6–0). Until recently, a set continued until one player earned a two-game margin. That is, if the games were tied 5–5, one player had to win two games in a row (to make it 7–5) or play continued until one player managed to win two in succession (creating a final score of 8–6, 9–7, or the like).

Now a tiebreaker system is used. Let's assume Smith wins a game to break a 5–5 tie. With Smith ahead, 6–5, Jones wins the next game to tie the score at six games each. Instead of continuing until one player earns a two-game advantage, a 12-point tiebreaker is played. The first player to earn 7 points wins the game provided there is a margin of at least 2 points (for example: 7–5, 7–4, 7–3, 7–2, 7–1, 7–0). If the score in the tiebreaker reaches 6–6, play continues until one player wins 2 points in a row. Conceivably, the tiebreaker could drag on to 16–14, 20–18, or whatever. Sometimes called "lingering death," if two players are evenly matched, the equivalent of another entire set could be played.

In a tiebreaker set, the score is recorded 7–6, with the tiebreaker in parentheses. (For example: 7–6 [7–1] or 7–6 [20–18].)

College and high schools always play a best of three sets contest. In major professional championships, such as Wimbledon, the men (not the women) play a best of five.

When newspapers print results in agate summaries, the scores for the winner are listed first, even if the winner has lost a set. Scores from an Arizona State–University of Arizona women's tennis match follow:

ARIZONA STATE 7, UNIVERSITY OF ARIZONA 2
SINGLES: 1. Leslie Hewett (ASU) def. Marsha Bladel, 6–2, 7–5; 2. Patti Schiff (ASU) def. Jane Klingaman, 6–2, 6–1; 3. Cheryl Hawkins (ASU) def. Casey Esparza, 6–3, 6–3; 4. Jennifer Bland (ASU) def. Joanie Lebedeff, 6–3, 3–6, 6–2; 5. Tracey Stern (ASU) def. Beth Siegler, 6–2, 7–5; 6. Debbie Brown (ASU) def. Karen Cooperman, 6–0, 6–2.
DOUBLES: 1. Lebedeff-Klingaman (UA) def. Hewett-Hawkins, 1–6,

6–3, 6–2; 2. Esparza-Bladel (UA) def. Schiff-Stern, 6–2, 6–3; 3. Bland-Brown (ASU) def. Cooperman-Siegler, 7–5, 5–7, 6–2.

Writing Match Stories

Butler covered the Arizona State–University of Arizona women's match summarized above. For her story, she chose a summary lead. Because there were no hotly contested matches to focus on, she built the story around interesting background and some excellent direct quotations. The story began:

> Leslie Hewett, a freshman from Birmingham, Ala., led a strong Arizona State University's women's tennis team to victory Friday over the University of Arizona, 7–2.
> Despite having two players on the disabled list, the Sun Devils swept six singles matches and one doubles in the Western Collegiate Athletic Association (WCAA) victory over the Wildcats at Whiteman Tennis Center.
> Formed in 1976, the WCAA includes California State University-Fullerton, California State-Long Beach, San Diego State, UCLA and 1979 national champion Southern California.
> "This is a really tough league," said Anne Pittman, ASU women's tennis coach since 1954. "The rivalry with UofA is tough enough but it's like that with every conference match."
> With a 4–3 conference record (24–6 overall), the Sun Devils rank 16th nationally.
> Patti Schiff, one of four freshmen on the Sun Devil squad, said she thinks the team is doing well in spite of the injured players.
> "We're such a young team and we're still winning conference matches in spite of having two players out for the season," she said.
> Hewett, ranked first in Alabama and the Southern section of the U.S. Tennis Association and who has been playing No. 1 singles and doubles at ASU, thinks the team's youth is an asset.
> "Freshmen are always eager and want to perform and practice hard," she said. "While seniors are a bit more lackadaisical after four years of collegiate tennis."
> The Sun Devils lost some of their enthusiasm two months ago when matches were interrupted by the rain and flooding.
> "We were competing against two opponents for a while—the weather and the other school," said Schiff, a native of Columbus, Ohio, who is ranked 29th in the nation in girls 18s and third in the Western section of the USTA. "It's taken us about a month to get into it."
> Hewett thinks the pressure is about equal on all six singles players— with slightly more on No. 1.

"It's sometimes tougher at No. 1 because the schools we play, even the less well-known ones, are going to have a good No. 1 player," she said.

The story went on to quote the ASU coach about her reaction to the relatively easy ASU victory and her feeling about the uncommon injuries that had plagued her squad.

When Butler covered an Arizona State–UCLA men's tennis match, she described in detail the most exciting match of an otherwise lopsided dual meet. After beginning with a summary lead, she provided an overview of the dual, direct quotations from the UCLA coach, and then she described the day's best match. She started her story:

> The UCLA Bruins shut out Arizona State University, 9–0, Saturday in a Pacific-10 Conference tennis match at Whiteman Tennis Center.
>
> Ranked No. 2 in the country in a pre-season coaches' poll, the Bruins displayed awesome talent, depth and consistency.
>
> All six singles were straight-set victories for UCLA.
>
> ASU is 0–4 in Pac-10 competition and 15–6 overall.
>
> Glenn Bassett, the UCLA coach for 15 years, had reason to be happy after his squad's first two confrontations in the Pac-10 this season. In addition to blanking the Sun Devils, the Bruins beat Arizona 7–2 Friday.
>
> UCLA has won more National Collegiate Athletic Association tennis titles (13) than any other school in the powerful Southern Division of the Pac-10.
>
> "I was really happy, especially with the singles," Bassett said after the match. "It's so tough playing away from home."
>
> The Sun Devils' No. 1 singles player, Paul Bernstein, had his chances against Bruin junior Marcel Freeman, but no-ad scoring, with sudden-death points, made the difference. Freeman won, 7–5, 6–4.
>
> In the first set, UCLA won two out of three crucial sudden-death points.
>
> Service breaks were traded in the first two games of that set, and in games nine and ten. Then, with Bernstein serving at 5-all, he got into a sudden death situation, and Freeman hit a superb volley to pull out in front 6–5.
>
> Game 12 also went to sudden death. Freeman clinched the set with a winning overhead.
>
> "Sudden-death points are so unbelievable," Bernstein said. "They turn the whole match around."
>
> In the second set, Bernstein lost his serve in the crucial ninth game, giving Freeman a 5–4 lead. Freeman blasted through the final game to give the Bruins the victory.
>
> Although the doubles were a formality after dropping all six singles, the Devils made a spirited stand at Nos. 1 and 2.

Butler's story continued with details of the doubles competition.

Clearly, the Phoenix writer adjusted her reporting strategy to fit the circumstances of the ASU-UofA women's match and the ASU-UCLA men's match. She concentrated on background information and direct quotations in the women's match because it did not produce any spirited head-to-head matches. Then, in the men's story, she used description to focus on the excellent match between the No. 1 singles players.

Butler also used description effectively in a story she wrote about a juniors tournament held in Phoenix. She began the story with a summary lead:

> Top-seeded Mike Velasquez of Albuquerque, N.M., playing his first year in the 18-year-old age group, won the boys' singles title Sunday in the Phoenix Junior Open-Mike Harden Memorial tennis tournament, beating No. 2 seed Jimmy Friend, 6–3, 6–4.
>
> No. 1 seeded Jackie Ranger won the girls' 18 championship at the Tempe Racquet and Swim Club, beating second-seeded Cindy Buchsbaum of Tucson, 6–4, 6–4.

Butler then listed the champions in other age groups and divisions.

By using descriptive writing and direct quotations, Butler brought to life the Velasquez-Friend match. She wrote:

> Velasquez, a left-hander who can blast the ball or drop it over the net with precise touch, won the first set over Friend with one service break in the sixth game.
>
> In the second set, Velasquez jumped to a 5–2 lead, breaking Friend in the first and seventh games. As Velasquez served for the match, Friend tightened his game, fought off three match points to break Velasquez, won his serve in the next game and narrowed Velasquez's lead to 5–4.
>
> But after playing those two loose games, Velasquez served out the match, sealing the set with a winning overhead smash.
>
> Citing his powerful forehand as his most reliable shot throughout the tournament, Velasquez said he felt he had "lucked out" by winning his semifinal round over his doubles partner, (Matt) Lofdahl, in three sets.
>
> "In the last set, I was serving a 4-all, ad out," he said. "Matt had a perfect forehand passing shot (that) he hit to the fence."
>
> Velasquez said this was his first out-of-state tournament in the 18s. He had won the boys' 16 title in the Fiesta Bowl Junior tournament last December, which he said was a "really big win for me."
>
> Asked about the eighth game in the second set, when he failed to win his third match point against Friend, Velasquez said, "I hit an overhead. I didn't want to let it go even though it might have been out. I was looking right in the sun and mis-hit it, then Friend passed me."
>
> Friend won the next two points making the score 5–3, Velasquez.

> Friend, who graduated from Phoenix Country Day School last spring, has been playing a U.S. Tennis Association satellite circuit in Texas. He said he plans to enter college in the second semester.

After the description of the Velasquez-Friend match, along with the explanatory quotations that added insight to it, Butler turned to the Ranger-Buchsbaum match, which she also described in detail.

In addition to extensive coverage of tennis matches, Butler also writes features and a weekly column. One of her features focused on some of the top senior women players who were in Phoenix for a tournament. Stories of this type can be written about senior players in most any city in the country. Butler began her feature with a direct quotation:

> "Tennis is the only sport in the world where you can hardly wait to get the next year older," said Betty Rosenquest Pratt, one of 164 women in Phoenix to compete in the national Senior Women's Hard Court tennis championships.
>
> Women have come from as far as Florida and Hawaii to take part in this event, which opens Tuesday and ends Nov. 21. Three age groups are represented—35, 45 and 55—and all the women are proud to announce their ages.
>
> Pratt, 57, from Winter Park, Fla., points out that she is being "shoved around by the young kids" in her age division and is looking forward to moving up to the next age group—60.
>
> Senior tennis starts at age 35 and is divided into five-year age divisions. To get a national ranking a player is required to play in two national events in one year. Four tournaments are offered on four surfaces—hard court, indoor, clay and grass.
>
> The women at Paradise Valley Tennis Club this week have a chance to win a gold ball charm, exactly like the one Chris Evert Lloyd won in the U.S. Open, but there the comparison stops.
>
> No prize money is offered these dedicated older players. No lucrative clothing or equipment contracts have been offered. Many have memories of junior titles as they come back to the sport. Some have turned to tennis after their children have grown up. All relish the exercise, sociability and skill involved in the sport.

After providing these details on the senior tournament, Butler closed with direct quotations from interviews with some of the competitors.

Stories about tennis are stronger and more appealing to readers if the writer goes beyond bare-boned statistics. Vivid description, analysis of turning points, and effective use of direct quotations—all carefully interspersed—make for good coverage and good reading.

Exercises

1. Discuss coverage given to college, high school, and summer youth tennis in area newspapers. Do some newspapers provide better coverage than others? What makes their coverage better?

2. Invite a local tennis coach to class. Ask the coach to discuss new rules or emerging issues. Does the coach have suggestions for feature stories or for ways coverage can be improved?

3. Write a feature about a local tennis player.

4. Cover a tennis match. Write a match story and compare it to stories published in area newspapers.

Sportswriters record the feats of talented track and field competitors.

(Photo by Henri Cohen)

CHAPTER ELEVEN

Track and Field

I n their book, *The Story of the Olympic Games*, John Kiernan and Arthur Daley wrote that athletes compete in dozens of sports. Still, "to the average man in the street the track and field program is the main point of interest and when it is said, for instance, that the United States has won or will win 'the Olympic Games,' the ordinary reference is to the Olympic track and field championships unless otherwise specified."

A recent survey of the nation's daily newspaper sports editors showed that, in their coverage of high school and college athletics, only football, basketball, and baseball receive more space than track.

In addition to coverage of high school district and state championships, many newspapers devote considerable space to dual meets. In college competition, with the possible exception of the National Collegiate Athletic Association's championships, four meets—the Texas Relays, Kansas Relays, Drake Relays, and Penn Relays—likely receive the most attention from the nation's newspapers.

The *Topeka* (Kan.) *Capital-Journal* provides complete coverage of the Kansas Relays. Coverage of the annual event actually starts about a month before the meet, according to Pete Goering, assistant sports editor. During the four weeks leading to the relays, the *Capital-Journal* publishes feature stories on top athletes who are expected to compete.

Premeet coverage builds to a crescendo the week before the relays. "We always hit the high school competitors hard in our newspaper," Goering said. "We publish stories that focus on the best prep athletes in Topeka and from around the state. Features also are carried about Kansas collegiate performers as well as other athletes coming in from around the country."

Coverage of one particular KU Relays was special, said Goering, a veteran of more than a decade of meet coverage. The Soviet Union sent a contingent; the *Capital-Journal* thus published more stories than usual.

The Topeka newspaper relied primarily on a University of Kansas correspondent for stories of the men's decathlon and women's heptathlon, which were held Wednesday and Thursday. The *Capital-Journal* expanded its coverage for the Friday-Saturday main meet. Four reporters and two photographers made the 20-mile trip to Lawrence for the Friday competition. Five reporters and three photographers from Topeka joined the Lawrence campus correspondent for Saturday's meet.

Goering, who coordinated the coverage for the *Capital-Journal*, said he enjoys track. "I consider myself to be knowledgeable, but I am not a statistical fanatic," Goering said. Indeed, reporters should understand some of the technical aspects of track and field and its rules. But readers should not be smothered with times, distances, and splits.

Goering said it is important for reporters to look at some times and distances "with honest skepticism." The reporter said that, particularly in high school competition, blazing times often are turned in early in the season. Reporters should determine if the performances were wind-aided. If so, this should be noted in the story. The Topeka reporter said track, in some respects, is easier to cover than football or basketball. "You are close to the athletes and they are usually accessible for interviews.

"If you really try, you can get some great stories and quotes from track competitors," Goering said. "But you need to keep your stories general. Pole vaulters, for example, like to talk about their poles, their test weights, and the length of their approaches. Most readers are not interested in this. Stories should emphasize personalities—not technical aspects. Technical information should be worked subtly into a story."

Often, in team sports such as football or basketball, the lead naturally focuses on victor and score. In some track meets, where no team score is kept, a reporter needs to decide what the most appropriate lead should be.

"You need to know which athletes are capable of top performances and to keep an eye on them," Goering said. "You never know which one—if any, will come through with a top time or distance."

Indeed, track and field is a curious blend of a team concept and an emphasis on individuals. "A lot of judgment is involved in selecting leads," Goering said. "At the *Capital-Journal*, we like to publish more than one story in our coverage of track meets. Sidebars are an excellent way to focus on individual performances."

The Scoring

In some meets, such as the major relays, team champions are not crowned. In duals, triangulars, conference championships, invitationals, and regional and national championships, team scoring is kept. Points are awarded in each event based on order of finish. In duals, for example, first place generally is worth five points, second place is worth three, and third place is worth one point. In relay competition in duals, the winning team gets five points; the second place team does not receive points.

In meets involving more than two schools, five or six places are scored. In five-place meets, first usually counts six points. Places two through five are worth four, three, two, and one. In six-place meets, first usually is worth ten points. Places two through six are worth eight, six, four, two, and one.

Points awarded for each place and the number of places scored can vary. Reporters always should check with meet officials to become familiar with scoring systems.

During the past decade, most high school and college meets have featured metric running events. Previously, running events for most meets held in the United States were measured in yards. Typically, though some meets still have running events measured in yards, college meets include the following track events: 100 meters; 200 meters; 400 meters; 800 meters; 1,500 meters; 3,000 meters; 110-meter high hurdles; 400-meter intermediate hurdles; 4 × 100 relay; 4 × 400 relay. The following field events are included: high jump, long jump, hammer throw, triple jump, discus, shot put, javelin, and pole vault.

High school meets generally include most of these field events. The shot put and discus, however, are lighter. Also, some states ban javelin competition, and the hammer is seldom thrown. On the track, high schools sometimes will run 1,600 meters and 3,200 meters instead of 1,500 meters and 3,000 meters. Preps often run the 300-meter intermediate hurdles instead of 400 meters. Prep high hurdles also are three inches lower than college high hurdles.

Special competition in high school can include the pentathlon (five events) or heptathlon (seven events). College women compete in either the pentathlon or heptathlon. College men compete in the decathlon (ten events). These events are scored on a point basis. A chart is used to convert times and distances to points. In college women's heptathlon competition, for example, a throw of 148 feet in the javelin is worth 844 points. A throw of 126 feet is worth 741 points and a toss of 113-4 is worth 678 points. Points from each of the seven events are totaled for each individual.

Newspapers should publish the event, names of competitors, distance or time, and points for pentathlon, heptathlon, or decathlon competition. For example, in the Kansas Relays' women's heptathlon long jump, these were the results:

Long Jump—1, Marjan Goedhart, Nebraska, 19-11½, 924 points.
2, Carla Battaglia, Indiana, 18-10¾, 853 points. 3, Margot Rogus,

Indiana, 18-3¾, 812 points. 4, Diana Elwer, Air Force, 15-11, 640 points. 5, Colleen Hobb, NW Missouri St., 15-5¾, 608 points.

After listing individual performances in each event, the totals for all events should be published:

Final Totals—1, Marjan Goedhart, Nebraska, 5,638 points. 2, Carla Battaglia, Indiana, 5,346 points. 3, Margot Rogus, Indiana, 5,335 points. 4, Diana Elwer, Air Force, 4,612 points. 5, Colleen Hobb, NW Missouri St., 4,256 points.

Places for regular meet competition are listed similarly:

Long Jump—1, Robb Schnitzler, Battle Creek, 22-8½. 2, Tim Dickey, Newman Grove, 22-7½. 3, Darren Cargle, Omaha Dominican, 22-6. 4, Jesse Thompson, Logan View, 22-3½. 5, Brent Harsin, Alma, 21-8½. 6, Brent Schott, Palmyra, 21-3½.

Point totals for teams also should be published in list form:

Battle Creek, 44; Alma, 34; Wisner, 34; Malcolm, 26; Ansley, 25; Imperial, 23; etc.

Writing Meet Stories

Track and field coverage requires diligence in recording precisely the times—to the hundredths of a second—and the distances—to one quarter of an inch, but runners can be so sleek and jumpers so graceful that it also is a sport that begs for descriptive writing.

Allen Quakenbush, a sportswriter for the *Capital-Journal*, mixed description, times, and direct quotations into a story about the distance medley (each of the four runners covers a different distance: 440 yards, 880 yards, 1,320 yards, and one mile) in the high school division of the Kansas Relays. Quakenbush began his article:

A Topeka West victory in the distance medley relay seemed inevitable at the Kansas Relays Saturday when Robbie Hays took a 20-yard lead into the final lap.

But Washburn Rural distance coach Chuck Copp, sitting in a corner of Memorial Stadium, wasn't so sure. A veteran runner himself, Copp had spotted potential disaster a lap earlier.

"I've seen it happen before," Copp said. "You put a runner way out in front on long relays (Hays' position after a fine 1,320 leg by Jeff Shelar), you don't get any splits and it's tough to tell how fast you're running.

"Chris (Junior Blue miler anchor Currie) went out in 2:08 through the first half, and he was still losing ground to Hays. He (Hays) just couldn't tell how fast his pace was.

"I was still scared at the three-quarter mark because Hays looked strong, but it finally caught up with him on the last lap."

That's when Currie, admittedly tired after a tough second-place finish in the Jim Ryun mile Friday afternoon, made his move.

In fourth place heading into the gun lap, Currie crept closer and finally passed Hays and the rest of the field on the final turn. The only question was whether he had enough strength to hold on the rest of the way.

He did it in style, winning going away to give Rural its first victory in a relay event at the KU Relays. The Junior Blues' winning time of 10:42.2 didn't break any records, but the pace suited Currie just fine.

"It ended up working in Chris' favor," Copp noted. "Because it was so early in the morning (8:15) and after that tough mile Friday, he was sluggish. He looked pretty good for the first 200, but then his stride changed.

"He's enough of a competitor that he stayed with it and hung tough. He's never been afraid to compete. If he loses, he remembers it for a long time."

"I was a little bit drained," Currie said, "but I felt better in the second half because I was using people for wind blocks most of the way. I was still kinda tired, but when I saw we could get it, I felt better in a hurry."

Currie, who ran a 4:26.4 split for his mile, received solid performances from his teammates, too. Half-miler Scott Groth went out in 2:03.3, then quarter-miler Brett Davis ran his leg in 51.3 and passed four runners down the stretch.

Steve Groth, a sophomore, ran a fine 3:20.5 split in the 1,320 and kept the Junior Blues within striking distance for Currie.

Quakenbush's story shows that he is knowledgeable about track. He carefully managed to weave split times into the story without bogging down the reader; he drew upon the track background of the Washburn Rural coach to help explain what can happen when one team gets a big lead in a distance relay; he made note of the resilience of anchorman Currie who had run a tough mile the afternoon before; and he selected the interesting quotation from Currie about using other runners as "wind blocks."

Track fans appreciate stories that go beyond the simple listing of winners and times. It also is good journalism to provide background, analysis, times, and direct quotations.

It is difficult to cover a major track meet with a single story. Quite often, the main story will focus on record-breaking performances. Sidebar stories, such as Quakenbush's, provide a necessary supplement.

Goering wrote the main meet story for the KU Relays that featured the Soviets. The lead was a natural: The Soviet Union, competing in the relays for the first time, made its imprint. Goering began his story:

> The Soviets didn't visit Kansas without leaving their mark. Well, actually, they left seven of them.
>
> Competing for the first time in the Kansas Relays, the Soviet Union athletes assaulted the Relays' record book Saturday with six record-setting performances. Grigory Degtyarev's decathlon mark on Thursday accounted for No. 7.
>
> "They competed a little better than I expected," Soviet Coach Igor Ter-Ovanesyan, a former Olympic long jump champion, said about his team. "I'm very glad their techniques are good because they didn't practice a lot outdoors."
>
> In fact, this was the Soviets' first outdoor competition of the year, but you wouldn't have known by the way they dominated their events Saturday.

After this lead, Goering used bullets to provide readers with a rapid-fire summary of the outstanding performances:

- Janis Bojars won the shot put with a record 68-7¾ heave, more than six feet farther than runner-up Gregg Bartlett of Kansas State.
- Nadezhada Raldugina whipped teammate Tatyana Pozdnyakova to win the 1,500-meter run in 4:08.94, knocking 12½ seconds off the old record.
- Nikolai Musyenko's record triple jump was 55-9¼. Teammate Gennady Valykevich was second at 53-11¼. No one else cleared 50 feet.

Exercises

1. Discuss coverage given to college, high school, and age-group track and field in area newspapers. Do some newspapers provide better coverage than others? What makes their coverage better?

2. Invite a local track coach to class. Ask the coach to discuss new rules or emerging issues. Does the coach have suggestions for feature stories or for ways coverage can be improved?

3. Write a feature about a local track and field athlete or a feature on some aspect of the sport, such as training procedures.

4. Cover a track meet. Write a meet story. You might want to use a descriptive lead by describing the closest race of the day or a record-setting performance.

Volleyball matches draw large crowds to many colleges and high schools around the country.   *(Photo by Irwin R. Daugherty)*

CHAPTER TWELVE

Volleyball

The sports editor of a medium-circulation daily once said, "You can give readers all they want to know about volleyball if you give them final scores." That option, presumably, is predicated on the principle that no one on the sports editor's staff is sufficiently indoctrinated to give readers a detailed—yet understandable—account of a volleyball match.

Much of the volleyball coverage in America's newspapers is limited to final scores or three-paragraph stories. It does not have to be this way. Volleyball is a fast-paced sport that is conducive to strong, vivid reporting.

"I think it is important to report *how* a volleyball match is won," said Gail Maiorana, a sports reporter for *The Mesa* (Ariz.) *Tribune*, a daily newspaper that provides considerable coverage of high school and collegiate volleyball. "There are turning points in volleyball matches—just as there are in football games—and I think readers should be made aware of them."

When Maiorana was assigned to cover her first volleyball match, she read a rule book, talked with coaches, and checked with the sports information office at Arizona State University.

"One of the assistant sports information directors was very helpful, particularly at the first couple of matches I covered," Maiorana said. "After covering a few matches, however, I got to the point where I not only understood the basic rules and scoring procedures, but I could spot alignments— just like in baseball where outfielders slide over to compensate for various hitters. I could tell which plays the teams were trying to set up."

A reporter does not have to be an expert on coaching theory to watch a volleyball match with understanding, but it is important to learn the scoring procedures and basic terminology. Also, a reporter should be able to determine—and, in turn, report—key plays.

"Volleyball is not like football, where it is easy to isolate major plays just by looking at a statistics chart,'' Dennis Brown, a sportswriter for *The Phoenix* (Ariz.) *Gazette*, said. ''There is nonstop action in volleyball. There are innumerable spikes, serves, and blocks. A reporter must be alert to what is happening on the floor. Scoring summaries should be kept—complete with notations on how the score came about. This helps a reporter isolate key plays.''

Still, reporters must be careful not to give too much play-by-play when covering volleyball. ''A feature angle often helps make volleyball more comprehensible to the average reader,'' Brown said.

The *Gazette* reporter said sportswriters always should be aware of what nonstar players do during a match. ''Volleyball is like baseball in at least one aspect,'' he said. ''The big hitters get lots of attention because they score most of the points. Often overlooked are the setters (players who get the ball to the spiker who then smashes it over the net) and the blockers. They don't have the opportunity to score a lot of points; they are unsung heroes like interior linemen in football, but many of them are fine athletes.''

The Scoring

In college and international competition, a team must win three games out of five to win the match. (A match is made up of a series of games; each game is equivalent to a set in a tennis match.) In high school competition, the number of matches varies. In some states, a team must win three of five; in other states, a team must win two of three. The winner of a game is the first team to score 15 points. To win, a team must be ahead by at least two points; thus, some games go beyond 15 points—until one team can earn a two-point advantage. Points can be scored only by the team that has the serve.

Volleyball terminology can be confusing, particularly to the novice. A logical first step is to purchase a book on the sport. *Winning Volleyball*, a book by UCLA men's coach, Al Scates, has a section on terminology. Reporters can, of course, cover volleyball effectively without becoming walking dictionaries; but an understanding of the basics—kills, service aces, and blocks—is essential.

A *kill* is the most common way for a team to score. The ball is passed to a setter who sets it up for a hitter who tries to slam the ball down on the floor past the opposing team's blockers. If the ball hits the floor in bounds, it results in a score for the serving team.

Service aces occur when the serve is placed in such a way that it is difficult, if not impossible, for the opposing team to return it. The official scorer determines this. If the other team simply mishandles a ''routine'' serve, it is not counted as a service ace—but it still counts as a point.

A *block*, according to Scates' book, is: "A play by one or more players . . . to intercept the ball over or near the net. Blocking is permitted by any or all the players in the front line."

These basic terms can be found in volleyball match stories written by Maiorana. They are blended into stories in ways that readers can understand.

Writing Match Stories

Maiorana, in the first three paragraphs of her story on an Arizona State-UCLA volleyball match, captured the emotion of the contest. She began:

> Arizona State volleyball coach Dale Flickinger knew it wouldn't be as easy to upset the fourth-ranked UCLA Bruins as it looked after the first two games in P. E. East Building.
>
> The No. 10 Sun Devils ran up two quick victories, 15–9 and 15–4, before falling behind, 14–11, in the third game.
>
> The serve changed sides eight times before ASU scored the decisive point, making it 17–15.
>
> "We're 5-0 against the Bruins now," Flickinger said. "I think it has something to do with their tradition. They're a power, and we're always up for them."

In the opening paragraphs, Maiorana told not only that ASU had won—but how it had won: It had fought back from a 14–11 deficit and, after the serve changed hands eight times, tallied the match point. Also, the reporter managed to weave quotations from the ASU coach into the early part of the story.

Maiorana continued her story with more direct quotations, more analysis, and more play-by-play. By blending these ingredients, Maiorana made the story more readable and comprehensive. She wrote:

> Flickinger said the timing of the matches against UCLA made a difference.
>
> "We always catch UCLA at a bad time," he said.
>
> Flickinger praised the play of middle blocker Terri Edison, a 6-2 junior.
>
> "Her hitting was incredible," he said. "And Tuesdi Valadez came off the bench to stabilize us there at the end.
>
> "In the past, we would have lost games we were behind in like that."
>
> In the first game, ASU fell behind, 8–5, after a series of errors. But the Sun Devils scored the next five points and held the lead.
>
> The Sun Devils surged ahead with six consecutive points behind the serving of Rebecca Koepke to open the second game. Trailing, 12–0, the Bruins scored the next four, but were handcuffed the rest of the way.

The third contest looked like it would be more of the same. But with a 9–5 lead, ASU committed enough errors to let UCLA tie the score at 10–10. Three reception errors and a Bruin kill put the visitors ahead 14–10.

With Heather Forbes serving, the Sun Devils regained their composure and pulled to within one. They went ahead on a UCLA kill error and scored the final point on a block by Suzy Boggess and Carla Greenup.

Clearly, Maiorana had taken good notes as the games progressed. Her description of the changing leads, reception errors, and kills helped to explain how the game was won. Just as key plays on a successful drive for a touchdown in a football game need to be reported, key plays in a volleyball match can be relayed to the reader.

Maiorana closed her story with an overview of individual performances. She wrote:

Valentina Vega paced the Sun Devils with 14 kills and Lisa Stuck chipped in 12. Forbes added four service aces, while Edison and Greenup combined for 10 block assists.

The win raises ASU's record to 20-7 overall and 3-2 in the conference. UCLA fell to 12-6 and 1-3.

In another match story, the *Mesa Tribune* reporter started with a summary lead before focusing on an outstanding individual performance. She wrote:

The No. 8-seeded Arizona State University volleyball team defeated Illinois State University in first-round NCAA regional tournament action in the P. E. East Building Saturday afternoon 14–16, 15–13, 15–8 and 15–13.

The Sun Devils play Cal Poly-San Luis Obispo Friday afternoon in San Luis Obispo.

Lisa Stuck, a first team All-Western Collegiate Athletic Association pick, set a school record for match hitting percentage. She was successful on 29 of 49 attempts.

"The way Lisa was hitting, we could have put her up against a 9-foot wall and she would have scored," said ASU coach Dale Flickinger, who also credited Suzy Boggess with good right-side hitting.

But ISU's first game victory had the Sun Devils coach worried.

"We had control of the game, but we still lost," he said. "But hanging in there and winning that second game made the difference.

"We hadn't played for two weeks and in that first game, you're jittery."

As she had done in reporting the ASU-UCLA match, Maiorana provided good play-by-play description. This time, since Stuck's play had been so outstanding, Maiorana's account of key plays followed the individual statistics and quotes about the Sun Devil star. The *Mesa Tribune* reporter continued:

> ASU lost the first game after leading by scores 10–4 and 14–11. ISU's Cathy Olson served the final five points.
>
> The turning point for the Sun Devils came with the score knotted 7–7 in the second game.
>
> ASU reeled off five consecutive points with a combination of two Boggess service aces, a Stuck kill, a Carla Greenup-Stuck block and a Greenup kill.
>
> The Redbirds made up three points, but ASU held on to win.
>
> Two ISU ball handling violations early in the third game set the momentum in favor of ASU.
>
> When the Redbirds pulled to within two points, Stuck turned on the power and helped to keep ASU ahead.
>
> With Valentina Vega serving, Stuck spiked a pair past the opponents and Terri Edison chipped in a kill to give the Sun Devils a 3–0 lead in the fourth game.
>
> But the Redbirds tied the score twice, at 8–8 and 13–13.
>
> The final two ASU points came on a Greenup kill and an ISU kill error.
>
> Vega finished the match with 18 kills, Greenup with eight and Heather Forbes, Boggess and Edison had seven apiece.
>
> ASU is now 31-15 while ISU, after its first NCAA tournament, is 29-18.

Again, Maiorana was specific. For example, readers were made to visualize the action as ASU jumped to a 3–0 lead in the fourth game. The reporter merely could have written that ASU spurted to a quick advantage. Instead, Maiorana used alliteration to tell how Stuck "spiked a pair past the opponents" and "Terri Edison chipped in a kill."

Maiorana used a contrast lead effectively in her story about an Arizona State-Southern Cal match. She began:

> While thousands of sports fans focused on Tempe last night for the Arizona State-Southern Cal football matchup, several hundred others were intent on Sun Devil-Trojan action of a different sort Saturday afternoon.
>
> The sixth-ranked ASU volleyball squad fell to No. 7 USC on Parent Appreciation Day, 15–10, 8–15, 9–15 and 7–15 in front of a packed house in the P. E. East Building.

No matter what type of lead is selected—summary, contrast, even anecdotal—it is important to get game scores high in the story. Maiorana did that in the paragraphs excerpted above. Before citing more statistics, however, the reporter provided direct quotations from the coach:

"If you look at those last three games, we were never really in it," ASU coach Dale Flickinger said. "This is the first year we've had the capability to win.

"I'd stem the whole thing from not playing good defense. If you play good defense behind the block, you win."

Lisa Stuck executed 26 kills for a .404 match percentage, a personal record, and made three service aces. Valentina Vega chipped in 22 kills.

After quoting the coach and isolating key individual statistics, Maiorana noted big plays. She wrote:

In the first game, ASU ran up a 4–0 cushion behind the serving of Vega and pushed it to 7–1 with Terri Edison serving.

The Trojans came back to knot the score at 8–8 and went ahead when they blocked an ASU kill.

But the Sun Devils regained the advantage as Suzy Boggess served two consecutives aces, Edison added a dink shot, and Vega made two kills. Stuck scored the final point.

It did not take long for Maiorana to report key plays in the second game—a contest USC used as a springboard to three consecutive wins. She wrote:

ASU scored the first point in the second game, but USC scored the next six. After ASU struggled for a second point, USC answered with five more. A USC kill error gave ASU a third point, a Rebecca Koepke ace provided the fourth and a Vega-Carla Greenup block was the fifth.

Then USC got down to business, fending off the Sun Devils for the rest of the game.

Maiorana's accounts illustrate that volleyball can be effectively covered— if the reporter has a working knowledge of the game. Her stories are a careful blend of results (which team captured three games to win the match and the scores of each game), direct quotations from coaches and players, basic statistics (kills and blocks), and play-by-play of turning points.

Exercises

1. Discuss coverage given to college and high school volleyball in area newspapers. Do some newspapers provide better coverage than others? What makes their coverage better?

2. Invite a local volleyball coach to class. Ask the coach to discuss new rules or emerging issues, and aspects of scoring and terms you do not understand. Does the coach have suggestions for feature stories or for ways coverage can be improved?

3. Write a feature about a local volleyball player or some aspect of the sport.

4. Cover a volleyball match. Be sure to work relevant statistics and direct quotations from coaches and athletes into the story.

Reporters can use descriptive writing in reporting action at high school and college wrestling matches.

(Photo by T. J. Sokol)

CHAPTER THIRTEEN

Wrestling

Westling is considered a major sport at many high schools and colleges. It has grown in popularity during the past two decades. Still, many college and high school coaches contend that they have to promote their sport extensively to draw crowds. Arizona State University Coach Bobby Douglas said he tries to "establish the wrestling team as an exciting, competitive source of spectator entertainment."

In some states, promotion is not necessary. It is not unusual for more than 10,000 fans to attend wrestling meets at the University of Iowa or Iowa State. Both schools perennially are among the nation's elite. Their fans expect—and receive—extensive coverage of the sport.

Veteran writer Buck Turnbull of the *Des Moines* (Iowa) *Register*, who first covered the National Collegiate Athletic Association's wrestling championships in 1973, strives to make his stories understandable to the "average reader."

"I don't get too involved in the technical terms because the average reader will not understand them," Turnbull said. "You have to keep it simple. It is important to tell a story that the reader can understand. Most readers, for example, know what is meant by a takedown, escape, or pin. But if you get involved in the technical jargon in a sport such as wrestling you are going to lose a lot of your readers after the first two or three paragraphs."

Turnbull keeps a running score as the meet progresses. He also does his homework before a meet. "You have to be prepared," he said. "It's just like covering any sport. You have to go in with a game plan. Know in advance the key matches that could be pivotal to the outcome of the meet. If you do not go into a meet with a good background, especially in championship competition, you will get bogged down as results are thrown at you.

Unless you are organized, you will get swamped. If you plan ahead, if you have talked with the coaches, if you have reviewed old clips, if you know key wrestlers and weight classes, you are less likely to make mistakes or overlook something.''

The Scoring

Wrestling meets are divided into weight classes. In college, for example, there are ten weight classes: 118 pounds; 126 pounds; 134 pounds; 142 pounds; 150 pounds; 158 pounds; 167 pounds; 177 pounds; 190 pounds; and heavyweight. High school meets also are divided into weight classes, with competition often starting in the 98-pound category. Weight classes are correspondingly smaller for junior high school competition.

Reporters need to check the guidelines for both individual and team scoring before covering a match. In college competition, there are three periods of wrestling in each weight class. The first period lasts three minutes, while the second and third periods are two minutes each. Points awarded in individual matches are: takedown, 2 points; reversal, 2 points; escape, 1 point; near fall (more than one second but less than five seconds), 2 points; near fall (more than five seconds), 3 points; and riding time (awarded to a wrestler who accumulates more than a one-minute advantage), 1 point. Points are subtracted for illegal holds or for false starts after one warning. The second offense costs the wrestler 1 point, the third offense costs 1 point, the fourth offense costs 4 points, and the fifth offense results in disqualification.

Points awarded after each match for team scoring are: draw, each team gets 2 points; decision, 3 points to the winner; major decision (a win by more than 8 points but less than 12), 4 points; superior decision (a win by 12 or more points), 5 points; pin, 6 points; default or disqualification, 6 points; and forfeit, 6 points.

The results of a dual meet between Arizona State and Athletes in Action, shown in figure 13.1, illustrates the scoring. After the first five matches, Arizona State held a 15–3 lead. Athletes in Action cut the lead to 15–7 after a major decision in the 158-pound class and to 15–13 after a pin in the 167-pound class. ASU's pin in the 177-class put the Sun Devils back on top 21–13. Athletes in Action won by a pin at 190 pounds to climb within two points, 21–19, going into the final match. AIA won the heavy-weight match by default when the ASU wrestler was injured. The 6-point heavyweight match victory pushed AIA past ASU 25–21.

After the match, the reporter should have checked the seriousness of the injury suffered by ASU's heavyweight before writing a story. The story could have started like this:

Figure 13.1
Results of a Dual Meet: Individual Match Score

ASU TEAM Score		ASU		AIA		AIA Team Score
3	118 — Don Mabry	13	vs.	10	Frank Harl	0
0	126 — Tom Graham	8	vs.	9	Greg Fetzer	3
3	134 — Gary Bohay	10	vs.	7	J. D. Hawkins	0
3	142 — Tom Riley	7	vs.	4	Jesse Castro	0
6	150 — Adam Cohen	—won by forfeit—				0
0	158 — Eddie Urbano	6	vs.	15	Steve Suder	4
0	167 — Dan Mear		vs.	won by pin	Jon Lundberg	6
6	177 — Tom Kolopus	won by pin	vs.		Dan Morrison	0
0	190 — Bob Barnes		vs.	won by pin	Greg O'Koorian	6
0	HWT — Mike Severn		vs.	won by default	Drew Whitfield	6
21		TOTAL TEAM SCORE				25

Arizona State wrestler Mike Severn suffered an incomplete separation of his right shoulder Friday night as ASU dropped an exhibition match to Athletes in Action. Severn will be out of action indefinitely.

Severn, last year's Pacific-10 Conference runnerup, appeared on his way to victory in the heavyweight match when he had to default. AIA, which trailed ASU 21–19 going into the last match, earned a 25–21 exhibition victory.

The Sun Devils got off to a fast start, winning four of the first five matches.

The early lead did not hold up, however, as AIA won four of the last five, two by pins and one by default.

After these early paragraphs, the story logically would flow into details of key weight classes, with references to fastest pin, most lopsided match, most exciting matches, and the like.

In big meets, such as conference and national competition, teams accumulate points each time their wrestlers advance; bonus points are awarded for pins, superior and major decisions. In the NCAA championships, for example, first place is worth 16 points, second place is 12, third place is 9, and fourth place is 7.

The scoring at all levels of competition is straightforward. Since there could be variations of the NCAA summaries listed above, however, the reporter always should check with meet officials before competition is underway.

Writing Match Stories

The *Des Moines Register*, with collegiate wrestling powers Iowa and Iowa State nearby, provides extensive coverage of the sport. Staff writer Turnbull tries to capture the emotion and intensity of the sport in his writing. His use of adjectives and strong verbs makes his match stories pleasures to read. When Iowa downed Iowa State in a dual match, Turnbull could have written:

> The University of Iowa's wrestling team beat Iowa State 24–11 in a dual match at Iowa State Saturday night.

The lead would have been grammatical and accurate. It would have been journalistically acceptable. But, Turnbull wrote:

> A dramatic pin by heavyweight Lou Banach climaxed a surprisingly easy 24–11 victory by Iowa's defending National Collegiate wrestling champions Saturday night over archrival Iowa State.

Notice the key words *dramatic pin, climaxed, surprisingly easy, National Collegiate wrestling champions*, and *archrival*. These key words bring to life an event that could simply have been reported as another ho-hum 24–11 victory.

After providing the most important information in the lead paragraph, Turnbull focused on the most exciting match of the evening. He wrote:

> The Hawkeyes were already assured of winning this early season showdown for the No. 1 ranking in the country when Banach suddenly found himself being mauled in the opening period against Wayne Cole, a Cyclone transfer from Iowa Central Community College in Fort Dodge.

With this paragraph, Turnbull effectively conjured up an image of the action: Banach was not merely losing in the early going, he was being *mauled*. Turnbull went on to provide more description:

> Cole scored a quick takedown and then stunned the near-silent crowd of 12,902 in Iowa Fieldhouse with another takedown and two-point near-fall just 30 seconds into the match.

That gave Cole a 6–1 lead and a three-point near-fall helped him increase the margin to an amazing 13–5 before Banach retaliated. He tossed Cole on his back and then finished him off after just 2 minutes 13 seconds.

After describing the action in the most exciting match of the evening, Turnbull provided an overview of the remainder. He wrote:

> Iowa won six of the 10 matches and got a draw by 126-pound Mark Trizzino in another to post its 49th consecutive triumph on the home mat.
>
> The other Hawkeye winners were Barry Davis (118), Lenny Zalesky (142), Jimmy Zalesky (158), Dave Fitzgerald (167) and Ed Banach (177).
>
> Fitzgerald furnished the key points that let Iowa pull away by beating Tom Pickard in a bout that figured to be critical in the premeet reckoning. He won it on an 11–2 major decision.
>
> "This was a big deal for me," said the elated Fitzgerald, a senior from Davenport. "I had never beaten a wrestler from Iowa State before. I figured that my match was going to be essential for us."
>
> Most of the wrestling was cautious and defensive, however, and had none of the excitement that Lou Banach and the unheralded Cole provided.

Turnbull provided descriptions of the remaining matches, interspersed with direct quotations from wrestlers and coaches, records of individuals, and national rankings. The story concluded with information on the Iowa-Iowa State rivalry: Iowa had taken command in the series 14–12–2.

Most newspapers do not cover a wrestling match in such detail. But Turnbull's story shows how the sport lends itself to descriptive writing, analysis of turning points, direct quotations, and background on competitors.

Turnbull's coverage of the NCAA championships also provided evidence of his knowledge of the sport and his ability to give readers accurate, informative, interesting, and descriptive coverage.

For the premeet story, Turnbull focused on the nation's No. 1 team—Iowa. He wrote:

> What it boils down to, Dan Gable said, Wednesday, will be his Iowa wrestlers against the rest of the country in the National Collegiate championships starting today in Ames.
>
> Everybody is laying for the top-ranked Hawkeyes, who are seeking their fifth straight NCAA wrestling title and their seventh in eight years.
>
> "I'm sure the Big Eight teams would really like to dethrone us," said Gable, "and it may come down to us against a Big Eight all-star team.

> "But my guys are ready. We're in good shape. I'd feel better if Lou Banach hadn't sprained his shoulder a few weeks ago, but I think he's recovered enough by now to make a good showing."
>
> The Hawkeye heavyweight and his brother, 177-pound Ed Banach, are among nine former champions in the 335-man field—eight from last season and one from the year before.
>
> Today's competition will begin with preliminary matches in Hilton Coliseum, followed by the first and second rounds this afternoon and tonight, trimming each weight class to eight title contenders.
>
> The quarterfinals will be staged Friday, starting at noon, and the semifinals that night. Consolation matches are slated for Saturday afternoon and the championships for Saturday night.

After writing a lead that focused on Iowa, its coach, and one of its top wrestlers, Turnbull provided basic meet information (sessions, times, and the like). The *Register* reporter then gave specifics on some contenders for the team and individual titles. The story concluded with the seeded wrestlers in each class.

For coverage of the first day of competition, Turnbull chose to focus his lead on Iowa's Banach brothers. He wrote:

> Those Banach brothers are at it again, getting favored Iowa off to a good start in quest of the school's fifth straight National Collegiate wrestling title.
>
> The two defending champions both scored pins Thursday night, with Lou putting a spectacular finish to the second round by flattening the heaviest entrant in the tournament, 407-pound Tab Thacker of North Carolina State, before a crowd of 11,718 in Hilton Coliseum.

After the lead, which drew readers' attention with mention of the state's best-known collegiate wrestlers, Turnbull gave details about the Hawkeyes and early team scoring. He wrote:

> Iowa had qualified its full 10-man lineup and moved eight into today's quarterfinals, taking firm command in the team race with 29½ points to 21 for second-place Iowa State. The Cyclones advanced six of their 10 through the early rounds.

Names and weights of individual Hawkeye and Cyclone wrestlers followed before Turnbull described the Lou Banach match with Thacker. He wrote how Ed Banach

> was the first person on the mat to lift brother Lou in a happy bear hug after the Hawkeye heavyweight did what seemed impossible by throwing the monstrous Thacker in 2:08.

Obviously, a good way to describe the win was to quote Coach Gable:

> "Holy mackerel, that was great," said Iowa Coach Dan Gable, who was almost beside himself with joy.
>
> "Lou did just what we told him. Thacker was almost ready to take him down, and Lou went for the headlock. We had warned Lou not to get his arms caught if Thacker tried to roll him.
>
> "So Lou pulled his arms away at just the right time, which gave him a brace when he took Thacker down. Actually, he got the pin off Thacker's move."

The remainder of the story described other key matches and evaluated the team scoring race. Complete results, by weight class, also were published in the *Register*.

Turnbull's second-day coverage of the meet logically continued to focus on Iowa. Readers naturally were interested in which wrestlers would advance to the finals. Turnbull provided the answer:

> Top-ranked Iowa continued to apply relentless pressure Friday night and send five wrestlers into tonight's championship matches of the National Collegiate tournament.
>
> Not even a semifinal loss by Lou Banach, the defending heavyweight king, slowed the Hawkeye charge as Barry Davis (118 pounds), Lenny Zalesky (142), Jimmy Zalesky (158), Ed Banach (177) and unheralded Pete Bush moved ahead to the final round.

After this general information, the reporter turned to the most exciting match of the night:

> Bush, a junior from Davenport, supplied the shocker before an evening crowd of 12,737 in Hilton Coliseum by pinning top-seeded Colin Kilrain of Lehigh in just 44 seconds. It was the first pin of Kilrain's collegiate career.

Turnbull continued his story by describing other key matches in the finals. The lead paragraph in the story of the finals was a natural. It told how the Hawkeyes had set a scoring record in winning the championship. Turnbull wrote:

> Iowa did the expected but with a couple of surprises Saturday night, winning its fifth straight National Collegiate wrestling championship by rolling up a record of 131¾ points.
>
> The biggest shocker was that the top-ranked Hawkeyes did it without getting an individual title from either of the Banach brothers.

But three other members of Iowa's star-studded lineup came through with title victories—Barry Davis (118 pounds), Jimmy Zalesky (158) and surprising Pete Bush (190).

Ed Banach, hoping to win a third 177-pound crown on the way to a possible four, saw that dream end when he lost a 16–8 decision to Oklahoma's Mark Schultz before a sellout crowd of 14,204 in Hilton Coliseum.

Turnbull quoted Gable high in the story:

"You always have your ups and downs," said Iowa Coach Dan Gable, who became the first coach in NCAA wrestling history to coach five consecutive championships.

"I was sorry to see Ed Banach lose. But there is one thing about the Banach boys. They thrive on motivation, and Mark Schultz will be back next year, so that should keep Ed motivated for next season."

Descriptions of all championship matches, more direct quotations, and complete team and individual results followed the story. Individual results were published in agate type. The *Register* provided a summary of each weight class. The 118-pound class, for example, showed:

Consolation final round—Bob Weaver, Lehigh, beat Joe McFarland, Michigan, 13–4; Bob Monaghan, North Carolina, beat Randy Willingham, Oklahoma State, 5–2.

Seventh place—Bob Weaver, Indiana State, pinned Charlie Heard, Tenn-Chattanooga, 4:26.

Fifth place—Willingham beat McFarland, 3–1.

Third place—Weaver beat Monaghan, 9–7.

Championship—Barry Davis, Iowa, beat Kevin Darkus, Iowa State, 7–5.

It is not difficult to dryly report winners and losers, by weight class, in a wrestling match story. But to cover the sport well, the reporter needs to buttress the scoring with vivid description, strong verbs, and effective use of direct quotations.

Exercises

1. Discuss coverage given to college and high school wrestling in area newspapers. Do some newspapers provide better coverage than others? What makes their coverage better?

2. Invite a wrestling coach to class. Ask the coach to discuss new rules or emerging trends, and aspects of scoring and terms that you do not understand. Does the coach have suggestions for feature stories or for ways coverage can be improved?

3. Write a feature about a wrestler or wrestling coach, or some aspect of the sport.

4. Cover a wrestling match. You might want to use a narrative or descriptive lead.

Coverage Beyond Stadiums and Arenas

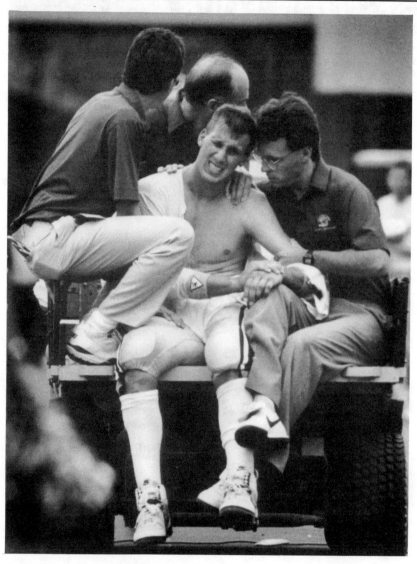

**Sports features can capture the pain and
frustration experienced by injured athletes.**

(Photo by T. J. Sokol)

CHAPTER FOURTEEN

Features

Sports reporters assigned to write feature articles can escape the restrictions of formula writing associated with the inverted pyramid approach to hard news stories. Features, which often emphasize a human dimension, might be categorized as personality profiles, trend stories, backgrounders, or analysis pieces. Seldom do features convey news firsthand. Rather, features illuminate a news event, add color to a breaking development, educate the reader, or simply entertain.

Sports pages are filled with both straight news stories and features. Mary Gillespie of the *Chicago Sun-Times* has said that feature writing is news writing with a heart. Indeed, the line that separates a straight news story from a feature has become fuzzier. Today, it is not uncommon for traditional hard news stories—such as the hiring of a new coach—to be softened with a featurized human angle.

The Story of a Playground Basketball Star

Steve Schoenfeld, the National Football League writer for *The Arizona Republic* in Phoenix, covers football almost year round. When searching for a summer feature project, he decided to select a nonfootball topic. "I wanted to do something different," he said. "I had read some playground basketball stories, and I thought it would be interesting to find the best playground player in Phoenix." He was given sixteen days to write the feature story. During that period, he was able to devote most of his time to the project.

The former *Tulsa Tribune* and *Dallas Times Herald* sportswriter started the story from scratch. "It was very frustrating at first," he said. "I had the idea for the story, but I had no clue about who the best players were or where the most competitive courts were located. I asked our high school writers to give me some suggestions on coaches who would know where the better players might be. Some of the high school coaches run summer recreation programs, but I had a hard time hooking up with them.''

The key to Schoenfeld's feature was finding the top playground players and locating the best courts in metropolitan Phoenix, which has a population of nearly 2.5 million. He was five days into his story when he accomplished that task. He had eleven days to conduct most of his interviews, visit all the playgrounds and gymnasiums, select the best player, and write his mainbar and sidebars. During that time, he drove nine hundred miles and visited sixteen parks.

The focus of his main story was clear: Feature the best playground player in Phoenix and incorporate how playground basketball works at the best places in town. Schoenfeld's sources were numerous. He interviewed more than a dozen top players, about fifteen playground supervisors, a handful of high school coaches, two college coaches, and former NBA star and assistant coach for the Phoenix Suns, Paul Westphal. In addition, he interviewed dozens of people at parks and gyms, seeking information on the best players and places to play.

"It was sort of scary in the beginning," Schoenfeld said. "I wasn't sure that I was ever going to get anywhere. A story like this is difficult in Phoenix because of the weather. During the late spring and summer months, people don't go out in the day much. I was trying to do my normal day workload and then I was having to make the rounds of the playgrounds at night. Because of the heat, a lot of the pickup players in Phoenix are gym players rather than asphalt players. I should have realized that in the beginning, but I didn't.''

Schoenfeld allowed himself two full days for writing, rewriting, and polishing. He produced a 58-inch mainbar, a 30-inch sidebar, a 7-inch informational sidebar, and information for graphics. "Once I began to write, the complicated part was to figure out how to profile this guy who we picked as the best player, but not to just make it a feature on him,'' Schoenfeld said. "I wanted to intertwine information about playground basketball and its characters with the profile of our top player.''

Schoenfeld's mainbar was an informative, human interest, quick read. Like all good features, it contained:

- A clear, tightly focused theme.
- A strong lead block.
- Effective transitions.
- Effective use of direct quotations from a variety of sources.

- Descriptive observation.
- A strong, logical ending.

The Lead Block

Schoenfeld's lead block focused exclusively on the man selected as the top playground player in Phoenix—Robert Spellman. In the lead block, Schoenfeld gave the reader a glimpse of Spellman's personality, his use of language, and his dedication to the game.

> To qualify as a "ball-a-holic," an asphalt animal, you must spend your youth waking up everyone in the neighborhood.
>
> That happened in Robert Spellman's south Phoenix neighborhood every morning at 4:30 when the alarms went off as soon as he took his first backyard dribble.
>
> He still gets up that early to shoot the rock and finishes late, often closing down Glendale's Harry Bonsall Sr. Park, known as the "Chicken Park" on the Valley's concrete circuit.
>
> On a typical day, he's also likely to play pickup games at Mesa's Broadway Recreation Center at 8 a.m.; the Student Recreation Complex at Arizona State at 11; Desert West Park in west Phoenix at 1 p.m.; and Indian School Park in Scottsdale at 5:30.
>
> One night last week, he played in a summer-league game at Mesa Community College at 6:30, in the Juneteenth Tournament at Eastlake Park at 8 and in a pickup game at Grand Canyon University at 9.
>
> Often, he leaves before games are finished.
>
> "If I'm winning, I leave at halftime," he said.
>
> "I'm a ball fanatic, a ball-a-holic. Wherever there is a run, I'll go. I don't care how far."
>
> A run is a full-court game in pickup lingo and nobody in the Valley does it better than Spellman, even though he is wearing out his family's automobiles in the process.
>
> He tries to drive a different car each time. Sometimes, he takes his mom's Plymouth Horizon. His brother lends him his Mazda RX7. He also bums rides from friends.
>
> "People come up to me and say, 'You're one of the best pickup players,'" Spellman said. "I don't like to hear that. I don't want to be just a pickup player. I don't want to be a playground legend."
>
> That's why Spellman plans to attend the Suns' rookie camp July 18-20 at Veterans Memorial Coliseum. He was invited by Suns assistant coach Paul Westphal, who recruited Spellman out of South Mountain Community College when he was coach at Grand Canyon.
>
> "A playground legend is somebody who never is going to get a shot," he said. "I'm getting my shot. I want to make some money playing."

Effective Transition

One of the most challenging aspects of writing a lengthy feature is connecting all the information, observation, and direct quotations. Schoenfeld chose to connect his story with quotations about basketball from well-known people. For example, after constructing a lead block that focused on Spellman, Schoenfeld wrote a twelve-paragraph section about playground basketball in Phoenix. He noted stars who had played on the Phoenix courts, some rules of the games, and playing styles.

The transition quotation—which was graphically displayed as a pull quote in larger, italic type—was this:

> "Ever play this game, Chief? C'mon, I'll show ya. Old Indian game. It's called, uh, put the ball in the hole."—Jack Nicholson, to Will Sampson in *One Flew Over the Cuckoo's Nest.*

That quotation led the reader into the next section that began with these six paragraphs:

> Sacramento Kings guard Steve Colter first experienced pickup basketball as an infant when his father, Andrew, brought him to Harmon Park's gym in a bassinet.
>
> Colter, a former Phoenix Union High School star, has been going there every Saturday in the summer ever since.
>
> "If you could play at Harmon, you could play anywhere," Colter said.
>
> The games there can get rough. Few fights erupt, but the meek should stay out of the paint.
>
> "I've seen a lot of friends go there and get hurt," Spellman said of Harmon. "It's wild."
>
> Connie Hawkins used to play there. So did Fat Lever and Byron Scott and Johnny Smith of the Harlem Globetrotters.

After detailing some rules—no credit is given for 3-point shots, dunking is allowed, and so forth—Schoenfeld ended the section with direct quotations:

> "The place (Harmon Park) has so much tradition," former South Mountain College player Karl Finley said. "Me and (former Grand Canyon guard) Rodney Johns used to just go to the gym as kids and watch. We weren't big enough to play, but you could learn so much.
>
> "A lot of moves come from street ball. You couldn't do them in a game. But in street ball, you can pretend you're Michael Jordan."

Schoenfeld's next section was introduced with a transition pull quote from Tom Heinsohn, former Boston Celtics forward, who had once commented on why he didn't play football:

> "If I was going to get beat up, I wanted to be indoors where it was warm."

Schoenfeld played off that quote to move into the heart of his piece: a description of the most competitive playgrounds in town; names of the most competitive players; and, of course, more direct quotes.

Effective Use of Direct Quotations from a Variety of Sources

Schoenfeld made good use of direct quotations, a common ingredient of good feature stories. For example, the writer passed on a quote from Chris "Backboard" Manning, a twenty-nine-year-old furniture builder and self-professed intimidator:

> "I'm the best (expletive) talker," he said. "They get so mad at me, it takes them out of their game. I don't have the jumping ability, so (woofing) is my defense."

In describing rough play at one court, Schoenfeld selected this quote for his readers:

> "I heard guys get fouls called on them and then get a gun on somebody," said Kevin Skinner, who plays at Cave Creek.

The following anecdote involving Spellman was enhanced by the direct quotes:

> Spellman likes nothing better than to play former and current (Arizona State University) Sun Devils.
> "I met this guy at ASU recently," Spellman said of guard Stevin Smith. "He told me, 'Just call me Hedake.'
> "I did well against him. Afterwards, I told him, 'Just call me Anacin.'
> "It bothers me when I go against Division I guys. I see guys out there that I crush. I play with a vengeance against them."

Descriptive Observation

Schoenfeld's story contained another essential ingredient of most good features—observation. For example:

> Encanto also is one of the Valley's loudest courts. Music boxes are allowed. Controversial rap group N.W.A. is the players' favorite.
>
> Two-year-old Cave Creek is the Valley's most modern outdoor facility.
>
> At a concession stand called "The Sports Cafe," players can eat an albacore tuna sandwich.
>
> As many as 750 to 1,000 players show up on a Sunday night, with losers waiting 30 minutes to return to action.

Strong, Logical Ending

Schoenfeld concluded his lengthy feature the way he began it: looking at Spellman. The writer provided background on the star (he was a gospel singer before he began playing basketball at age seven; he was an all-state high school player who starred in junior college but didn't shine when he transferred to Idaho, which played a slow-down offense) and more description ("He has great vision, plays pressure defense for 94 feet, can pound the ball with either hand, penetrate and dish. In one summer league game, he drove to the hoop, did a 360 and passed under his legs to a teammate for a lay-up."); and a concluding quote. The closing quote, in fact, tied back to the lead block:

> Spellman will get that chance (to play against first-rate competition) next month at the Suns' camp. Until then, he will continue to give his neighbors early morning wake-up calls.
>
> Does he worry that he will become a nuisance?
>
> "You don't make any noise when you hit nothing but net."

Writing Sidebars

When writers tackle a major feature story, such as Schoenfeld's piece on playground basketball in Phoenix, they will gather a lot of information, and it is not possible to weave it all into the mainbar. In most instances, they write sidebars. Schoenfeld's sidebar featured a handful of other Phoenix playground stars and legends, many of whom boasted descriptive nicknames ("Fin-Rock," "Pickpocket," "Flakes," and "Mr. C."). The focus of the sidebar was Mr. C.—fifty-four-year-old Andrew Colter, father of Sacramento Kings guard Steve Colter. The elder Colter had been spending his Saturdays at Harmon Park gym for more than thirty years.

The accompanying artwork included photos, a map highlighting all the courts Spellman played on in one day, a list of the best places to play, and miscellanea such as best music (Encanto Park), best food (Cave Creek Sports Complex's Sports Cafe), best T-shirt (Encanto Park, "Smile if you're not wearing any underwear"), and best rules (Blue Gym at ASU Student Recreation Center, $10 fine, and one-week suspension for anyone opening doors to allow unauthorized access).

Clearly, Schoenfeld's hard work was apparent. He came up with a good idea for a feature; he diligently scoured knowledgeable sources; he set aside time for intense writing; his free-flowing style matched the subject he was writing about; and he packaged the material to make it easy for the readers to comprehend. Indeed, his feature bared the heart and soul of playground basketball in metropolitan Phoenix.

Black Basketball Coaches: Climbing the Ladder of Success

Too often, journalism students take writing features for granted. After all, what could be simpler than conducting an interview or two and building a story around direct quotations? Good features, though, are often predicated on sound research as well as good interviewing.

Solid research was evident in a story by J. A. Adande that was published in *The Daily Northwestern*. That story, which won a sports writing award in the William R. Hearst Foundation's intercollegiate writing competition, examined the challenge faced by blacks who aspire to head coaching positions at large universities.

The Lead Block

Adande's first three paragraphs outlined the parameters of his story without giving away the specific peg.

> Northwestern assistant basketball coach Tim Carter's share of Welsh-Ryan Arena is more of a stopping place than an office. Only the essentials—desk, chairs, bulletin board, calendar and a few notes—are there. A picture of his family serves as the only decoration.
>
> His stint at NU, the fifth coaching job of his career, is just another stop on his way to what he hopes will someday be the big office: a head coaching position at a Division I school.
>
> "There's no question that I want to be a head coach," Carter says. "If you don't have aspirations of being a head coach, you're wasting your time."

Head coaching jobs, though, are not easy to come by—and virtually every college assistant aspires to one. But, Adande's story featured this twist: head coaching jobs are particularly hard to come by for blacks.

The Nut Graphs

In his fourth and fifth paragraphs, Adande told readers precisely what his story was all about. Usually, the peg of a feature story is revealed in a single "nut graph" or "so-what" graph as the writer makes the transition from the lead block to the body of the piece. In essence, the writer says to the reader: I've set you up with the lead block, and now I'm going to usher you directly into the heart of the story. Occasionally, though, it takes two or three paragraphs to lead the reader into the body. Here are Adande's "nut graphs":

> But if you are an African-American like Carter, the odds are not in your favor.
> Of the 290 NCAA Division I head basketball coaches, only 50 are African-Americans, 18 of them at historically black colleges. The number is disproportionate, considering the fact that 56 percent of college basketball players are black.

Readers now know what this story is all about. It's not merely a general feature about assistant basketball coaches who aspire to head jobs; it's a story that focuses on the odds faced by black assistants who want to be head coaches.

The Importance of Research

Clearly, Adande had done his homework. Northwestern's Carter was the local source; but this was not a one-source story. Adande interviewed black coaches who brought their teams to Northwestern to play. But, in order to build a firm foundation for the story, the writer also consulted reference material and an academic source.

The next ten paragraphs of Adande's story were based upon an interview with Ohio State head coach Randy Ayers and upon research.

> "You have to remember that college athletics has been a 'good-ol'-boys' network, much like Corporate America," says Charles Farrell, a special projects coordinator at the Northeastern University Center for the Study of Sports and Society in Boston. "Blacks can't get into the 'good-ol'-boy' pipeline as easily as whites."
> Randy Ayers is one of the lucky few. An assistant at Ohio State for

six years, Ayers was given the job when head coach Gary Williams left for the University of Maryland in 1989. Ayers now has his Buckeyes ranked No. 2 in the nation in his second year as head coach.

"I was very lucky," Ayers says. "I was in the right place at the right time. I feel very fortunate to be in the position that I am."

Ayers knows who he owes his debt to.

"I think you have to give credit to some of the old black coaches— John Thompson (at Georgetown), John Chaney (at Temple)—that opened the doors for some of us young coaches," Ayers says. "Coach (Clarence) Gaines down at Winston-Salem—all those guys have done some big things for us over the years and I think it's starting to pay off a little bit."

Clarence (Bighouse) Gaines is an institution at Winston-Salem, an NCAA Division II school. He has been there for nearly half a century and has more than 800 career victories. He won the Division II title in 1967, making Winston-Salem the first black college to win an NCAA title.

Ten years earlier, John McClendon, Jr., won the first national title for a black college when he guided Tennessee State to a National Association of Intercollegiate Athletics tournament victory.

At the time, black colleges were the only option for blacks who wanted to become coaches. In "Art Rust's Illustrated History of the Black Athlete," Chuck Cooper, the first black player drafted by the National Basketball Association, shows how frustrating it was to try to find a job: "I felt I knew the game and how to handle young men. But there were no opportunities for black coaches then. When my alma mater (Duquesne) was looking for a coach, they approached me in a roundabout way, but it was only for a position as an assistant coach. If I was white, they would have offered me the top spot."

"The earlier trailblazers like Gaines and McClendon helped open the doors for black coaches to get jobs at predominantly white schools. The next wave, including Thompson and Chaney, who played for Gaines, helped keep the doors open by winning. Thompson's Georgetown team won the NCAA Division I tournament in 1984.

"Had the pioneers not been successful, it would have been very difficult for many others to follow," Farrell says. "All coaches have to have success, but blacks have to be twice as good."

After enlightening readers with relevant background on black basketball coaches, Adande made good use of direct quotes from Minnesota coach Clem Haskins. The story then examined the Black Coaches Association, an organization that provides a network for coaches.

The next major section of the story explored what Adande called "one of the biggest advantages and drawbacks for black coaches": many have reputations for being good recruiters. Having a reputation as a good recruiter, of course, is fine—to a point; the problem occurs when coaches get categorized as "recruiters" rather than multidimensional coaches.

The final section of the story discussed what the future held for black coaches. Like many good features, the story ended with a strong direct quotation:

> "I hope people think of me as a good basketball coach who happens to be black," says Clem Haskins of Minnesota. "Don't get me wrong. I'm happy to be black; I'm proud to be black. But if I win, it's not because I'm black. I know what I'm doing."

Adande's feature was a calculated blend of background information, direct quotes, and contemporary issues—all neatly tied together with logical transitions.

Putting a Personality with the Voice

Some of the most readable features are personality profiles. Writers have the opportunity to probe beneath the surface demeanor of famous people as well as not-so-famous people to tell readers what they are really like.

One of the best known voices in metropolitan Phoenix belongs to Al McCoy. But most people would not recognize him if they met him on the street. McCoy, the radio-television announcer of the Phoenix Suns, has a smooth-as-silk delivery and a colorful vocabulary. English professors can quote Shakespeare. Students of basketball in Arizona can quote "McCoyisms."

Joel Horn, a journalism student at Arizona State University, was captivated by McCoy's delivery and on-air presence. He sat by McCoy during an NBA game, talked to scores of players, coaches, and fans, and took notes of patented McCoy phrases during a series of Suns games. The result was a lucid, fast-paced personality profile of McCoy that was published in the *State Press*, ASU's campus daily. The story won a national award in the William Randolph Hearst Foundation's intercollegiate writing championships. Readers got a good look at McCoy in Horn's smoothly flowing ninety-two paragraph profile that was tied together with highlighted quotes from the announcer's play-by-play repertoire.

The Lead Block

Horn started his story with two paragraphs of narration, a nut graph that told readers who and what the story was all about, and several direct quotations from McCoy. The writer pulled readers into his story with this eight-paragraph block:

> Arizona Veteran's Memorial Coliseum at 19th Avenue and McDowell
> is rapidly becoming a sea of purple and orange as coaches for the

Phoenix Suns and Denver Nuggets, tonight's National Basketball Association opponents, mingle at courtside moments before tipoff.

The players glide through their pregame warmups as dozens of well-dressed, suntanned, mostly affluent people file by the scorer's table. Many extend a hand or a pat on the back to the impeccably groomed man sitting just to the left of the Suns bench. He smiles and welcomes them warmly.

Those who don't know his face surely recognize the voice, for he is Al McCoy, "the Voice of the Phoenix Suns" for the past 18 years. To those in the arena and tens of thousands of basketball fans throughout Arizona, McCoy is much more than an announcer. He **IS** the Phoenix Suns.

McCoy doesn't enunciate words. They ripple from his lips; in the heat of a game, he's calm; the words flow, as if his mouth is on automatic pilot.

Turn on the radio. McCoy is always enthused, always under control, no matter if the Suns are ahead or behind.

"There's so many great plays every single night in pro basketball, I think more than any other sport," the bespectacled 56-year-old McCoy said as he adjusted his seat behind the announcers table. "If you make every one of those plays sound like the end of the world, you have no place to go.

"You've got to maintain a certain amount of composure while you're doing the game. If you start off the game and everything is bang, bang, bang and everything is fantastic, then everything sounds the same."

McCoy's office is in the Suns Executive Office on Central Avenue in Phoenix. He is employed by the team to broadcast their games on KTAR Radio and KUTP-TV in Phoenix.

Transition to the Lingo

Horn interspersed a series of twelve italicized quotes from McCoy's play-by-play to provide logical transitions throughout the story as well as to entertain readers. The first quotation in the series was McCoy's description of the tipoff: "Rasmussen against West and the Suns control the tip. So we're underway here at the Madhouse on McDowell."

That quote introduced a twelve-paragraph section that focused on McCoy's most famous trait: his terminology. Here are the first six paragraphs of the section:

Another announcer would be called the "king of cliches" if he spouted the descriptives that drip from McCoy's lips. But not McCoy. Somehow, his language—always spontaneous and colorful, yet somehow controlled—transcends the cliches. A cliche from McCoy sounds almost lyrical. "Twine time!"

"A lot of announcers are statisticians and color commentators," said

> Jim Taszarek, general manager of KTAR Radio and an acknowledged expert in the broadcasting industry. "Al is more of a reporter. He paints word pictures."
>
> Through the years, McCoy has been identified by his colorful lingo: "Pigeon" Paul Silas, Alvin "the Space Needle" Scott, "Leapin'" Lamar Green and current player "Thunder" Dan Majerle have all donned the Suns purple, orange and copper.
>
> Suns career scoring leader Walter Davis, now with the Nuggets, was never simply "Davis." He was either "Sir Walter," or "Sweet D," or—if he was on a shooting binge with his satiny-soft outside jumper— he was "the man with the velvet touch."
>
> "Dunk" is not in McCoy's vocabulary. When former Sun Garfield Heard rattled the rim with a stuff, it was a "wham bam slam by the Thundering Heard!"
>
> A "basket?" Uh-uh. Try a "hoop-de-doo for two." Or a "swisheroo for two." A three-point basket? Too tame. It's "the NBA supershot" or "Shazam!"

Another italicized quote provided the transition to the next main section of Horn's story: "Pass to Majerle, right side . . . he slashes into the key . . . It's Thunder Dan for a Thunder Slam!"

Effective Use of Description

By now, readers are caught up in the fast-moving story about the well-known—but not widely recognized—announcer. Horn provided a section of description that began with this paragraph:

> McCoy sits at the scorer's table with neatly organized notes strategically placed before him—a schedule for the Suns Warmup Show broken down into 30-second intervals, media guides, a list of tonight's officials, the disclaimer (This copyrighted program is presented . . .), advertisements typed out on notecards, a wristwatch, the all-important stopwatch and current statistics for both teams.

Horn's description of McCoy's mannerisms was vivid; readers were made to feel as if they, too, were sitting courtside. The middle sections of the profile provided background on McCoy's career with the Suns (he had missed only two regular-season games in eighteen years, once running up a string of 1,385 consecutive games broadcast), his family, and his entry into broadcast journalism via his youth in rural Iowa and college at Drake. Horn also quoted former Suns players who spoke highly of McCoy.

Horn ended his story with a McCoy direct quote about how going to ball games remains a thrill to him and with this final McCoy observation as the buzzer sounded to end the Suns-Nuggets game: "Suns 112. Nuggets 108. We'll be right back."

The McCoy profile contained all the crucial ingredients of a good personality profile: an intriguing introduction, strong transitions, vivid description, smooth narration, meaningful direct quotes, and well-researched background. Horn built the story around a theme—McCoy's colorful use of language—in such a way that readers actually could have fun working their way through the lengthy profile. When readers put down the newspaper, they *knew* Al McCoy.

A Quaker at the Academy

Colorado Springs Gazette Telegraph sportswriter Terry Henion effectively combined description, vivid quotations, and a staccato writing style in a profile of Air Force Academy quarterback Marty Louthan. Henion began his story describing Louthan the player; the next block of paragraphs focused on Louthan the person and his Quaker faith; the third section was a blend of description and statistics, which helped readers to visualize Louthan the athlete; the story closed with a news peg, the upcoming Air Force-New Mexico game and the role Louthan would play in it.

Henion began his story:

> His eyes are strikingly gray, the color of a mountain lake frozen solid in the dead of winter. But beneath that tranquil surface, deep inside Marty Louthan, there are fires that burn white-hot.
>
> Fire and ice.
>
> Louthan, Air Force's junior quarterback, rapidly is becoming one of the nation's finest players. Arguably, he's already the best at handling the wishbone offense, the kind of wishbone Air Force has ridden to the top of the Western Athletic Conference.
>
> Louthan is a master at running the wishbone option, a task that requires precision-like timing and decision making. It takes a cool customer, one who won't crack under duress. One who will make the right choices.
>
> Louthan always seems to make the right choice, select the right option. On the field and off. Keep or pitch? Run or throw?
>
> Fire and ice.

After this brisk, descriptive block of lead paragraphs, Henion described Louthan's inner turmoil. He quoted Louthan:

> "It was kind of a crisis time for me," said Louthan. "It was simply this—what did I want to do with the rest of my life? I talked to my parents a lot. It was too big of a decision for me.

"Did I want to give eight or nine years of my life to the Air Force?
That's a lot to put on the line. I needed all the help I could get. I prayed
a lot."

Drawing a parallel between Louthan's decision on what to do with his
life and his ability to play football, Henion wrote:

Should he stay at home and go to the local Christian college? Or
should he take the offer he'd gotten from the Air Force?
Keep or pitch? Run or throw?

Louthan decided to return to the academy. In the next section of his
story, Henion described Louthan's playing style:

What Louthan does never brings the crowd to its feet. His style isn't
flashy. But the chains keep moving. Louthan's runs, throws and pitches
are deadly, though. Subtly so. Like a dirk slipped under the fifth rib.

Henion gave the readers statistics about Louthan the player and then
more insight into Louthan the Christian. The *Gazette Telegraph* writer closed
the story with a quote from Louthan about the role he would play in the
Academy-New Mexico football game:

"I like to be in a position where I can have a direct effect on what
happens. I have faith that I can do the job."
Faith. There it is again. Louthan is proof that life is full of options,
on the field and off. Keep or pitch? Run or throw? Fire and ice.

Henion's story is a good example of how a writer can take an ordinary
feature (a look at a football quarterback) and mold it into a probing,
descriptive, human account. It takes hard work, planning, and an eye for
detail.

How Strong? She Puts Dents in a Volleyball

Dennis Brown, a sportswriter for *The Phoenix Gazette*, has watched a lot of
volleyball. He knows the game well. When he decided to do a feature on
Arizona State's Lisa Stuck, one of the country's best players, he focused on
her most striking characteristic: strength. The *Gazette* headline was vivid:
"Pure power: Lisa Stuck puts dents in a volleyball."

The lead block of paragraphs on a feature is important; if the first few
paragraphs are well written and interesting, readers likely will want to know

more about the subject. Brown adroitly captured the attention of readers with
this lead block:

> Pure power: It fascinates us.
> Finesse is fine, but the power people of sports make us shudder.
> Lisa Stuck is pure power.
> Stuck, a junior at Arizona State, hits a volleyball as hard as or harder
> than any woman in college today. She doesn't just spike the ball, she
> crushes it.
> "Power-wise, she's as good as anybody," says Sun Devil Coach
> Dale Flickinger.
> ASU assistant coach Steve George adds, "When she gets a good set
> and is going well, she hits as well as anyone."
> There are major college players who can read a block better and who
> have a wider variety of shots, but when a Stuck spike hits the floor it
> rattles the rafters.
> "I just want to kill it," said Stuck. "I don't want anybody to be able
> to return it. I don't want it to be blocked or dug.
> "It's the best feeling," she says of spiking the ball. "Especially
> when there's no block up. Then you can just crunch it."
> As you might expect, Lisa Stuck is no petite woman. At 6-foot-0,
> 175 pounds, Stuck is an imposing figure. Yet, she isn't overweight.
> What she is, is a well built athlete—among the finest to come out of
> Arizona.

Most readers, even if they knew nothing about volleyball, likely were
pulled into the story. They wanted to know more about this athlete. In the
next block of paragraphs, Brown used quotations from Stuck and her
coaches to explain how she decided to enroll at Arizona State after an
outstanding career at a local high school. Brown also inserted a paragraph
about Stuck's credentials—the honor teams she had been named to. He then
used a transition paragraph that led to a discussion of how she could improve
her game:

> But, as good as Stuck is—and as much as she has improved—most
> feel the best is yet to come.
> "She's a marvelous athlete," Flickinger said. "Once she's able to
> appreciate her athletic ability, she'll be better."
> ASU assistant George adds, "She has a lot of pure athletic potential,
> most of which is untapped."
> There are several areas of her game which, on a technical level, need
> work. Though she is one of the better passers for the Sun Devils, Stuck
> has trouble on defense. Her size is part of the problem, but there is
> more, according to Flickinger.
> "I don't see it as a lack of quickness," he says. "I see it as
> hesitation. We regard her as an excellent passer. You can crush the ball

at her and she'll get it. It's the off-play—the tip or dump—that gives her trouble."

With her spiking, Stuck needs to become more aware of when to kill the ball and when to take something off her shot.

The above paragraphs are illustrative. They show that a sportswriter can construct an excellent, positive feature about an athlete without cheerleading. Brown was candid in analyzing Stuck's weaknesses—as were her coaches. Brown also quoted Flickinger, who said that Stuck, when she became frustrated, was prone to make mistakes. Brown asked Lisa about it. He quoted her:

Stuck is aware of her moodiness. And, too, she knows that, as the dominant figure on the team, her attitude rubs off on everyone.

"I tend to doubt myself," she admits. "But, I know that when I'm up, other people get up."

Brown used the direct quote as a transition to the next paragraph:

Of late, both Stuck and the Sun Devils have been very up. After a good start, ASU slumped badly through most of September. Three weeks ago, however, Flickinger and George began to push their players harder in practice. The results have been excellent.

The *Gazette* sportswriter provided details on the ASU season before closing with several paragraphs of direct quotations from Stuck that dealt with her future in volleyball. It takes skill to piece together probing features such as the Stuck story. Writing features on minor sports athletes, though, is an excellent way to focus on subjects that most newspapers do not ordinarily cover extensively.

Writing in the First Person

An emerging sports feature form is the first-person account. *Sports Illustrated* has published first-person accounts from athletes in "as told to" formats. Sometimes, though, athlete and writer are one. Cassandra Lander, a star women's basketball player at Arizona State University and a broadcast journalism major, combined her skills in a story that was published in *The Phoenix Gazette*.

When preseason basketball practice opened for Lander's senior season, she started a diary. The diary closed with the center jump of the season's first game. *Gazette* readers got an inside glimpse of Lander the athlete and

Lander the person. Lander told them how it sometimes hurt to practice; how she sometimes wished she was merely a student, not a student-athlete; and how desires of coaches and players sometimes conflicted.

Diary dates were the bold-face transitions that tied the story together. It began:

> Sunday, Aug. 22—Tomorrow is the first day of class at Arizona State. More than 39,000 students are going to be frustrated in finding parking places, locating classrooms, and standing in long lines at the bookstore.
>
> I, too, will face those frustrations, but I am preoccupied with one thing today: The start of pre-season basketball training.
>
> Frankly, I'm a little frightened. Coach (Juliene Simpson) made clear to me last May what she expected: I was to practice every day all summer and hit the weight room religiously.

Lander said she did not train as much as she should have. She continued:

> The summer slipped away. Suddenly, I was three weeks from pre-season training—and I was nowhere near the shape I had to be in. Potential All-America? I knew deep down I was a long way from that.

Lander said she was apprehensive about preseason practices:

> Why can't it be like high school? I never worried about preparing for the season. When basketball came, there was excitement. We practiced, we played—and it was over.
>
> In college, it's a year-round thing. Coaches expect it and I guess you have to do it if you want to be the best. For some reason, I never have adjusted to playing basketball all 12 months.
>
> I can envision all the work and running I will be doing tomorrow. I know I'll make it, but I don't know how much it will hurt.

Lander laid off basketball for a few days in mid-September to go to Nashville to play in a softball tournament. She felt great—until she returned to school. Lander wrote:

> Back on the court again. My trip to Nashville was great. My team won the national championship and I was named first-team All-America, but the greatest thing was seeing my family. I hadn't seen them in more than a year. Evansville, Ind. (Cassandra's hometown), is only two hours from Nashville, so it was an easy trip for them.
>
> My whole body was aching. Every muscle hurt. My trip away from

Tempe was so good I didn't want to return. I was depressed; I wanted to be out enjoying life. I've been going to organized basketball practices for eight years.

I prayed for help to get through another practice. I might sound like I'm really religious. I am not a zealot, but I really believe God controls everything and does everything for a reason.

Two years ago in the National Women's Invitational Tournament, I was named most valuable player. It was the first national tournament the ASU women's team had ever played in.

All that year, I had been inconsistent. I had lost some confidence in my coach and myself. But, in the NWIT, I was unstoppable. I did things I didn't know I could do. How many times do you see someone shoot a 360-degree, full-spin layup?

I had all the confidence in the world. I also was hurting tremendously from a groin pull (no one knew) and in three tournament games I averaged 28 points. That's the work of God.

Now I was calling on Him once more to get me through practice.

As the days passed, Lander freed herself from depression. She wrote on November 11:

We are only a week away from our first game. We have learned three offenses, three defenses and a press.

I get excited thinking about our first game. I am really glad to be rid of the depressing feelings I had in the beginning. When school started, I was ready to get on with my life, to find a job and get into my career (broadcasting).

All that will come in time, I'm sure, but now it's basketball. My heart is in it once again.

On November 18, the season opened. Lander wrote:

It's here. The day of our first game. I was awake at 7 a.m. I was excited. At 1 p.m., we would meet our first opponent—Santa Clara (in the Straw Hat Classic tournament in San Luis Obispo, Calif.).

The team ate breakfast (omelletes and hot chocolate) at the Apple Farm at 9 a.m.; everyone still was talking and laughing. At 10:30 I had to be taped, and at 11:30 we left for the game. The gym reminded me of a high-school facility; it was chilly. We met in a locker room; it was cold, too, and in the process of being refurbished. Coach reviewed our game plan.

I began putting on my game shoes. All the smiling faces had turned serious and determined. I led the team from the locker room. After our 20-minute warmup, we ran to the bench and began taking off our warmup suits.

It was only seconds before tipoff. Our bench was cheering and clapping as the announcer began introducing the starters: "For the Devils, a 5-6 guard from Evansville, Ind.—Cassandra Lander."

I ran onto the floor. My teammates quickly joined me. Suddenly it was time for the tipoff. I couldn't help but smile as the official tossed the ball in the air.

Sometimes, first-person accounts can be powerful. They can be descriptive and captivating—just as Lander's story was. This writing style, however, is not appropriate for most stories. Some first-person approaches can be almost juvenile: "My first day of bowling" or "How I learned to skate." But a sports reporter should remember that the first-person account is an acceptable feature form that sometimes can be effective.

Exercises

1. Clip three sports features from an area newspaper. Analyze each of the features. Describe the type of lead each writer used. For example, is it narrative, descriptive, anecdotal, or summary? Isolate the transitions that make the story cohesive. Underline the transitions. Isolate examples of descriptive observation. Does the author make good use of vivid direct quotations from a variety of sources? Does each feature have a strong, logical ending?

2. Clip a major feature from an issue of *Sports Illustrated*. Analyze it the same way you analyzed the features from the newspapers. What are the similarities and the differences—in regard to approach and style—between the newspaper features and the magazine feature?

3. Write a personality profile. The subject does not have to be a major sports star. The subject, for example, could be an honor student who persevered through four years of collegiate competition without ever seeing much playing time. Be sure to talk to several sources about your subject. Make sure your feature contains the elements of most effective stories: a clear, tightly focused theme; a strong lead block; effective transitions; effective use of direct quotations from a variety of sources; descriptive observation; and a strong, logical ending.

4. Write an analysis piece. You might want to select a sports event that recently has been in the news—such as the signing of a letter of intent by athletes to play football or basketball at your school—and then, based on extensive interviews with knowledgeable sources, analyze the quality of the recruiting class.

Columns often focus on the personalities of
demonstrative coaches.

(Photo by T. J. Sokol)

CHAPTER FIFTEEN

Columns

Columnists are the most visible members of daily newspapers' sports sections. Leonard Koppett, a columnist for the *Peninsula Times Tribune,* Palo Alto, California, wrote in the *Bulletin,* a publication of the American Society of Newspaper Editors: "The reader turns to the news, features, and box scores to find out what's going on. He turns to the columnist to see what the columnist has to say about what's going on."

A national survey of sports editors, published in *Journalism Quarterly,* showed that 27 percent of their daily newspapers published locally written sports columns each day. Twenty-three percent published columns once a week and 50 percent published them two to four times each week.

Larger circulation newspapers are more likely to publish locally written sports columns each day. The survey found that 75 percent of the newspapers that circulate more than 50,000 publish columns each day; the remainder publish them two to four times a week.

Forty-five percent of the newspapers that circulate between 25,000 and 49,999 publish daily sports columns; 14 percent of the newspapers that circulate between 10,000 and 24,999 publish daily columns; and 7 percent of the newspapers that circulate under 10,000 publish daily columns. All sports editors who responded to the survey reported that their newspapers publish sports columns at least once a week.

Bob Hentzen, who has been writing a regular sports column for the *Topeka* (Kan.) *Capital-Journal* since 1960 and who has been writing five a week since 1968, believes that "even a mediocre column is better than no column."

At the *Capital-Journal,* which circulates 73,000 on Sundays, all sports staff members write at least one column a week. "We'll have two or three locally written columns in every day's paper," Hentzen said. "I believe that writers take pride in columns and enjoy the freedom they don't always have in news stories and features. I feel that readers like them, too."

Hentzen said he believed that sports columns help sell newspapers. "But I have never thought my role in today's society was very important," he said. "In the majority of things I write, I try not to take myself too seriously. I remember a few years back I wrote a series of columns advocating the building of a civic center sports complex here. I thought I did a heckuva job of presenting convincing arguments. Voters turned it down by a 2-1 margin."

Joe McGuff, longtime sports editor and columnist of the *Kansas City Star,* who now is editor of the newspaper, said the "role of the columnist is to inform, explain, and provide commentary, and, if possible, to entertain."

"These are games we are dealing with, not Armageddon," McGuff said. "The sports columnist is often the most visible member of the staff and as such he carries a special responsibility for fairness in his commentary and for doing his homework. Too many sports columnists comment on complicated subjects without taking the time and trouble to become familiar with the intricacies of their material.

"Now that we have to deal with trials, contracts, labor negotiations, and municipal affairs, it is important to be conversant with these matters before writing."

Sports columnists indeed have an obligation to their readers. McGuff summarized this observation well: "Even though most of us don't think of ourselves as sports experts, the public does and the public wants to know what we think. In this respect I'm reminded of something that happens every year when I come back from baseball spring training and a friend or someone in the office asks, 'How did the Royals really look?' Just as people want to know what a reviewer thought of a play or movie they saw, they also want to know what the sports columnist thinks (about sports events)."

Every time he sits at a video display terminal or typewriter, a columnist must ponder two basic questions: What am I going to write about and how much time do I have to write it?

Hentzen spends at least "a couple of hours" writing the "average column"—if there is such a thing. "The interviewing or thought process preceding a column can take from a few minutes to hours or even days," Hentzen said. "A good 'notes' column, while it does not take long to write, usually takes a half day to assemble because other papers must be perused and notebooks checked for appropriate items."

McGuff also said the time spent writing a column varies. McGuff was reminded of the late Red Smith's answer when asked how long it took him to write a column. Smith replied: "How much time do I have?"

"If I have two days, I'm afraid I take two days," McGuff said. "If I have two hours, I take two hours. Think columns take longer. Interview columns take longer to gather, but are faster to write. But you have to guard against doing too much quoting. Most columns probably take me three or four hours once I start writing. Getting the first three or four paragraphs is the most time-consuming part. Once I get that done I move pretty quickly, but if I have time I'll probably rewrite the column once.

"The hardest thing when you are under the gun is making yourself take the time to think the column through and get off to the right beginning. I'd say the least amount of time you need to do a quality column after an event is two hours. Columns are personalized and they take longer than game stories to write."

Personalized they are. Koppett, in his *Bulletin* article, wrote: "With respect to the writer, the first consideration is personality. Over a period personality will come through whether the writer likes it or not. It cannot be concealed or falsified. The whole point of a signed column, with or without mug shot attached, is that the reader identifies the columnist as a specific person—knowledgeable, witty, profound, stupid, insufferable, or illiterate, as the case may be."

Columnists always need to be alert to topics. "The search for topics is something you carry with you wherever you go," McGuff said. "Some topics flow from events that you attend and they are relatively simple to write, but on the days when there are no games and you are barren of ideas, well, those are the times you pay dearly for the job. I do a lot of reading—magazines, other papers, the wire reports. You never know where a column idea will come from. I also like to talk with other sports people as much as possible because a lot of ideas also come up in conversation. You can't be a hermit and write a column."

Sports columns can take a variety of forms. These include feature, postcontest analysis, personality profiles, personal reflections, and letters from readers.

Features

Feature columns possibly are the most widely published. Columnists often elaborate on information that is in a straight news story. For example, when pro golfer Jim Colbert, who attended Kansas State University in Manhattan, returned to his alma mater to help raise money for Wildcat athletics, Hentzen used an approach in his *Capital-Journal* column that explained how football initially lured Colbert to the campus. Hentzen wrote:

> MANHATTAN—Labron Harris, remember him? The man who built
> a golf dynasty at Oklahoma State?
> A number of years ago Harris had a private airplane pick up a young

golfer from Kansas City and bring him to Stillwater. In fact, the day Jim Colbert was scheduled to enroll he was staying at Harris' house.

Golf, though, wasn't the only sport on Colbert's mind when he was preparing to start school at O-State. He had been a high school football star, too.

"I asked him if I could try to play football," Colbert related, "and he said, 'You play golf down here. You don't play football.' I wasn't sure I could get along with Labron. (They wound up good friends.)"

So it was that Colbert got on the phone and called Bebe Lee, then the Kansas State athletic director, and asked if a football scholarship might be available. It was, and Colbert was soon on his way to Manhattan.

"I don't even remember how I got here," he said. "Maybe my folks came and got me. I don't know that. I didn't hop a bus."

It worked out that Colbert didn't play much football at Kansas State. He was injured his freshman year.

But the decision he made that day in Stillwater was one of the good things that's happened to K-State athletics.

Sure, Colbert turned out to be the best golfer ever to play for the Wildcats—finishing second in the 1964 NCAA tourney. But the neat thing is that Jim Colbert, on the pro tour since he graduated . . . , never forgot where he started.

This week, for the eighth time, he was back in Manhattan to serve as host for a golf bash to raise money for K-State athletics.

He doesn't come alone, either. A virtual "About to be Who's Who" on both the men's and women's tours have accompanied him here to mingle with K-Staters and show off their golf games.

David Graham ("Nobody had heard of him"), Hubert Green, Fuzzy Zoeller, Andy Bean, Craig Stadler, Bill Kratzert and Phil Hancock are among the now household names in golf that Colbert has lured to small-town Kansas.

In the first half of his column, Hentzen painted a vivid picture of Colbert the person: loyal and down to earth. Hentzen then went on to explain how the Colbert golf classic came about:

> The idea for the Jim Colbert Celebrity Golf Classic was not Colbert's.
>
> "Vince Gibson—I stayed in his house last week when we were in New Orleans—is the one who said, 'We're gonna do it,' " he said.
>
> But the former K-State football coach didn't have to do a lot of talking to coax Colbert into making it happen.
>
> "It's the people here I really cherish," said Colbert. "The people of Manhattan always have been great to me.
>
> "And the thing that's great is this club. I worked here five years for Ron Fogler (the former Manhattan CC pro-manager, who now runs Colbert's public course in Las Vegas). It's a combination of Vince Gibson, Ron Fogler and the people here in town."

Those are the reasons why Colbert, as has been his custom this time in May, jumped on a private jet Sunday after shooting a 70 that gave him a share of 10th place in the Byron Nelson Classic in Dallas.

Hentzen closed his column with Colbert's comments on his future in professional golf.

The column is a good blend of the past and the present. Thousands of Hentzen's readers follow the progress of Colbert; most of them probably had read news stories about Colbert's golf classic in Manhattan. But it was Hentzen's column, a careful combination of direct quotations and anecdotes, that enabled the readers to get to know Colbert—the man—a little better.

Bob Hurt, sports columnist for *The Arizona Republic,* is known for his ability to attend a football game—the same game watched by thousands of fans and dozens of reporters—and develop an angle that no one else recognized. At an Arizona State-University of Southern California football game, action was fierce on the field. But Hurt found a feature column angle in the press box. His column began:

TEMPE—You can judge a football game by the company it keeps.

Arizona State and Southern California kept 71,071 around Saturday in ASU's 17-10 victory until the end. The crowd, the second largest in Sun Devil Stadium history, included Don Coryell, head coach of the San Diego Chargers. He was one of 15—yes, 15—scouting for pro prospects.

And what brought Coryell?

"Players, big bunches of them, both sides," he said.

Coryell was asked to identify the best players.

"Ask him," said the coach, nodding toward Gil Brandt, Dallas Cowboys vice president and pro football's most widely publicized talent hunter.

So I did.

"Out there," Brandt said, "are 25 to 30 players who will be drafted or who will be signed as free agents this year."

Gulp. How many for each team?

"About evenly split," he said. Brandt dug into his notes and extracted a white card. In red ink, he had listed USC prospects on one side, ASU prospects on the other. Each team appeared to have 15 to 20 players on the Cowboys' wanted list.

"Look at this," Brandt said, and his finger traveled down the program to USC offensive guard Darryl Moore. "He's a second-teamer, but he will be drafted."

Hurt shifted to the importance of the football game and the rivalry that was developing between the two institutions. He closed with an analysis by

Brandt of the blitzing ASU defense, which then was rated among the country's best.

These feature columns show that ideas can be found most anywhere—at a fund-raising golf tournament or in the press box at a big-time college football game. Astute sportswriters will capitalize on the ideas.

Postcontest Analysis

Columnists may analyze isolated occurrences in contests. Often, these occurrences are reported in straight news stories, but a good columnist will provide additional background to explain the significance of the happening.

David Casstevens, a gifted columnist for *The Arizona Republic,* provided a thoughtful analysis of an NCAA Final Four basketball shocker: Duke's stunning upset of heavily favored Nevada–Las Vegas. Casstevens' opening paragraphs made it clear to readers that the ramifications of UNLV's loss extended beyond the parameters of the basketball court.

> INDIANAPOLIS—His father could be Boris Karloff, his mother a troll. He has peach fuzz for hair and the strangest dopey grin.
>
> But it's those eyes, those hollow eyes with the shades pulled halfway down as if to conceal some secret behind them that distinguishes him from every other figure in sports.
>
> The NCAA doesn't trust those eyes, and you can bet that Saturday night the NCAA privately celebrated the sadness that was in them.
>
> It is unfair to label Duke's 79-77 upset of top-ranked UNLV a victory over good vs. evil. But the NCAA must be pleased Duke, with its squeaky-clean image, eliminated Tark The Shark and his band of Runnin' Rebels.
>
> For 20 years, Tark has battled the NCAA in and out of court. The NCAA's latest investigation charges UNLV with 29 new violations. Tarkanian has called the NCAA vindictive. Witch hunters. "If Joe McCarthy were alive today," the Vegas coach said, "he'd be working for the NCAA." At this moment, David Berst, NCAA director of enforcement, is raising a toast, "To Duke!"
>
> Certainly, the drama that unfolded in the Hoosier Dome seemed surreal for the Blue Devils, who capered about the court, gulping in the pure oxygen of victory.
>
> As upsets go, this one ranks right up there with some of the shockers in modern Final Four history. Villanova over Georgetown. North Carolina State over Houston, with Akeem Olajuwon and Clyde Drexler.
>
> No one, including yours truly, gave Duke much chance. A year ago, UNLV beat Duke, 103-73, in the most lopsided NCAA championship game in history. The Blue Devils figured to be competitive, but to pick Duke to avenge last year's loss required an athleticism of the mind.

Casstevens went on to observe the age differences of the Duke and UNLV players; to discuss that all of the pressure seemed to be placed on UNLV, with Duke being such a big underdog; and to analyze UNLV's inability to go on a big scoring run, which it had been doing all year. The column concluded with two sentences that summarized the analysis that had preceded them:

> The team that plea-bargained with the NCAA to play in this year's tournament simply got beat, fair and square. It's a tossup who felt more satisfied, Duke or the long arm of college athletic law.

Personality Profiles

Among the most difficult types of columns to write is the personality piece. It is a challenge to capture a person's personality in a few hundred words. It is all the more difficult when the subject is reserved, soft-spoken, and values his privacy. Mike Kelly, sports editor of the *Omaha* (Neb.) *World-Herald,* seized upon a public event to paint a portrait of Nebraska's football coach Tom Osborne. The column also drew upon the perceptions of Johnny Rodgers, former Nebraska All-American and Heisman Trophy winner. Writing in the first person, Kelly began:

> I was telling Johnny Rodgers how I didn't really know his friend Tom Osborne, and how the Nebraska football coach was in some ways both the best known and the least known person in Nebraska.
> Perhaps no one in the state has a name more widely known than Osborne. No one, I'd bet, is asked more questions, or more often quoted, or more frequently praised, or more frequently criticized, or more talked about. But very few people, I think—probably because Osborne wants it that way—really know him well.
> "You're not supposed to," Rodgers said. "He's always trying to do the best he can, always trying to do the right thing. No matter what pressure he gets from the press or the fans or whoever, he consistently tries to do the right thing."
> Well, I sure don't doubt that.
> In any case, I was asking Johnny Rodgers about this because J.R. had stood in front of 1,175 men and told them that he loved Tom Osborne. It was very sincere and touching. I know it's 1983 and all that, but there still aren't a lot of men who could stand in front of a lot of men and say that they love a man.
> Johnny Rodgers did. And by the time he was finished speaking, a fellow who sat close to Osborne told me the Husker coach was misty-eyed.
> The occasion was the annual B'nai B'rith Charity Stag last week in

Omaha, and it was an unusual night. Rodgers, the former Nebraska All-American and Heisman Trophy winner, put it another way.

"There was a lot of positive energy in the air," he said.

For starters, the Jewish organization's guest of honor was Osborne, who doesn't belong to B'nai B'rith but does belong to the Fellowship of Christian Athletes. That's not such an unusual combination, of course, but it was kind of nice.

And then there were Osborne and Rodgers. Bob Devaney, now the NU athletic director, was head coach when Rodgers played at Nebraska, and Osborne was an assistant coach. But Devaney called Rodgers "the finest protege of Tom Osborne."

They would seem an unlikely pair:

Osborne, a serious, cerebral type with a Ph.D. in educational psychology, a tenured assistant professor who gave up teaching to coach football players: a red-headed, small-town Nebraska guy who's a conservative dresser and said recently that "My social life is zero."

And Rodgers, a city kid who came to the university with a master's degree in streetsmart, but who says he wasn't a serious student; a flashy dresser who had the reputation of a social life on the opposite end of the scale from zero.

Rodgers, who now publishes a cable television magazine in San Diego called "Tuned-In" (weekly circulation: 65,000) got up and recited some of Osborne's accomplishments in 11 years as an assistant coach and 10 years as head coach.

"I respect Tom Osborne for those reasons," Rodgers said, "but I love him for the time and knowledge he has contributed to my life. He taught me not just how to be a great athlete; he taught me how to use my mind."

Later, in a conversation, Rodgers tried to explain:

"Tom happened to come into my life at my lowest point, when people had reason—because I was wrong—to kick me out of their lives," he said. "My life was crumbling. I did not know what to do or say. You have a million friends when you are doing well and on top, but there were people who were glad to see me down. I admitted what I did because Tom told me to tell the truth."

What he admitted was his part in a gas station holdup his freshman year. He got probation, stayed on the team, won the Heisman, played pro football and got into a successful business. Rodgers said Osborne showed him the way.

To those of us who cover Nebraska football, Osborne is an intriguing and sometimes puzzling man. He gives a lot of time answering writers' questions but, I think, would be glad if he never had to answer another.

If something gets in the paper that he thinks reflects poorly on the program, or that he thinks is plain wrong, he'll let us know, as he should. A recent example was when Ernie Chambers, the state senator from Rodgers' old Omaha neighborhood, said that football players receive special "favors." Osborne said we shouldn't print something like that when Chambers won't substantiate it. Chambers said he wouldn't say it if he didn't know from players that it's true.

Did Rodgers receive things from fans at Nebraska? "People did not give me things so I would go there," he said. "I wanted to be there. All my life, from my mother and a lot of others, people have given me things."

It's difficult. These things are complicated and they are sensitive, and there are many shades of gray. It's not as easy as saying that one's totally right and one's totally wrong.

"I believe they're both right," Johnny Rodgers said. "Tom's right, but Ernie's right, too."

Kelly's column did not answer all questions readers might have had about Osborne; it did not provide any insights to explain precisely what Osborne is really like—deep down. But it did paint a realistic picture of a conservative man who every day is under a microscope, being scrutinized by thousands of Nebraska football fans and football detractors. Readers certainly would have had a better perception of Osborne the person after reading the column.

Personal Reflections

Writing a reflection column is delicate. If the column is not thoughtfully composed, readers often will not go beyond the second paragraph. Some reflection columns are as interesting as listening to a neighbor articulate in boring, excruciating detail what he did on his vacation. Columnists must have the sensitivity to choose topics carefully. A fine line exists between entertaining and boring readers with such tales.

Joe McGuff chose to write a column about Red Smith, one of the country's best sportswriters. Many of McGuff's readers would have read some of Smith's columns and most all of them would have read of his death. McGuff carefully combined first-hand experiences with Smith and background on the writer. The personal touch is what made this column particularly interesting. McGuff wrote in the *Kansas City Star:*

I'm not quite sure how to begin a column about the death of Red Smith because he handled the English language with such purity and grace that anything written about him will be clumsy and inappropriate by comparison. Writing about Red Smith is like singing at Caruso's funeral or delivering a eulogy at Bishop Fulton J. Sheen's services.

I suppose the best thing is to come right to the point and say Smith is the greatest talent our field of journalism produced. No one—Damon Runyon, Paul Gallico, Grantland Rice or anyone else—has written about sports with the humor, inventiveness and literary skill of Red Smith.

Those of us making this judgment are not without authoritative support because when Ernest Hemingway was searching for the ultimate sportswriter, he settled on Smith.

This is not to say Smith did not have his peaks and valleys or that in his latter years he was writing as well as he once did, but over the course of his lengthy career no one has written so well so consistently. If someone picks up one of his anthologies 50 years from now, he will be as delightfully readable as he is today.

I first began to read Red Smith when he joined the old *New York Herald Tribune* in 1945 and I was working as a fumbling apprentice at the *Tulsa World*. He immediately became one of my heroes. I was imitating other writers in those days, a phase every writer goes through before settling into a style of his own, but unfortunately Smith's skills were so exceptional they defied imitation.

I first became acquainted with Red more than 25 years ago. The Dodgers and Yankees were playing in the World Series, and the Dodgers had their hospitality room in the Bossert Hotel in Brooklyn.

I introduced myself to Red there, and he invited me to sit down and have a drink. That was typical of Red Smith. Red was not without ego, but he abhorred pretense and was one of the most approachable celebrities I have ever known.

Through the years we became good friends. Not close friends, but good friends. Red was a delightful raconteur and he spoke with a gracefulness and wit that matched his writing. Staying up late in the bar with Red Smith was one of life's most enjoyable experiences. Red despised hypocrites and bullies and could lacerate his enemies with words honed to a sharp edge.

Speaking of a writer he disliked, he observed, "It's hard to understand how such a small brain could nourish such a large ego."

After describing other personal experiences with Smith, McGuff closed his column with reflections on Smith's writing talents:

There is no "best" Red Smith column because so many of them were so good, but the quintessential Smith can be found in the opening paragraphs of his story on the 1944 Notre Dame-Army game:

"Quiet country churchyards from Killarney to Kimberly gave off a strange, whirring sound this afternoon as departed Irish whirled and spun and did flipflops under the sod.

"In the most horrendous Gaelic disaster since the Battle of the Boyne, the Celtic Szymanskis and Dancewiczes of Notre Dame were ravaged, routed and demolished by Army's football team by the most garish score in history—59–0."

Smith saw nothing demeaning about committing his talents to sportswriting and contended that if athletes have been blown up into false heroes they are not alone.

"When you go through Westminster Abbey," Smith said, "you'll find that except for the Poet's Corner all of the statues and memorials are to killers. To generals and admirals who won battles, whose specialty was human slaughter. I don't think they're such glorious heroes."

Red had a way of putting everything in perspective. With his passing, a luminous talent has been extinguished.

Arizona Republic writer David Casstevens provided a deft personal touch on a column he wrote in reaction to an announcement by baseball Commissioner Fay Vincent that he wanted to remove the asterisk beside the name of Roger Maris, who hit 61 home runs in 1961.

Casstevens addressed his column to the late Maris:

Roger Maris
Holy Cross Cemetery
Fargo, N.D.

Dear Roger,

You don't know me. We never met. I was 15 the year you hit 61 home runs, but I can close my eyes and it all comes back to me, like a Technicolor dream.

What a season.

Who could forget the Summer of '61?

Since you've been gone, only one player in baseball has created as much excitement and controversy as you did that historic summer.

Six years ago, the game was ready to usher Charlie Hustle into the Hall of Fame, then and there.

You wouldn't *believe* what's happened to Pete.

Baseball is a funny game. But who am I to tell *you* that? Misery. Bitter memories. And a lousy asterisk beside your name.

Baseball made you a lifetime member in the Yes But Club. You know how it works. Tom Dempsey kicked a 63-yard field goal in an NFL game. *Yes, but he wore a special shoe.* Johnny Miller shot a record 63 in the first round of the U.S. Open at Oakmont. *Yes, but heavy rains the night before left the course defenseless.* Forward Pass won the 1968 Kentucky Derby. *Yes, but Dancer's Image finished first and was disqualified.*

Roger Maris hit 61 homers. *Yes, but it took him 162 games. Ruth hit 60 in a 154-game season.*

It never seemed fair. You hit your 61 homers in 684 plate appearances (at-bats, plus walks). Ruth hit 60 in 687 trips to the plate. But baseball purists chose to ignore that fact.

What was it Rogers Hornsby, a Ruth contemporary, said after you hit No. 55? "Maris has no right to break Ruth's record."

No *right?* Good grief.

What Ford Frick did to you was unforgivable. The commissioner ruled there would have to be some "distinctive mark" in the record book alongside your name. A qualifier. A Yes, But.

Baseball was determined to defend the memory of The Babe. So you wore an asterisk, like a scarlet letter, for 24 years, until the day you died.

I cannot imagine what it must have been like closing in on the sacred record of the most beloved baseball player in history. What was it like living in an aquarium? How could any man handle the pressure of knowing an entire nation was watching him every time he came to the plate? The questions. And more questions. Probing. Insensitive. Insulting.

When that New York reporter asked, "How's this affecting your sex life, Rog?" what kept you from decking him? They said you became sullen and withdrawn. Who wouldn't?

Casstevens then closed his column by giving Maris the good news:

I don't know if you've heard from your family. If so, I'm sure they told you the news. Baseball Commissioner Fay Vincent said this week that he supports the single-record thesis. He wants to remove the asterisk beside your name.

Roger Maris hit more home runs in a single season than any player in history. Period. No ifs, ands or yes buts. . . .

The record will be yours and yours alone assuming the commissioner's recommendation is approved by—and you'll get a laugh out of this—the Committee for Statistical Accuracy.

Only baseball would have a Committee for Statistical Accuracy. Two of the eight members are college professors. Wonder if the committee will double-check every Yankees box score and recount your home runs, just to make *sure* you hit 61, before they take a vote.

You once said of the Summer of '61, "Maybe I wouldn't do it all over again if I had the chance. I don't think it was worth the aggravation." Would this change anything? About the way you feel? Do you care anymore?

This much we know. Whatever is decided won't change how people feel about Maris vs. Ruth and the record. An asterisk is just a printer's symbol. It carries whatever value and weight one chooses to give it.

Even so, I, for one, am pleased. In its own curious way, baseball is considering righting a wrong. It's 30 years too late, but better late than never.

Rest in peace.

Casstevens, through his column, tied a contemporary development to its historical antecedents. The writer's "voice" made the column special. Casstevens used a "personal reflections" approach to effectively convey to readers not only a point of view but also an appropriate tone.

Letters from Readers

Printing letters from readers is a staple of some sports columnists. Readers often make significant points or raise interesting questions. Columnists generally respond briefly to the points made or the questions raised. Letters and responses usually are serious. However, Jim Murray of the *Los Angeles Times* occasionally will blend letters from readers with his well-considered responses. The combination of letters from readers and responses from Murray makes for pure enjoyment for readers. The beginning of one Murray column was a delight:

> As the old saying goes, if you can't say anything good about a person, write it down. I think it was Alice Roosevelt Longworth who said, "If you can't think of anything good to say about anybody, come sit by me."
> Alice would love my mail. . . .
> "Jim:
> "What do you do well? Anything? You certainly don't have talent when it comes to writing articles about sports. Jealously (sic) will only get you enemies. You need an 'attitude adjustment,' you jerk. The worse to you and yours."—B.W.
> —*OK, I'll go to the same place where you got yours.*

Obviously, most letters columns will be more serious. Murray is one of the few columnists who can blend letters and responses so cleverly. Attempts by others are not necessarily as effective.

Exercises

1. Clip what you consider to be the three best sports columns written by area newspaper journalists during a one-week period. Then, go to your school's library to read sports columns that recently have been published in out-of-state dailies that you do not normally see. Select several of the best columns in those newspapers. Categorize the columns—features, postcontest analysis, personality profiles, personal reflections, letters from readers, and others—and analyze the writing styles. Who do you consider to be the best columnists based on your limited sample of selections? Consider making a call to the columnist you found to be the best and discuss with him or her writing strategies.
2. Invite one of your state's most highly regarded sports columnists to class. Discuss the columnist's work habits, writing schedule, and ways of generating topic ideas.
3. Write a column.

Stu Pospisil of the *Omaha* (Neb.) *World-Herald*
rates high school teams and selects all-state
squads.

CHAPTER SIXTEEN

Ratings and All-Star Teams

W hich institution has the best college football team in America? For more than a half century, that has been determined by media members from around the nation who have voted in the Associated Press poll.

The shortcomings of writer polls are well known. Voters could have regional biases or soft spots in their hearts for their alma maters. Certain teams get Top 20 votes based on reputation, even when they get off to bad starts; other teams without reputations as big-time football powers sometimes do not get votes, even when they are having outstanding seasons.

Occasionally, this perplexing dilemma surfaces: An 11-0 squad is voted the national championship because it is the only undefeated, untied major college team in America. But an examination of its schedule reveals that its opponents have been, for the most part, lackluster and limited to one geographical region. Is this squad, then, really better than a team with one or possibly even two losses that has played several schools that are, or at one time were, in the nation's Top 20 ratings? Granted, this is not the most burning issue facing American journalists. But one undisputable fact remains: millions of readers and listeners turn to the media each year to see where the "experts" rate their teams.

The *New York Times*, during the late 1970s, started to explore ways to apply social science methods (quantitative approaches in which numbers, aided by computer analysis, are used to measure and evaluate) to all aspects of reporting. Management of the *Times* reasoned that computer-generated assistance need not be limited to the business, production, and circulation departments.

Henry Lieberman, who then was head of the special projects department at the *Times,* said he coordinated an effort to develop a model that would be objective in the sense of determining what criteria should be examined to rate the quality of an athletic team. The *Times* decided to enlist the aid of a computer to rate college football teams.

The *Times'* college football ratings are based on an analysis of each team's scores, with an emphasis on three factors: who won the game, by what margin, and against what quality of opposition. According to the *Times'* explanation of its system:

> The quality of an opponent is determined by examining its record against other teams.
>
> The *Times'* computer model collapses runaway scores and takes note of a home-field advantage. As the season progresses, results in recent games count more than results in earlier games.
>
> The top team is assigned a rating of 1.000; the percentages of all other teams are percentages reflecting their strength relative to the top team.
>
> The opponents' won-loss record and average margin of victory show how each ranked team's opponents performed in all their games before they played the ranked team.

The *Times* releases its Top 20 ratings using this format:

	Record	Average Win Margin	Rating	Opp. Record	Opp. Average Win Margin
1. Virginia	7-0-0	36.7	1.000	11-8-0	11.3
2. Washington	7-1-0	19.8	.994	17-9-2	5.9
3. Georgia Tech	6-0-1	15.9	.953	20-10-0	7.8

There are those, of course, who would argue that sportswriters and college coaches have a better "feel" for ratings than a computer that merely is fed raw data. The *Times'* ratings nevertheless have generated much interest.

The "big four" of big-time college ratings consists of the AP poll, the *USA Today* poll, the United Press International poll, and the *Times* poll. Until the late 1970s, the two wire services—AP and UPI—had a lock on the rating business. AP relied on a panel of the nation's media members for its ratings; UPI relied on a panel of college coaches representing all regions of the country.

In the spring of 1991, however, the American Football Coaches Association (AFCA) announced that it was going to move its Top 25 poll from UPI to *USA Today*. UPI said that it would continue to rate teams. *Editor & Publisher* magazine quoted Charles McClendon, the executive director of the AFCA, who said: "We just decided this would be the greatest move for us. We felt like we could get the greatest amount of publicity with *USA Today.*"

The magazine noted that *USA Today* listed a daily circulation of more than 1.3 million and a daily readership of nearly six million. The *USA Today* poll is based on votes of sixty college coaches and one randomly selected fan. *E&P* quoted *USA Today*'s managing editor/sports Gene Policinski, who said: "They (the coaches) were seeking more publicity for their poll as the number of UPI clients dwindled. Clearly *USA Today* is a very visible billboard for the coaches' poll."

Most daily newspapers do not have the resources to engage in sophisticated rating procedures, but most of them publish high school ratings. A national survey of daily newspaper sports editors, published in *Journalism Quarterly,* showed that 63 percent selected and published high school ratings in football and basketball. The study found that newspapers that circulated between 25,000 and 49,999 were most likely to select and publish high school ratings. Seventy-five percent of the sports editors who worked for newspapers in this circulation category said they publish prep ratings. In the under 10,000 circulation group, 57 percent reported that they published prep ratings; 60 percent in the 10,000 to 24,999 circulation range reported publishing prep ratings; and 69 percent of those editors who worked for newspapers that circulate more than 50,000 reported publishing high school ratings.

The study showed that publication of high school all-state and all-area teams is even more popular. Seventy-eight percent said their newspapers published lists of these honor teams. Again, newspapers in the 25,000 to 49,999 circulation range led with 95 percent. Ninety-four percent of the sports editors of papers that circulate more than 50,000 said their newspapers published prep all-star teams. Seventy-nine percent of the sports editors of papers in the 10,000 to 24,999 circulation range and 57 percent of the sports editors of the newspapers that circulate under 10,000 reported publication of prep all-star teams.

Clearly, sports editors are convinced that high school ratings and all-star teams are of interest to readers. Stu Pospisil, prep writer for the *Omaha* (Neb.) *World-Herald,* is experienced at assembling high school ratings and all-state teams.

Rating the Preps

Among Pospisil's primary responsibilities is rating high school teams. This is no small task; 348 Nebraska high schools field athletic teams. In 1991, the schools ranged in size from Lincoln High, with a sophomore-junior-senior enrollment of 2,095, to the Nebraska School for the Visually Handicapped, with eight students. Pospisil records scores of *each* game played in the state during football and basketball seasons.

Pospisil, who works seven days a week during football and basketball seasons, has been with the *World-Herald* full time since 1985, shortly after his graduation from the University of Nebraska—Lincoln. The National Merit Scholar worked for the *World-Herald* part time during his last semester.

There are no major league sports in Nebraska. Thus, the state's dailies devote considerable space to universities, colleges, and high schools. Few metropolitan newspapers in the country match the *World-Herald*'s coverage of prep sports. "To an extent, high school sports results are the only way a small town in Nebraska sees its name in print," Pospisil said. "Their local high school is a source of pride. This, of course, has caused problems as schools get smaller and smaller."

Nebraska has seven classifications for schools that field football teams: A, B, C-1, C-2, D-1, D-2, and six-man (the D-1 and D-2 schools play eight-man football). Classifications are based on enrollment. The thirty-two largest schools are in Class A, the next sixty-four in Class B, the next sixty-four in C-1, the next sixty-four in C-2, and the remainder spread among the lowest classifications. "Some people say Nebraska should just do away with the smaller classes and thus force schools to consolidate," Pospisil said. "But it's a matter of name recognition. If there were not small-school athletics, people in Nebraska would never hear, for example, about Elba, Guide Rock, or Rising City."

Indeed, Nebraska is a state of 1.6 million people. But most of them live in eastern Nebraska, with residents of Omaha and Lincoln accounting for more than one-third of the state's population. Western Nebraska has scores of towns and high schools, but the area is sparsely populated. The density of much of western Nebraska averages fewer than five persons per square mile. Pospisil's job is to keep track of the nearly 350 sports-playing high schools that are spread across Nebraska's 77,355 square miles, which make it the fifteenth largest state in the union.

Residents of many of Nebraska's small towns have been tenacious in holding on to their schools and their sports teams. A few high schools, however, have consolidated, and others have entered into cooperative arrangements where towns maintain their individual high schools but combine resources for athletics and some academic programs. "Longtime rivalries hold some schools back from consolidating or cooperating," Pospisil said. "But those are slowly starting to drift away as people see the economic reality of trying to keep a high school open. The cooperatives have been beneficial to communities wanting to keep a sense of identity. You haven't seen many co-ops dissolve because they haven't worked out."

The *World-Herald*'s dedication to extensive coverage of prep athletics is apparent. The tradition was started in the 1920s by the late Gregg McBride, who served as the newspaper's prep sportswriter for nearly a half-century. McBride began the practice of rating prep teams and selecting all-state teams.

Recording the scores for all high schools in the state is no easy chore. Rating the schools in such a geographically large state is no less difficult. Many of the top teams in the smaller enrollment categories do not play each other during the regular season. After compiling scores, talking with coaches, and watching several teams play, Pospisil nevertheless is in position to compile his ratings.

Pospisil's weeks are busy:

Sunday. The *World-Herald* reporter sifts through Friday's and Saturday's results, posting them in his records. "I chart wins, losses, points scored and points given up," he said. "Our files date back to 1941. We are the only paper in the state that has such extensive statewide files. I don't know if that is what a newspaper's function is to be, but, in this state, we've assumed the responsibility."

It takes Pospisil more than two hours to post results each Sunday. Once he has completed that task, he puts together his Top-10 ratings for Monday's editions. "If things go smoothly, it's a four-hour process," he said. "Sometimes, though, it can take twice that long."

Pospisil's ratings are accompanied by a story that contains analysis and often a feature angle. The stories usually include direct quotations from coaches of the top teams. The stories always are preceded with the list of Top-10 schools, their records, the points they have scored, and the points they have allowed.

As the football season was winding down one year, this was Pospisil's Top 10 that preceded the story:

Top 10

	W	L	Pts.	O.P.
1. Papillion-La Vista	6	0	239	56
2. Grand Island	6	0	209	21
3. Om. Cr. Prep	5	1	188	69
4. Bellevue East	6	0	132	47
5. Bellevue West	5	1	181	71
6. Lincoln SE	5	1	107	13
7. Omaha Burke	4	2	98	110
8. Millard North	4	2	130	57
9. Omaha Benson	3	3	94	105
10. Omaha Westside	5	1	110	68

Top games this week—
Friday: Bellevue East vs. Omaha North at Omaha Northwest, Omaha Westside vs. Bellevue West at Bellevue East, Lincoln High at Lincoln East, Omaha Benson vs. Omaha Creighton Prep at UNO.
Saturday: Grand Island vs. Lincoln SE at Seacrest.

Pospisil's story focused on fifth-rated Bellevue West, which was making a run for the playoffs for the first time. High in the story were direct quotes from the Bellevue West coach. Here are the first seven paragraphs:

> Bellevue West will have a great deal to say as to which teams make this year's Nebraska Class A state football playoffs.
> The Thunderbirds, which remained fifth in this week's unchanged World-Herald Top 10, improved to 5-1 after Friday's 23-16 victory over No. 9 Omaha Benson. They will play host to No. 10 Omaha Westside this week and will close their season with road games with No. 3 Omaha Creighton Prep and Omaha Central.
> West, Benson and Westside, along with No. 7 Omaha Burke, are in powerful District 2.
> Bellevue West has perceived recent games to be playoff contests. The Thunderbirds have never been to the playoffs, despite several 7-2 seasons.
> "Since we lost to Bellevue East," West Coach John Faiman said, "basically we feel we've been under the gun as far as not losing. It's so even that not any of the top teams can be counted out until the last week."
> West defeated Benson, breaking a 16-16 tie by scoring on all-state quarterback Clester Johnson's 5-yard pass to Don Kiviniemi with 1 minute, 21 seconds left.
> "It definitely was a big win for us," Faiman said. "At this time of year, winning is as much mental as physical. If you think there's nothing at the end of the rainbow, teams give up that shouldn't."

Pospisil's story concluded with an analysis of teams in the other five districts. That analysis was introduced with this transition paragraph:

> Playoff berths are Class A's rainbow jackpot, and this weekend's football games begin the sorting process.

Ratings naturally are a source of controversy and pride for Nebraska high school athletes and fans. The fact that such a high percentage of the nation's dailies publish prep ratings, however, attests to their readership value.

Monday. Pospisil's Class A ratings are published in *World-Herald* editions, and he begins work on his Class B ratings, which will appear in Tuesday's newspaper. He also starts gathering information for a feature—called "Prep Notables"—that is published at the end of the week. "We take nominations for prep athletes who had exceptional performances," Pospisil said. "We've had as many as twenty formal nominations. We take them from interested fans, community leaders, and even parents. I haven't had a kid nominate himself, yet."

Pospisil skims *World-Herald* issues and other state newspapers for accounts of exceptional prep performances. "I try to get a good selection from Omaha to the Panhandle," he said. "I try not to feature the same athletes week in and week out. Sometimes, though, athletes have great seasons and do merit mention in several weeks." "Prep Notables" is a popular *World-Herald* feature that also can give readers a preview of athletes who likely will be named to all-state teams. One week's list featured more than fifty athletes in girls cross country, girls volleyball, boys cross country, and football. Written in a punchy style, here is a selection of some "Prep Notables."

> **Susan Schmidt, Bennington**—The Badgers' junior won the girls' race in the Capitol Conference cross country meet at Fort Calhoun, leading Bennington to a meet-tying record score of 14 points. It was the fifth title of the season for the second-year runner.
>
> **Debbie Thies, Clarkson**—The 5-foot-8 senior led Clarkson to a 15-10, 15-11 volleyball victory over Humphrey St. Francis by having a hitting efficiency of .640 on 16 kills in 25 attempts. She added four ace blocks.
>
> **Kathy Kearns, Ginny Hoefer and Andrea Felton, Millard North**—Cross country trio capped season of steady improvement in placings by leading Mustangs to their first Metro Conference title in the sport. Kearns, a ninth-grader, was third at Metro, Hoefer, a junior, was fourth and Felton, a freshman, fifth. The Mustangs have three wins, two seconds, and two thirds entering districts.
>
> **Doug Anderson and Rich Still, Anselmo-Merna**—Anderson accounted for four touchdowns, three by rushing, 221 yards of total offense, nine tackles and an interception in 40-20 victory over Dunning Sandhills. Still, a defensive end, had five tackles for 32 yards in losses, 17 tackles overall and a 3-yard TD run.
>
> **Lane Werner, Tilden Elkhorn Valley**—Starting his third game at quarterback, the junior threw for 202 yards and three touchdowns and ran for 101 yards, two touchdowns and a two-point conversion in a 34-21 victory over O'Neill St. Mary.
>
> **Cindy Bosak, Papillion-LaVista**—The 5-6 senior had a total of 75 set assists as her team defeated then No. 1 Bellevue West in the semifinals and defending champion Millard North in the final of last week's Metro volleyball tournament.

Clinton Childs, Omaha North—Junior rushed for 226 yards on 22 carries in the Vikings' 39-14 victory over Millard South. The performance vaulted him to the top of the Metro rushing chart with 894 yards.

Debbie Evans, Omaha South—The 5-10 senior has ascended to the top of the Metro volleyball chart in service aces. In 32 games, Evans has 45 aces, 1.4 a game.

Melvin McPhall, Omaha Flanagan—Junior quarterback rushed for 125 yards and two touchdowns to lead the Chargers to a 24-15 win over Omaha Roncalli.

Mike Pszanka, Scottsbluff—Wide receiver caught three passes for 111 yards and two touchdowns in Scottsbluff's 26-0 win over Gering. On defense, he intercepted two passes, returning them for 37 yards.

Kevin Crosgrove, Allen—Middle linebacker had 30 tackles—five unassisted, 25 assisted—and two interceptions, with one returned 47 yards for a touchdown, in a 56-6 victory over Walthill. Also blocked Walthill's extra point. Has 124 total tackles in six games.

Brendan Holbein, Cozad—Holdrege was chasing the 5-11, 175-pound junior all night in a 39-0 loss. He scored on 97- and 92-yard runs in the first half, when he carried just nine times but gained 274 of his career-best 310 yards. Teammate **Corey Barnes,** who threw a 72-yard TD pass, had three of Cozad's six interceptions.

Marc Hultquist, Minden—By winning the Southwest Conference boys cross country meet, the senior became a rare four-time winner. On his home course, he ran the 3.1 miles in 16 minutes, 39 seconds.

Tuesday. Pospisil continues to work on his "Prep Notables" list and to compile his Class C-1 and C-2 ratings, which will be published in Wednesday's editions.

Wednesday. The *World-Herald* prep sportswriter finishes up his ratings for eight-man and six-man teams which will be published Thursday. He also enters into his computer all Friday night games, which will be published in Thursday's editions, with his selections in boldfaced type. "If I can pick winners in three-fourths of the games, that's pretty good," Pospisil said. "That's the benchmark I shoot for."

Thursday. Pospisil devotes part of the day to writing his weekly prep column, which is published Fridays. The column often is part feature and part notes. "The column usually contains as much information as it does opinion," he said. "I try to feature anything that has happened during the week that I think belongs in the paper." Pospisil also puts the finishing touches on "Prep Notables" for the week and makes sure he hasn't missed coverage of newsworthy events in other sports. Even though football dominates the fall sports pages, golf, volleyball, and cross country also have to be covered.

Friday. This is a travel day for Pospisil, who selects a top game to cover. In an average year, he puts more than 25,000 miles on his company car. "I try to be seen around the state," he said. "Naturally, I try to cover the best games. But I also like to spread some newspaper goodwill. I always make contact earlier in the week with the coaches, athletic directors, or principals of the schools I'm going to cover. Ninety-nine percent are glad to see me; they like to get publicity in the state's largest newspaper." Pospisil must file his stories by 11:15 Friday night.

Saturday. This serves as a catch-up day for the prep sportswriter. He also sketches out his schedule for the next week and, occasionally, has a Saturday night contest to cover.

Methodology for Ratings

Pospisil considers a team's record, its schedule strength, and its momentum. He talks to coaches around the state. He also relies, to an extent, on his instincts. "Some schools perennially have good football records," he said. "They might be 8-0 or 7-1 year after year when the playoffs begin. But they usually lose in the first round. That says something about the competition in that part of the state."

The *World-Herald* writer likes to see as many of the top teams in action during a season as he possibly can. The miles mount up during football playoffs, when games are played on weekdays as well as weekends. One Tuesday, for example, Pospisil drove nearly 300 miles from Omaha to Ogallala, a western Nebraska community of 5,600 people, to cover an evening game. He filed his story, spent the night, and drove about 100 miles the next morning to Gering (population 7,760) for a Wednesday afternoon game. After writing the game story in his car in the parking lot after that contest, he headed down the interstate to Chappell (population 1,270), about a two-hour drive, for an eight-man night game. After filing his story, he drove nearly an hour back to Ogallala, where he spent the night. He returned to Omaha on Thursday.

Selecting All-State Teams

Few honors a high school athlete can earn are more coveted than being named all state. The *World-Herald*—in football, soccer, baseball, boys and girls basketball, and girls volleyball—selects an All-Nebraska first team and second team. The newspaper also selects first and second teams for each of the enrollment classes in football, basketball, and volleyball. In addition, honorable mention lists are compiled for each class.

Pospisil relies, to a certain extent, on nominations from coaches when he selects his teams. He sends out nomination forms to every athletic director in the state before year-end tournaments or playoffs; the athletic directors then distribute them to appropriate coaches.

Nomination forms are mailed about two weeks before the end of regular seasons. That way, athletes whose teams do not qualify for the playoffs or state tournament will not be overlooked. Pospisil asks that the forms be returned within two days of the conclusion of the playoffs or state tournament. Coaches are invited to nominate players, including those from their own teams. They are asked to provide statistics as well as observations. "We ask the coaches to start with the player they consider to be the best and to work on down," Pospisil said. "They also can nominate players for honorable mention. Usually, every team in the state has at least one player worthy of being recognized with a mention."

The *World-Herald* publishes its all-state teams the week following the playoffs or state tournament. Pospisil does not rely totally on nominations from coaches. He watches many of the state's top players sometime during each season. Basketball and volleyball teams often are easier to select than football. It is difficult, for example, to ferret out names and accomplishments of outstanding interior linemen, especially in the smaller-school classes.

"Because I have seen players throughout the year, I have a pretty good idea who is going to be All-Nebraska," Pospisil said. "At least I have a good feeling about at least some of the spots. I put down the 'locks' and then check the ballots to see what the coaches have to say." At that point, Pospisil tallies the nominations by the coaches and fills out his teams. Because he writes several paragraphs on the accomplishments of the All-Nebraska players, he relies on the information provided on the nomination forms, on information provided on the preseason fact sheets coaches earlier had returned, and on telephone calls to coaches and athletic directors.

Compiling information for all-state teams is a major task, as is writing the stories and inputting all the information. Pospisil devotes a full week to the job. "Then I sit back and wait for the hate letters," he said with a smile. "We always receive a handful of letters from people who disagree with our selections."

The *World-Herald* gives prominent play to its all-state teams, always carrying a full-color photo of the All-Nebraska units. Here, for example, is one of Pospisil's first teams for boys basketball:

Player, School	Ht.	Cl.	Avg.
Erick Strickland, Bellevue West	6-3	Jr.	26.3
Jason Glock, Wahoo	6-4	Sr.	30.0
Curtis Marshall, Omaha Creighton Prep	6-0	Sr.	30.5

Andy Woolridge, Omaha Benson	6-1	Jr.	26.5
Terrance Badgett, Omaha South	6-6	Sr.	24.5

Honorary captain—Jason Glock, Wahoo.

In his accompanying forty-nine-paragraph story, Pospisil's lead block focused on four characteristics the stars had in common: their potential to be major-college players; their scoring ability; their expertise from three-point range; and their passing prowess. Here is Pospisil's lead block:

> All will be major-college players. All should end their high school careers as the No. 1 or No. 2 all-time scorer in school history.
>
> In those two highly noticeable ways, this year's World-Herald All-Nebraska boys basketball team will leave its mark.
>
> Consider two more ways that the five players—seniors Jason Glock of Wahoo, Curtis Marshall of Omaha Creighton Prep and Terrance Badgett of Omaha South and Juniors Erick Strickland of Bellevue West and Andy Woolridge of Omaha Benson—will have an effect on future stars in the state.
>
> They are the first All-Nebraska class able to take advantage of the three-point shot throughout their careers. This season, Glock shot 48 percent, Strickland 43 percent and Marshall 42 percent from three-point range. Woolridge, a 38-percent shooter from three-point range, made 57 three-point baskets and Badgett, at 6-foot-6 the tallest All-Nebraska selection, made 28.
>
> The five also were accomplished passers, able to excite a packed gymnasium with lookaways and thread-the-needle assists.
>
> "They all pass a little differently," said Bellevue West Coach Lanny Richards. "Erick, Andy and Curtis are willing to gamble. Sometimes you can see they wish they had the pass back.
>
> "Erick is a good passer in the lane, best at the wraparound. Woolridge is a good passer from halfcourt on. He sees a hole and zips it in. Marshall can do both.
>
> "As for Terrance and Jason, they're a bit more sure with their passes. They'll check a little closer than the other three."
>
> Their credentials suggest this All-Nebraska team can take its place among the best in state history.

After his lead block, Pospisil used a transition paragraph to put the team in historical perspective:

> Is it as good as the fabled 1982 team, which honored Dave Hoppen, Ron Kellogg, Kerry Trotter, Bill Jackman and Mike Martz?

Pospisil then quoted a Nebraska coach who was familiar with players on the 1982 team as well as players on the dream team of nearly a decade later.

After explaining how the All-Nebraska team was selected, Pospisil devoted more than six inches of copy to each of the five athletes, beginning with the team's honorary captain. Pospisil's handling of the honorary captain—Jason Glock—illustrates the type of overview he provided on the other four players:

> Glock's versatility allowed (his coach, Mick) Anderson to use him as a perimeter player until needed this season as a post player.
>
> "Down the stretch we kept him inside, taking advantage of some teams at district and state," Anderson said. "He had been playing a lot on the perimeter and shot 51 percent on threes last year and 48 percent this year. It's an area where he'll have to continue to improve in college."
>
> Glock entered the state's all-time charts for single-season scoring, 15th with 779 points, and career scoring, seventh with 2,167. He averaged more than 20 points a game in his 101 varsity games. The only game Glock didn't play was a 48-45 loss to Syracuse his freshman year, the lone loss for Wahoo during its four title seasons.
>
> Glock, 6-4, was a 67-percent career field-goal shooter on 868 of 1,293 attempts and improved his free-throw average from the low 60s as a freshman to 85 percent as a senior. An All-Nebraska tight end in football, his 889 career rebounds are another school record.
>
> "It's no secret how he's been such a big part of our team the past four years," Anderson said.
>
> In January, Glock said he would sign a letter of intent with Nebraska.
>
> Glock will need to release shots quicker in college, Anderson said, plus improve his foot speed and lateral quickness.

Clearly, Pospisil had done his homework. He mixed the contemporary with the historical. The theme was clear: This was an All-Nebraska unit of significance.

In the same issue, Pospisil named boys all-state first and second teams for Class A, Class B, Class C-1, Class C-2, Class D-1, and Class D-2. Mug shots of players who were named to the first teams were included. Extensive honorable mention lists—for all classes—contained the names of hundreds of the state's better players.

World-Herald sportswriter Daryl Blue provided equally complete information on the girls All-Nebraska team and the all-state teams for each of the enrollment classifications.

It is no wonder that most newspapers publish all-star teams and ratings. They represent earned recognition for top athletes and teams. Sports fans across a state open their newspapers with anticipation when the top teams and players are announced. The responsibility that rests with the newspaper also is clear. The reporter who compiles ratings, assembles all-star teams, and covers prep contests should approach the task with organized diligence. Pospisil provides these pointers:

- *Give the ratings and all-star teams good play.* Stories and photos should occupy a prominent place on the page. Recognition given to the state's top teams in all classes and to the best players brings honor to the communities they represent. For some of the smaller towns in the state, communities that seldom rate mentions in daily newspapers, having their teams and players listed as among the best is a matter of particular pride.
- *Gain a knowledge of your state or area.* The athletic cultures of states and areas vary. Prep sportswriters who rate teams and select all-star teams need to have an appreciation for the historical as well as the contemporary. "It's best if you can spend some time with your predecessor," Pospisil said. "He or she can fill you in on the situation you are walking into. You also need to spend time reviewing old clippings and microfilm. I feel I have a handle on Nebraska prep sports because I grew up in the state. I have followed high school sports here all my life. Because this state is so large—geographically— that background is an advantage to me."
- *Keep good records.* Maintaining accurate, complete records on all the teams and top individuals is imperative. This aspect of the job is not glamorous, but it is essential.
- *Stay in touch with coaches and athletic directors.* Conversations and interviews with coaches and athletic directors around the state help to provide writers with information on the top teams and players, as well as the trends and undercurrents sweeping the high school sports scene.
- *Emphasize the human side of sports and athletes.* Prep sportswriters have difficult issues to report and discuss: use of steroids, school suspensions of top athletes, car accidents that claim competitors, and so forth. "But it's important to tell the human side of events," Pospisil said. "I try to convey the joys, the triumphs, and the disappointments of individuals and teams."
- *Write with balance.* "All teams can't be winners," Pospisil said. "But they all expect to be treated fairly. Sportswriters who cover profession-al and collegiate teams often have to be critical in their writing. But my philosophy in covering the preps is to let the players and coaches tell their own stories through their actions and quotes. I feel I owe it to my readers and the players and teams I cover to write balanced, fair accounts."

Exercises

1. Clip from major sources—the Associated Press poll, the United Press International poll, the *New York Times* computer-generated ratings, and the *USA Today* poll—the top twenty or top twenty-five ratings for a given week during a college football season. Examine and discuss the similarities and differences.

2. Invite an area sportswriter who has a vote in the Associated Press poll to class. Ask the writer to explain the process and the role he or she plays in it.

3. Invite an area sportswriter who is responsible for rating high school teams and selecting all-area or all-state teams to class. Ask the writer to explain how the selections are made.

Game coverage might dominate sports pages, but sportswriters increasingly are finding themselves reporting off-the-field developments.

(Photo by Jeorgetta M. Douglas)

CHAPTER SEVENTEEN

Courtrooms and Boardrooms

Davit Shaw, media critic for the *Los Angeles Times,* alerted readers in the middle 1970s that the sports pages of most American newspapers were undergoing a metamorphosis. No longer would sports sections be filled only with stories about baseball heroes who could do no wrong, basketball players who burned the nets on Saturday nights and escorted elderly widows to church on Sunday mornings, and kind, grandfatherly athletic directors, who always looked out for their boys. No indeed. Shaw wrote that contemporary sports page readers were "sophisticated and literate." They wanted to know more than the score. They wanted "to know *how* it happened and *why* (or why not), as well as what may have happened before (or after) the event, in the locker room, the courtroom, the boardroom and the bedroom."

The staple of sports pages remains contest coverage, personality profiles, statistics, and features. But sports pages are increasingly providing readers with accounts of the off-the-field exploits of their heroes. Who could ever forget these thirty words from a *Sports Illustrated* story?

> There are a few things a University of Colorado campus policeman won't leave the office without: handcuffs, his copy of the Miranda warning and a University of Colorado football program.

Sometimes, sports page readers must think they have inadvertently stumbled into the business section. For example:

> NEW YORK (AP)—Baseball's annual joint winter meetings were called off Wednesday while negotiators for the major leagues and minor leagues again met in an attempt to reach a new Player Development Contract.

The PDC is the deal that binds the majors and the minors. Major-league owners want to lower their subsidy to the minors; minor-league owners, represented by the National Association of Professional Baseball Leagues, want the amount to stay the same.

High finance is often the subject of a lead story, as illustrated by the first seven paragraphs of a story by *Arizona Republic* sportswriter Lee Shappell:

On Thursday, the NBA will become the first professional sports league to pay its players an average of $1 million a year.

Even the Players Association grudgingly admits the primary reason for that is the nebulous, misnamed, misunderstood salary cap.

The cap is regarded by many as a three-headed monster. But it never could have three heads. That would be two over the cap.

The "cap" is more of a salary framework, or salary guideline, or salary agreement. It is anything but an absolute ceiling as the name implies. There are many, many ways for a team to be over the cap and still be within the rules.

The cap is an outgrowth of the collective bargaining agreement of 1983, revised in 1988, and due for another round of talks. It was implemented during the 1984-85 season, at a time when the NBA was a minor professional league in terms of fan support, and when about one-third of its franchises appeared ready to fold.

It provides for a revenue-sharing plan in which players are guaranteed 53 percent of the league's gross revenues for salaries. It has kept competition more or less equal between big-city teams and those in smaller, less-profitable markets. It has mandated fiscal responsibility to some degree.

David J. Stern, the NBA commissioner who was chief legal counsel when he dreamed up the cap in 1983, has been credited with transforming the league to major status. The game is becoming popular worldwide. NBA players will be permitted to take part in the Olympic Games next summer. Stern's manifest destiny seems to be globalizing the sport.

Even sportswriters for college newspapers recognize that their beat no longer is limited to playing fields. Here is the lead block from a story by Oklahoma State's Kyle Newkirk that was published in the *Daily O'Collegian* and won an award in the William Randolph Hearst Foundation's intercollegiate writing championships:

No university can compare with the success Oklahoma State has had in wrestling and baseball. The Cowboys have won 29 national titles on the mat and have been to the College World Series 21 times and won one national title in baseball.

Between the two sports, 204 athletes have been named All-American.

This season, the second-ranked wrestling team and the 13th-ranked baseball team again are challenging for national titles, but their fate might not depend on how well the Cowboys perform in post-season play.

It might depend on decisions in courts of law.

The best athlete from each squad, defending NCAA champion wrestler Pat Smith and All-American second baseman Mitch Simons, lost their eligibility this year for different reasons, but both filed lawsuits in Payne County District Court to regain their eligibility.

Stories about off-the-field exploits don't dominate sports pages, but, on given days, they almost seem to. Here, for example, are the tops of two Associated Press stories that were transmitted the same day:

LOS ANGELES (AP)—Two former University of Southern California football players were sentenced to 15 years in prison after pleading guilty to reduced charges stemming from a series of robberies and beatings.

STILLWATER, Okla. (AP)—NCAA investigators have returned to Oklahoma State amid allegations that wrestling coach Joe Seay told his players to lie during an investigation into the program.

The Daily Oklahoman cited unnamed sources inside and around the program as saying that Seay called a meeting to make sure everyone had their stories straight.

The newspaper reported Wednesday that eight wrestlers, told their eligibility was in as much danger as the wrestling program, later told NCAA investigators that they lied the first time around.

Sometimes, stories about dollars and the courts converge. Note the first three paragraphs from a story published in the *Fort Lauderdale* (Fla.) *Sun-Sentinel:*

Tony Russell, the target of a criminal investigation into an illegal financial aid scheme at the University of Miami, said this weekend that a $60- to $100-a-week cocaine habit caused him to begin charging students a fee to falsify their applications.

Speaking publicly for the first time about the investigation, he said he acted alone, submitting Pell Grants for about 50 athletes during his two years as an assistant to the Athletic Department's academic coordinator.

In an hour-long interview at his home with the *Sun-Sentinel,* Russell also said he had filed about 600 Pell Grant applications in the past 12 years, falsifying many of them, to get students money that they were not entitled to at schools across the country.

Clearly, it is no longer sufficient for sportswriters merely to understand the athletic events they cover. They also must have knowledge of finance, courtroom procedures, boardroom practices, and NCAA regulations.

NCAA Investigations

With increasing frequency, NCAA investigations are being reported extensively by the print media. NCAA enforcement procedures state: "All representatives of member institutions shall cooperate fully with the NCAA enforcement staff, Committee on Infractions and Council to further the objectives of the Association and its enforcement program. The enforcement policies and procedures are an essential part of the intercollegiate athletics program of each member institution and require full and complete disclosure by all institutional representatives of any relevant information requested by the NCAA enforcement staff, Committee on Infractions or Council during the course of an inquiry."

The NCAA can assess penalties against member institutions for secondary violations. A secondary violation is defined as "one that provides only a limited recruiting or competitive advantage and that is isolated or inadvertent in nature." Penalties can range from none to such actions as forfeiture of contests in which an ineligible student athlete participated or a reduction in financial aid awards.

Penalties for major violations are more severe. The NCAA defines major violations as "those that provide an extensive recruiting or competitive advantage." Penalties can include reprimands and censures, probation for specified periods, or ineligibility for NCAA championship events. Repeat violators can be dealt with more harshly, including having their teams in specified sports banned from some or all outside competition.

Member institutions have the right to appeal findings and penalties. In June 1991, federal legislation was introduced that would require the NCAA to afford due process to its members. Florida, Nebraska, and Nevada already had enacted similar state measures. The NCAA has maintained, however, that it has taken steps to ensure greater due process, thus rendering any legislative enactments unnecessary. Figure 17.1, which is taken from the *NCAA Manual*, illustrates the processing of a typical infractions case.

The Long-Running NCAA-UNLV Battle

Possibly no feud is chronicled more extensively than that between the NCAA and Jerry Tarkanian and his University of Nevada—Las Vegas basketball program. Bruce Pascoe, who covers UNLV for the *Las Vegas*

Review-Journal, said that writing NCAA-related stories constitutes roughly one-third of his work covering the Rebels. "In fact, while I cover everything on the court, I share off-the-court business with Greg Bortolin, who covers UNLV football in the fall," he said.

Pascoe possesses the skills to cover UNLV on the court and off it. He grew up in the San Francisco Bay area, where he devoured the local sports pages each day. He attended Northwestern University, where he double majored in journalism and economics. "When I started college, it was my intention to one day work for a bank," Pascoe said. "But, I got serious about journalism when I was a sophomore."

Pascoe worked on the staff of *The Daily Northwestern* during his four years in college. As a senior, he served as managing editor while continuing to write sports. He also interned at *The Washington Post,* where he wrote sports. Pascoe took his first full-time job at the *Review-Journal* in January 1988. Since then, he has come to know the NCAA and UNLV well.

Pascoe, who said he is "still learning," provided these tips to sports-writers who cover NCAA investigations:

- *Talk to as many sources as possible.* University attorneys, Las Vegas lawyers who have had dealings with the NCAA, athletic department officials, school administrators, coaches, and players form his nucleus.
- *Become familiar with the NCAA Manual.* "I didn't know that much about NCAA procedures when I started my job," Pascoe said. The *NCAA Manual* is logically and efficiently indexed; thus, reporters easily can find sections that relate to stories they are writing.
- *Maintain good records.* "I keep a list of all allegations and proceedings," Pascoe said. "That way, I can periodically check with university and NCAA officials. The school is not likely to formally announce the results of all internal investigations."
- *Stay in touch with NCAA officials.* "I have found the NCAA to be helpful, though dealing with it occasionally can get frustrating," Pascoe said. He tries to develop contacts in various wings of the NCAA—enforcement, legislative, and communication, for example— so he can make quick calls while on deadline. "NCAA officials often talk like lawyers," Pascoe said. "But the staff-level people can be very helpful, even though they rarely comment on specific cases."
- *Don't take criticism personally.* "When you are working on investigative or NCAA stories, you often don't have a lot of friends out there," Pascoe said. "You have to develop a thick skin when you write stories that are critical of players or programs."
- *Feed off of support from management.* "UNLV basketball is big in town," Pascoe said. "Management really supports our efforts to cover the beat extensively—on and off the court."

Figure 12.1
Processing of a Typical NCAA Infractions Case

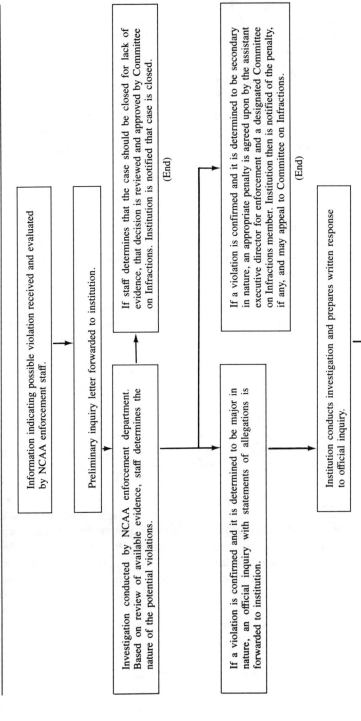

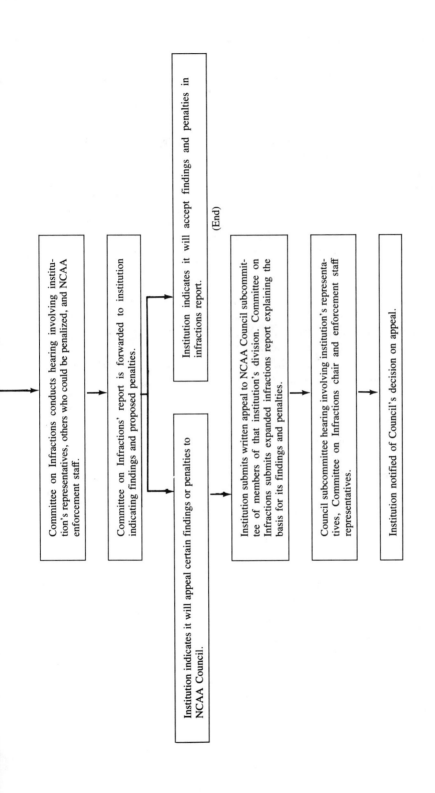

Committee on Infractions conducts hearing involving institution's representatives, others who could be penalized, and NCAA enforcement staff.

Committee on Infractions' report is forwarded to institution indicating findings and proposed penalties.

Institution indicates it will accept findings and penalties in infractions report.

(End)

Institution indicates it will appeal certain findings or penalties to NCAA Council.

Institution submits written appeal to NCAA Council subcommittee of members of that institution's division. Committee on Infractions submits expanded infractions report explaining the basis for its findings and penalties.

Council subcommittee hearing involving institution's representatives, Committee on Infractions chair and enforcement staff representatives.

Institution notified of Council's decision on appeal.

Pascoe said, however, that his aggressive coverage of off-the-court activities sometimes hinders his beat coverage. "The players look at you as the bad guy," Pascoe said. "Ninety percent of the players don't understand journalism. They don't understand my job."

Coaches and university administrators do not appreciate negative stories about their programs. "You don't have a lot of friends within programs that you cover," Pascoe said. "But, you try to generate respect. Some of the lawyers and central administrators at the university, I think, know we shoot straight and that we have a job to do."

UNLV's altercations with the NCAA, of course, preceded Pascoe's arrival at the *Review-Journal*. Here is a streamlined chronology, based on a *Sports Illustrated* story by William F. Reed:

- Aug. 25, 1977: The NCAA announced that it had found UNLV guilty of recruiting and organizational violations; it banned the Rebels from television appearances and postseason play for the next two seasons. The NCAA also requested that UNLV show cause why the university should not discipline Tarkanian.
- Sept. 7, 1977: The UNLV administration suspended Tarkanian for two seasons. As a result, Tarkanian filed suits against UNLV and the NCAA, temporarily blocking the suspension.
- Sept. 26, 1977: A Nevada state district court judge issued a permanent injunction preventing UNLV from suspending the coach.
- June 25, 1984: A Nevada state lower court judge ruled that the NCAA had violated Tarkanian's due process rights.
- Aug. 27, 1987: The Nevada Supreme Court upheld that ruling.
- Dec. 12, 1988: The U.S. Supreme Court ruled 5-4 that the NCAA had a right to discipline its members. The Court said that, as a private organization of voluntary members, the NCAA had the right to make UNLV show cause why Tarkanian should not be penalized.

At an NCAA meeting in Kansas City in June 1990—four months after the Rebels had humiliated Duke to win their first national championship—the NCAA Committee on Infractions asked UNLV to do what had been requested thirteen years earlier: to show cause why Tarkanian should not be suspended for two years. Then, on July 20, 1990, the NCAA banned UNLV from the 1991 NCAA tournament.

Shortly after that, UNLV asked the NCAA for a special hearing on the basis of "new information." That fall, the university's request was granted. Here are the first four paragraphs from Bruce Pascoe's story in the *Las Vegas Review-Journal:*

UNLV's basketball team, its hopes for the chance to defend its national championship still in the air, was pleased but cautious with the announcement Tuesday that the NCAA Infractions Committee would rehear its case later this month.

UNLV Coach Jerry Tarkanian met with his players before their afternoon conditioning class Tuesday and told them the news. He said the team received it guardedly, and then echoed the sentiments of many of his players.

"I think everyone was pleased," he said. "This gives us another opportunity. . . . Hopefully, when we go back this time, we'll be more successful."

Tarkanian also praised the efforts of UNLV legal counsel Brad Booke, who has been handling the school's NCAA matters and was preparing to present its arguments next week in a scheduled appeal at Kansas City. The appeal has since been postponed to January, pending the outcome of the new UNLV-NCAA meeting Oct. 28.

The remainder of Pascoe's story contained several direct quotations from Rebel players.

In a companion analysis piece, *Review-Journal* sportswriter Greg Bortolin credited a Las Vegas lawyer for devising the plan that got UNLV the rehearing. Analysis pieces—which provide background on and put in perspective news events—have become common on sports pages as business and legal issues are covered more extensively. Here is Bortolin's lead block:

> Until Tuesday, the consensus was that UNLV's basketball program faced the same odds of participating in the postseason as Saddam Hussein did of running for president of the United States.
>
> But, that was before Tuesday's revelation that UNLV Counsel Brad Booke had talked the NCAA Infractions Committee into rehearing a case in which it banned UNLV in July from postseason basketball play.
>
> After a persuasive appeal written by Booke in August and direct negotiations with the NCAA for three weeks, the doomed UNLV basketball program suddenly has a chance it never appeared it would get.
>
> The argument that the NCAA penalty hurt the players who would be denied the chance to defend their championship, not the targeted UNLV Coach Jerry Tarkanian, has been effective, President Robert Maxson said. Booke argued that the ban would penalize players who were in elementary school when the original infractions occurred.
>
> Instead of appealing to the NCAA Council, which has never overturned its infractions committee, UNLV will get a second chance to have its case heard before the original committee. UNLV will still have the opportunity to appeal to the NCAA Council.
>
> Different arguments will be made at O'Hare International Airport in Chicago on Oct. 28. Bluntly, it will be Let's Make a Deal time between the NCAA and UNLV.
>
> By its actions, the NCAA is second-guessing itself.

Maxson is cheering Booke on and praising NCAA administrators for being fair-minded.

The *Review-Journal* covered developments in the case leading up to the October 28 meeting. At that meeting, Maxson asked the NCAA to consider alternatives to the absolute ban on UNLV's participation in the 1991 tournament. In addition, Tarkanian also promised not to take further legal action against the NCAA or UNLV.

One month later, the Infractions Committee made its decision. Bortolin's lead block summarized the "Rebel Reprieve":

> UNLV basketball fans will be able to add the word "repeat" to their Rebel chants after the university received word Thursday morning from the NCAA that the national championship team can defend its title and Jerry Tarkanian will be allowed to coach it.
>
> "We received two alternatives and we accepted no live television during the 1991-92 season and the team will not be allowed to play in the postseason next year," said UNLV President Robert Maxson from his conference room, which was packed with university regents, media and fans.
>
> "Everyone is in agreement. The coach feels good about this second alternative as does our athletic director and legal counsel.
>
> "It took about 30 seconds before Coach locked on to alternative No. 2."
>
> Fans standing in the president's office reception area cheered the announcement.
>
> Las Vegas television station KLAS-TV, Channel 8, broadcast a videotape of Tarkanian's reaction from Vancouver, British Columbia, where he is promoting Saturday's UNLV–University of Alabama—Birmingham game.
>
> "No, it's not what we wanted, but I'm glad to get it over with," he said. "Sometimes I feel the NCAA is the only organization that is above the law."
>
> Maxson also said the NCAA's decision to modify its penalty officially ended 13 years of litigation between Tarkanian and the NCAA.
>
> The NCAA alternative UNLV did not accept included:
>
> "The university will suspend its men's head basketball coach from engaging in any coaching activities, including participation in or attendance at formal or informal strategy or planning sessions, practices, or competition, following the 1990-91 regular season; and the University of Nevada, Las Vegas, men's basketball team will not participate in any postseason competition following the 1991 regular season, including the NCAA men's basketball championship tournament."
>
> Maxson said he thought both alternatives were fair, but one of the goals of the university presenting new information was to get the NCAA to allow this year's team into the postseason tournament.

Naturally, as word of the NCAA's offer and UNLV's choice started to sink in, reaction stories dominated sports pages around the country. Jim Fossum, a *Review-Journal* sportswriter, interviewed several coaches and basketball analyst Dick Vitale. Fossum's story, which contained several direct quotations, began this way:

> The NCAA's decision Thursday to modify UNLV's ban from postseason play in 1991 may signal a change in direction designed to enhance the image of the governing body of intercollegiate athletics, people in the college basketball community said Friday.
>
> While some coaches expressed apparent disagreement with the decision through an unwillingness to comment, others expressed optimism in what the decision may mean to their future dealings with the NCAA.
>
> "I think that as one views the NCAA since (executive director) Dick Schultz took over (in 1988), it's not very difficult to conclude that the organization has taken on a whole new posture," Southern Cal Coach George Raveling said from Los Angeles. "I think regardless of what one thinks about the decision, to me some bottom-line conclusions are that as an organization they want to be flexible, fair and realistic in the way they govern so that it's done in a manner that allows the rules to be apropos to contemporary times."

About one week after the NCAA announced its decision, the Associated Press moved a story that focused on Schultz's response to the reaction of others:

> KANSAS CITY, Mo.—Just about everybody whose school ever went on NCAA probation were indignant when UNLV was given an alternative penalty, allowing it to defend its basketball championship this season.
>
> But there has never been a case quite like UNLV, which reached all the way to the U.S. Supreme Court, NCAA executive director Dick Schultz said.
>
> "Everybody wants to compare this to their own situation," Schultz said this week in response to criticism of last week's decision by the NCAA infractions committee.
>
> "This is not a normal infractions case. People don't realize UNLV served an institutional penalty 13 years ago. This is not a normal infractions case. It's really a show-cause situation, and it's complicated by the permanent injunction."
>
> The infractions committee told UNLV in July it would not be able to defend its title as an outgrowth of the 1977 case. But after listening to the school offer four alternative penalties, the committee came up with a couple of alternatives of its own.

The story went on to quote the head coach at Kansas, which had been banned from defending its national title two years earlier:

"I sure wish they'd given us a multiple choice penalty," Coach Roy
Williams said last week.

Clearly, sportswriters around the country—and particularly those on the
staff of the *Review-Journal*—followed the NCAA-UNLV case with the same
diligence that court reporters on the news side of newspapers exercise when
they cover litigation. Indeed, sports departments no longer can be referred to
accurately as the "toy departments" of newspapers. Sportswriters increasingly are dealing with many of the same challenging issues that face city
room reporters.

A New Controversy Emerges

Just when the dust had cleared from the infractions committee decision on
UNLV's participation in the 1991 postseason tournament, the Rebels were
hit with a new inquiry from the NCAA. Less than a week before Christmas,
Greg Bortolin's story in the *Review-Journal* informed readers that the
off-the-court activities of the Rebel basketball program would continue to be
in the spotlight.

Here is Bortolin's lead block:

> UNLV officials confirmed Tuesday evening they had received a letter
> of inquiry from the NCAA Enforcement Staff.
>
> However, President Robert Maxson, interim Athletic Director Dennis
> Finfrock and counsel Brad Booke would not reveal the contents or
> confirm reports from KVBC-TV that the school was charged with 29
> NCAA violations—some of which were considered major.
>
> According to reports aired on the local NBC affiliate Tuesday, Coach
> Jerry Tarkanian wasn't implicated, but some of the charges against
> UNLV included:
>
> —A lack of institutional control stemming from the handling of the
> recruitment of Lloyd Daniels.
>
> —Mismanagement of scholarship funds to players in which coaches
> handled cash.
>
> —Illegal tutoring of a recruit, believed to be redshirt Barry Young.
>
> —Six infractions that named assistant coach Tim Grgurich.
>
> If it is revealed today that these are some of the violations included in
> the letter of inquiry, they are still only allegations at this point which
> will be responded to by UNLV and reviewed by the infractions
> committee before a decision is rendered.

The story went on to note that some of the allegations could be considered
nondisclosable under the Nevada Open Record Law and under the Buckley
Amendment, which protects student records as privileged information.

As it turned out, UNLV did withhold names of UNLV players, employees, and boosters listed in the letter. That action immediately brought cries of censorship from Las Vegas journalists. Pascoe followed developments in the case closely. In a mid-January story, he wrote:

> UNLV may become the first school in NCAA history to relinquish a national basketball championship if current charges are proven against its basketball program.
>
> Precedent has been established of the NCAA forcing schools to vacate final championship standings.
>
> In a letter of inquiry delivered to UNLV last month, the NCAA accused the school of providing illegal tutoring to two students, who are believed to be Barry Young and former Rebel recruit Lloyd Daniels.
>
> Young, who is redshirting this season, played in last year's NCAA Tournament and the final game against Duke. If he is ruled ineligible, under NCAA sanctioning rules, UNLV's 1990 title could be vacated— and if it is ruled the school knew or had reason to know about the tutoring, it might be forced to return up to 90 percent of the nearly $1 million it received by reaching the title game.
>
> UNLV interim Athletic Director Dennis Finfrock called the possibility of a vacated Rebel title a worst-case scenario, but he and UNLV legal counsel Brad Booke declined to comment in specifics on the Young case.

Pascoe went on to detail five instances when the NCAA previously had vacated the spots of Final Four teams. He also cited relevant NCAA bylaws, thus illustrating the importance of reporters keeping abreast of regulations that govern intercollegiate and interscholastic sports.

UNLV spent the next three months gathering information and preparing a response to the NCAA inquiry. In late April, the university announced its intentions. Here is the lead block from Brock Mullins' story in the *Review-Journal:*

> UNLV will plead guilty to unspecified rules violations alleged in the NCAA's 20-count letter charging improprieties in the Rebel basketball program, according to UNLV legal counsel Brad Booke.
>
> However, UNLV will vigorously contest other allegations made by the NCAA that were contradicted by the school's internal investigation, Booke said Wednesday.

Reporters must remember to bring readers up to date on stories. Because the NCAA-UNLV story was long-running, it was important for reporters to provide background information in each story. Mullins, for example, closed his story by noting that UNLV already was on NCAA one-year probation after settling the thirteen-year ordeal between the governing body and Tarkanian less than six months earlier. The story also reiterated that apparently there was nothing in the new NCAA inquiry that was tied directly to Tarkanian.

Troubles, though, continued to mount. Less than a month after Booke outlined the university's intentions in the pending NCAA inquiry, the *Review-Journal* obtained photographs that linked a convicted sports-event fixer with some UNLV players. A.D. Hopkins' story in the *Review-Journal* featured a straight news summary lead.

> Richie "The Fixer" Perry entertained at his home three key players on UNLV's 1990 national championship basketball team.
>
> Photographs obtained by the *Review-Journal* confirm the convicted sports-event fixer associated with players near the start of the 1989-90 season.
>
> Perry is under investigation by state gaming investigators for inclusion in Nevada's so-called Black Book, the list of people banned by law from Nevada casinos. Perry also figures in the National Collegiate Athletic Association's current inquiry into the UNLV basketball program.

The story went on to note:

> The players' association with Perry may pose grave problems for the Rebel basketball program with the NCAA.
>
> NCAA bylaws prohibit any involvement in gambling activities or any conduct that the association deems unethical. Violations of the bylaws could cost players their eligibility.
>
> Use of ineligible players could force the university to forfeit its 1990 basketball championship.

Within a week, Tarkanian spoke out on the controversy. The first three paragraphs of Pascoe's story made it clear that the off-season was not providing much respite for Tarkanian:

> UNLV basketball Coach Jerry Tarkanian, seething over negative publicity involving ties between his players and convicted sports fixer Richard Perry, said Friday the recent stories could cost him his job.
>
> Tarkanian, who is scheduled to discuss his case with the University of Nevada Board of Regents on Monday, maintains that the only connection between his program and Perry came through former Rebel Moses Scurry, who played for Perry in a New York City summer league.
>
> "When you stop to analyze everything, what is the worst thing I've done?" Tarkanian said. "The worst thing is, I've got a New York City kid like Moses who didn't obey my orders (to stay away from Perry). I

may be out of a job Monday over this. Look what they've put me
through.''

Indeed, one week later, the winningest coach in college basketball
called it quits. Here are the first four paragraphs from Pascoe's story:

> Jerry Tarkanian, a fiercely successful competitor on and off the
> basketball court, put an end to his fights Friday: The longtime Rebel
> coach announced he will retire next spring after a final season.
> Tarkanian, who has won 82 percent of his games at UNLV and
> brought the school its first-ever national championship in 1990, cited
> off-court struggles as the final blow to a long career.
> Tarkanian and UNLV President Robert Maxson held a news confer-
> ence Friday morning on the university's campus, with both saying they
> were pleased with the decision.
> "This is an end of an era at UNLV," Maxson said. "There is no
> question Jerry Tarkanian is a legend. He has established himself as a
> legend while he is still an active coach, and I think sports history will
> record him as such."

Pascoe went on to provide details on Tarkanian's contract, to relay direct
quotations from the coach, and to cite precise statistics on Tarkanian's
coaching record.

The story examples in this chapter illustrate that sports reporters must
be prepared to cover off-the-field developments with knowledge and
aggressiveness. Indeed, the *Review-Journal*'s Bruce Pascoe made significant
contributions to his newspaper. His contributions, though, were not limited
to covering Rebel basketball games with finesse, but also included his ability
to report with accuracy on UNLV's altercations with the NCAA.

Exercises

1. Clip stories that focus on off-the-field sports issues from area
newspapers. Discuss them in class.

2. Analyze the content of the sports section of an area daily newspaper
for a one-week period. Determine the number of stories that deal with
on-the-field activities and the number of stories that focus on off-the-field
issues. Calculate column inches devoted to both types. Discuss in class.

3. Invite to class a coach or athletic director who can provide a
personal assessment of the relationship between his or her program and the
NCAA.

4. Invite a sportswriter who has had experience writing stories dealing
with finance, corporate procedures, or the court system to class.

Sportswriters often have to look beyond the
playing fields and sidelines to report in depth
on issues and controversies.

(Photo by T. J. Sokol)

CHAPTER EIGHTEEN

In-Depth Reporting

Sports reporters have an opportunity to thoroughly explore topics when writing in-depth stories. Unlike game stories that are written on deadline, in-depth pieces often are the result of weeks or even months of work. And unlike features that are written after interviewing a handful of sources, in-depth stories usually are based on interviews with dozens of people. The best in-depths also are fortified with extensive research.

Those who run 100 meters are sprinters; those who compete in the 10,000 meter events are long-distance runners. In-depth writers are journalism's long-distance runners. They often must survive without the daily gratification of by-lines for several weeks while working on major articles or series. They immerse themselves in their topics.

Suzanne Halliburton, a tenacious sportswriter for the *Austin American-Statesman* in Texas, enjoys the challenge of writing in-depth stories, many of which are the products of investigative reporting. She got her start as a sportswriter at the University of Texas at Austin on the staff of the *Daily Texan*. She worked two years at the *Beaumont* (Texas) *Enterprise,* first as a general assignments reporter concentrating on features and then as a business writer. In 1986, she joined the *American-Statesman*'s sports staff. For three years, she covered the Dallas Cowboys, Dallas Mavericks, and Texas Rangers while living in Dallas. Since 1989, she has served as a general assignments sports reporter, concentrating on investigations, enterprise reporting, and special projects.

A member of the Association for Women in Sports Media and the Investigative Reporters and Editors, Halliburton has won several national, regional, and state writing awards. "I have covered a beat," Halliburton said. "That gets boring. In-depth and investigative reporting doesn't." Halliburton said her years working exclusively on enterprise and investigative stories have been enjoyable. "I seem to stumble upon things," she said. "The more you stumble on them, the more tips you get." Her major stories include college athletic slush funds, gambling, steroid use, and eating disorders of University of Texas women athletes.

Reporting Tips

Halliburton provided these tips to sportswriters who are working on in-depth pieces:

- *Talk to as many people as you can.* "After one person tells you something, don't assume that it is accurate," Halliburton said. "Instead of talking to three people, talk to fifteen or twenty."
- *Be willing to put in a lot of hours.* Comprehensive in-depth stories require systematic, painstaking gathering of information and the scheduling and rescheduling of dozens of interviews.
- *Be familiar with state open-records laws and the Freedom of Information (FOI) Act, which can be used to gain access to federal information.* State laws vary, but most contain statements that the law should be construed liberally in favor of persons seeking records, information on the types of records that generally can be obtained, and information on appeal processes available to those who are denied access.
- *Develop a good working relationship with your supervisor.* "It is good to sit down every week or two during long-running projects and have brainstorming sessions," Halliburton said. "It is important to always keep the lines of communication open."
- *Beware of people who will try to make you feel guilty about writing the story.* In-depth and investigative stories often contain information that subjects would prefer remain unpublished. Be prepared to deal with their calls.

Without doubt, writing in-depth stories is hard work. Reporters must:

- *Select a topic worth exploring.* Not all ideas will result in major stories. Reporters must pursue their ideas aggressively, exploring all available avenues to put meat on the bones of the story skeleton.
- *Conduct extensive research.* The best in-depth stories are based upon vast amounts of background information, which comes from printed sources and from interviews. Electronic data bases are effective tools for writers who are searching for information on topics or people. Reference librarians can be valuable allies to reporters who are working on in-depth stories.

■ *Rely upon observation whenever possible.* Strong narrative leads and other descriptive story passages often are based upon observation.

Writing Tips

Once information has been gathered, it is time to write the story. Reporters must:

■ *Organize the material.* If reporters have done a good job gathering information for a story, they will find that only a fraction of it actually will be used in the story. The information must be reviewed carefully. Initially, some reporters like to categorize their background material and interview notes. One stack, for example, could include material that almost assuredly would be used in the story. Another stack might contain material that likely would not be needed. A third stack could contain material that may or may not be used, but a final decision would not be made until the writing process progresses further.

■ *Organize the story.* In-depth and investigative stories almost always are longer than news or feature stories. In order to hold the reader, stories must be organized logically and efficiently. Some reporters like to work from note cards, organizing a lengthy story much as they would a college term paper. The note cards can be shuffled until a logical order emerges. Lengthy stories need a strong introduction, a meaty body, and a logical conclusion.

■ *Make effective use of transition.* Lengthy stories must be tied together with transitions. Transitions can be words, phrases, sentences, or paragraphs that usher readers from one section of a story to the next. Transition words include *meanwhile, however,* and *also.* Examples of transition phrases are *in other action* and *in addition to.* Transitions are the cement that bonds lengthy stories together. All parts of the story must be connected smoothly and unobtrusively.

■ *Make effective use of direct quotations.* Strong, vivid direct quotations— gleaned from interviews—breathe life into a story.

■ *Realize that most first drafts are woefully inadequate.* The best writers know that their early drafts are never good enough. Most passages of in-depth stories must be rewritten several times; then they are polished and edited.

Anatomy of a Series on Eating Disorders

Suzanne Halliburton and Shelly Sanford combined on a three-part series that explored eating disorders among female athletes at the University of Texas.

The series, published in the *American-Statesman*, won national awards from the Associated Press Sports Editors, the Women's Sports Foundation, and the Center for the Study of Sport in Society at Northeastern University.

The Idea

An *American-Statesman* columnist was talking to an Olympic-caliber athlete who mentioned that he knew of several UT women who were undergoing treatment for eating disorders. The columnist mentioned the tip to Sanford, who was working part-time at the newspaper while going to school. At about this time, Halliburton moved to Austin after a stint in the Dallas bureau. Sanford and Halliburton were assigned the story.

Gathering Information

During the next six months, the two reporters interviewed nearly forty sources—many of them on several occasions—and scoured written sources. A turning point came when the reporters used the Texas Open Records Act to pry loose information from the UT athletic department. "We wanted to see if UT was paying any outside organizations for nutritional information," Halliburton said. "We found through the records that two private nutritionists were doing counseling to UT athletes on nutritional guidance and eating disorders. This opened the door to more sources."

The Time Frame

Halliburton and Sanford started gathering information in March; they began writing about ten days before the early August publication. "The six-month time frame is somewhat deceiving," Halliburton said. "I was working on other things, as was Shelly. We didn't work on the series full time, but it was a cloud hovering over us for a half year."

The Writing Process

The reporters first transcribed all their notes. They read them and highlighted all the information they intended to use. "All the while, we were thinking of what the focus of the series should be," Halliburton said. Then they developed an outline. "Because it was to be a series, we had to organize how we wanted to divide it up," she said. "We also had to think about sidebars and graphics. We spent a day just brainstorming about the graphics."

The first installment, a forty-five-column-inch story, went through several editors. "I don't think we realized just how powerful the story would turn out to be," Halliburton said. The reporter credited her sports editor,

John Triplett, for strong support. Halliburton said that Triplett, who had done investigative reporting before he got into management, is a strong believer in in-depth reporting. "Our sports department has a reputation for doing good in-depth work," she said. "We often put new twists on old topics. That requires hard work."

The Series

Halliburton and Sanford put together a three-part series and several sidebars on the eating disorder issue. The lead block in the first installment summarized the severity of the problem:

> During the past 18 months, more than a dozen University of Texas women athletes, including some of the best swimmers in the world, have been diagnosed as having severe eating disorders traceable in most cases to the pressures of their sport and the training methods of their coaches.
>
> In virtually all of the cases, the athletes have received specialized counseling and treatment. Two Olympians and an All-American have had hospital treatments, sometimes as expensive as $500 a day.
>
> Swimmer Tiffany Cohen, an Olympic double gold medalist, was hospitalized for nine weeks; All-American swimmer Kelley Davies was hospitalized for six weeks; and Olympic swimmer Kim Rhodenbaugh went through a six-month outpatient treatment program.
>
> Two of the most common eating disorders are anorexia and bulimia. People with anorexia literally starve themselves skinny. They do not recognize how thin they are becoming and in some cases starve themselves to death if they do not receive counseling. Bulimics go on eating binges, then get rid of the food by artificial means, such as forcing themselves to vomit and taking laxatives.
>
> One of every 10 female athletes at UT has been diagnosed as having an eating disorder and referred to a specialist for treatment, according to university documents and officials. Another 20 to 30 percent show signs of a disorder, according to a UT survey.
>
> A study several years ago indicated 4 to 5 percent of UT's female student population suffered from eating disorders.

The story, which continued to focus on problems at Texas, put the UT situation in perspective by noting that "examinations of UT records by the *Austin American-Statesman* and recent interviews with dozens of current and former athletes show the problem is not limited to UT or its swimming program. It is a growing concern facing female athletes in many nationally competitive programs where training emphasizes body weight."

Halliburton and Sanford used a transition paragraph to move into the body of the first installment, which included background on NCAA legislation concerning outpatient treatment of eating disorders and numerous vivid direct quotations from former swimmers, eating disorder specialists, and an athletic department administrator at UT.

The transition paragraph effectively set the stage for that which followed:

> In separate interviews, athletes told the *Statesman* they've been secretly fasting, making themselves vomit, taking laxatives and diuretics, and exercising excessively on top of their everyday training. They said they have been doing this to meet weight goals set by coaches who are pushing them to be No. 1.

Certainly no one could argue with the success of the UT swimming program. Indeed, the second installment of the series focused on several former UT women swimmers and former coach Richard Quick, who the year before had left to assume the head coaching job at Stanford. During his six years at UT, Quick won five NCAA championships.

The engaging lead block on the second installment pulled readers into the story:

> Tucked away in a corner of the women's dressing room at the University of Texas swim center is what appears to be an ordinary freight scale with digital readout.
>
> But to many recent UT swimmers, some of them among the finest in the world, and to some of the university's athletic officials, it has been anything but an ordinary device to measure body weight.
>
> To the athletes, it often has been a critical measure of self-esteem and the coach's approval. To school officials, it has become a symbol of the high human and institutional costs that can come with an intensely competitive sports program.
>
> During the past 18 months, one of every 10 female athletes at UT has been diagnosed as having a serious eating disorder. Another 20 to 30 percent have shown signs of eating disorders. Among all women at the university, a study has shown that roughly 4 to 5 percent have these disorders.
>
> In most of the cases involving female athletes, the disorders are traceable to the pressures of the sport and training methods. Virtually all of the athletes have been referred to specialists for counseling and treatment. Some have been hospitalized.

Next came the nut graph, which provided the thrust of the second installment:

> Although the problem involves athletes in a number of sports, the impact has been particularly acute among members of the nationally

ranked swimming teams produced by Coach Richard Quick during the 1980s.

The story went on to quote several former UT women swimmers who told of predawn runs and extensive laxative use—all to make weight and not be relegated to "The Fat Club."

The story also contained numerous direct quotations from Coach Quick, who had directed the 1988 U.S. Olympic team in Seoul, South Korea. Many of the direct quotes played off of one another. For example:

> "We never, ever encouraged them to lose weight in an unhealthy manner. We never wanted them to lose weight faster than it was medically safe because it wasn't beneficial to their training," Quick said.
>
> Still, swimmers say they left those meetings feeling a lot of pressure to make the weight goals or else. Some felt the "or else" meant the "Fat Club"; others felt the "or else" meant they would fail to reach the highest levels of the sport.
>
> "I think in Richard's case, you came to Texas knowing you were swimming for the best coach in the United States," said Olympian Kim Rhodenbaugh. "I think there were mixed emotions. Most of the people thought that he has to know what he is talking about because he has produced a lot of incredible swimmers."

Later in the story, another former swimmer struck the issue head on:

> Ann Drolsom, a two-time All-American and current UT law student, remembers how Quick's message about weight could get twisted.
>
> "He would always explain it in terms of your body working efficiently— there being a perfect line, and that was goal weight," she said. "But it's easy to cross the line.
>
> "Primarily the pressure came from the coach, until you started to internalize it. Then it became self-inflicted—torture almost—where some people would weigh themselves three or four times a day."

The well-written installment led directly to the final story that focused on the extent of the UT problems and possible solutions. The lead block illustrated the human dimensions of the problem:

> Four-time All-American Kara McGrath listened to the painful confession of a University of Michigan swimmer who forces herself to throw up so she can stay skinny.
>
> McGrath, an assistant coach at Michigan, was a borderline anorexic

during her freshman year at the University of Texas, so she could draw on her own experience to comfort the swimmer.

"This girl came to me because she had a problem. She was not thin, and I never suspected it. The girl really didn't want anybody to know," McGrath said. "She swam for a team in Germantown, Pa., so she was around a lot of elite swimmers, and she said that is where she learned about bulimia. I'm anxious to get back with her and see what has happened."

The frustrating part for McGrath is that all she can do is share her experience. She cannot force the swimmer to stop throwing up or seek professional help. She cannot even be sure that the swimmer who came to her is the only one with a problem because most people with eating disorders keep them secret.

What to do about female athletes with eating disorders is becoming an issue at universities with highly competitive programs. Problems such as anorexia (starvation) and bulimia (eating binges followed by vomiting or using laxatives and diuretics to purge the food) are on the rise, especially among athletes in swimming and track, where weight goals are enforced.

The remainder of the story told about "The Performance Team" that had been assembled at UT to address the problem associated with eating disorders. The director of the team, an exercise physiologist at UT, was a primary source for the story. The reporters also interviewed counselors and former swimmers, making heavy use of direct quotations from them.

The conclusion of the final installment of the series left the reader with the impression that there is some hope to remedy the dilemma now that it has been openly and directly addressed. Here are the final three paragraphs:

> McGrath, who swam for Quick for four years, said she wishes she had known in her freshman year that other people had similar problems. She lost 15 pounds in one season and, like the swimmer who approached her at Michigan, thought she was alone.
>
> 1984 Olympian Kim Rhodenbaugh, 23, went through six months of outpatient treatment for bulimia at the Austin Eating Disorder Clinic. She said she would like to find a way to reach athletes who have eating disorders and help them build their self-esteem, an underlying problem that contributes to the disorders.
>
> "It has changed my life," Rhodenbaugh said. "I believe I can set out to conquer anything. I have conquered something that was my enemy for years."

The powerful series, which included sidebars that summarized eating-disorder issues in rapid-fire fashion and additional details on individual athletes and treatment programs, contained a unique blend of information gleaned from public records and intimate, personal reflections.

Reporters should take advantage of opportunities to work on in-depth stories. Through these stories, writers have the opportunity to inform readers about significant issues and problems that should be addressed. But these stories do not come easily. Effective in-depth stories, such as the series on eating disorders, require diligent reporting, exhaustive information gathering, and careful, precise writing.

A Look at the Recruiting Business

Paul Coro, sports editor of the *State Press,* the campus daily at Arizona State University, wanted to examine the lifeblood of his institution's nationally prominent athletic program: recruiting. The headline over his story, which won a national award in the William Randolph Hearst Foundation's intercollegiate writing competition, summarized the 103-paragraph in-depth account: "Coaches roll dice on top prospects while playing by the rules."

When the story was merely an idea tucked in the back of his mind, Coro asked the NCAA to send him brochures and literature on recruiting guidelines. He also:

- conducted preliminary interviews with some of ASU's coaches
- examined budgets
- spent a weekend following a group of high-school recruits during their campus visit
- spent a day with ASU's football recruiting coordinator
- interviewed recruits who eventually signed with the Sun Devils
- interviewed parents of athletes

He asked one of ASU's assistant football coaches, known for his recruiting prowess, to keep a diary of his travels for an entire week.

From the mounds of notes that he assembled over a two-month period, Coro crafted this lead block:

> Big-time collegiate sports programs—with all their glamour and glitz—must be constantly nourished by infusions of prized high school recruits in order to ascend to the levels expected of them.
>
> Coaches, with their careers riding on their winning percentages, perpetually wade through a swamp of NCAA rules while feverishly courting teen-age heroes.
>
> Recruiting is hard work. Hauling in major prep talent while staying

within the rules is no easy task, but coaches must reel in their share of blue-chippers if their programs are to be competitive.

Make no mistake, recruiting powers major college sports.

Each year coaches at 296 NCAA Division I schools spend 365 days and nights trying to lure the nation's best prospective student-athletes to their institutions.

Recruiting makes or breaks teams' and coaches' futures. Some say recruiting is more important to a program's prosperity than is coaching. So there is no doubt coaches will do everything allowed by NCAA rules and sometimes outside them to get the players they want.

"I hear and read where coaches say they like everything about coaching except recruiting," Arizona State University head football coach Larry Marmie said. "I don't understand how you can expect to be successful if you don't like the recruiting process."

After the lead block, Coro used two transition paragraphs to move into the next major section of his article:

On Feb. 6, the first day recruits could commit to a school, Marmie and his staff signed a highly touted class of 25 players. One year ago the Sun Devil staff was looking at nearly 700 prospects.

By last autumn, the number had been whittled to 200 and then again to around 70 for the 85 allowed paid campus visits of prospective student-athletes at the beginning of the year. While the process is year-round, crunch time for football recruiters is in January and February when choices are made.

The transitional paragraphs were followed by Coro's description of the weekend activities of high-school recruits who visited ASU. Coro then moved to a discussion of ASU's head basketball coach, Bill Frieder, who is known as a "manic recruiter." Coro provided some recruiting anecdotes about Frieder as well as direct quotes from him. Coro also inserted details on the basketball budget for recruiting. Throughout the lengthy in-depth story, Coro inserted direct quotes that were bordered and set in italic type. The quotes provided transitions to alert the reader that the story was moving from one section to the next.

The next section of Coro's story was based on observation of and direct quotes from ASU's recruiting coordinator. It started with these two paragraphs:

It's 6 a.m., the Monday morning after the last January weekend visit by the 15 football recruits. ASU recruiting coordinator Dr. Ronnie Cox's sixth-floor office is the only one lit in the Intercollegiate Athletic Building that closes off the stadium's south end.

He is there at 6 a.m. because it is 8 a.m. on the East Coast, where recruiting activity is happening. His office has dozens of recruits' highlight tapes scattered on the floor, a giant board on the wall structuring visits, and piles of papers and faxes cluttering the desk.

The next section, which Coro based on assistant football coach Don Bocchi's diary of his travels during a hectic first week in February, painted a vivid picture to readers of the eighteen- to twenty-hour days that recruiters endure during the push period just before recruits can commit.

The article wound down with a look at the most important NCAA guidelines, the most common problems that confront schools that tangle with the NCAA, and proposed rule changes. The story ended the way many good in-depths do—with direct quotes:

> "I'm for anything that will take our coaches off the road and allow them to spend more time with the kids on campus and their families," Marmie said.
> "But then again, if (UCLA coach) Terry Donahue is on the road, I'm going to be on the road because somebody will use that against you. It's a 12-month job."

No one could have read Coro's story without gaining a feel and understanding for the hectic endeavor that propels big-time collegiate sports: recruiting. Coro's story also illustrates the necessity of consulting numerous sources—human and written—when working on lengthy in-depth stories.

The Role of University Presidents in Big-Time Sports

Change was in the air when the NCAA held its annual convention in Nashville, Tennessee. It was clear that university presidents no longer were willing to entrust athletic programs solely to athletic directors and coaches. Impending reforms were the subjects of articles in newspapers and magazines leading up to the convention. Joel Horn, who had worked as a sportswriter for Arizona State's campus daily, the *State Press,* and as a student intern in the university's sports information office, was captivated by the speculation. He decided to explore the changing relationship between university presidents and athletic departments and to examine new NCAA guidelines.

Horn spent more than a month after the NCAA convention gathering information, interviewing coaches, athletic directors, and presidents, and attempting to make sense of the legislation and determining the effects it would have on big-time collegiate sports.

Horn decided to organize his story around six rule changes that would have a significant impact on ASU and other major sports schools: a reduction in mandatory practice time for student-athletes, cuts in scholarships, the imposition of stricter academic standards, a reduction in the size of coaching staffs, the phasing out of athletic dormitories, and cuts in training meals.

Horn, in an award-winning story published in the *State Press,* lured readers with this lead block:

> After three consecutive "losing" seasons (7-4-1, 8-4, 8-4), former University of Oklahoma football Coach Barry Switzer was summoned to the home of Bill Banowsky, the school's president.
> Wade Walker, the OU athletic director at the time, was there.
> In his book, "Bootlegger's Boy," Switzer related what transpired:
> "Barry," said Banowsky, a Church of Christ preacher and real charmer, "if you start going to church every Sunday morning and Sunday night and Wednesday night and marry that little girl you're dating, you could lose four games again next season and still be my coach as long as I'm here, but I can't guarantee you how the board of regents will feel.
> "However, if you go 10-2 next season and beat Texas and Nebraska, you don't have to attend church or get married and we won't fire you.
> "But, Barry, if you win the national championship, the regents won't fire you even if we catch you smoking dope."
> When he and Walker walked out of the president's house, Switzer said, "Wade, what the hell kind of a profession is this?"

Next came Horn's nut graph, which told readers precisely what this ninety-seven-paragraph in-depth story was all about:

> That was 1983, but today's university presidents are still flexing their muscles in front of athletic directors and coaches. In the 1990s, however, they are not necessarily looking for victory at any cost. The presidents of the country's NCAA Division I institutions, including ASU, are trying to clean up their athletic programs and give sensible boundaries to those that are out of control.

Like all good stories, Horn's article contained several strong direct quotations, many of them high in the story. He used a quote from ASU's president and a paragraph of background to move into his discussion of the major reform areas:

> "Intercollegiate athletic policy is responsible to the president of the university," said ASU President Lattie Coor, a former Division I chairman of the Presidents Commission. "The NCAA is an organiza-

tion that properly has coaches, athletic directors, everyone else but the presidents as well, and what has happened successively now over the last several years is that presidents have come to take a fuller and more complete role. So I agree that presidents have fully, tangibly this year asserted their rightful role in the policy-making process.''

If viewed as a struggle between college presidents and athletic directors for control of sports programs, January's 85th annual NCAA Convention in Nashville, Tenn., was a clean sweep. On virtually all 182 proposals, resolutions and amendments, including a so-called ''reform package'' sponsored by the Presidents Commission, the presidents outmuscled the ADs.

In the body of his story—which elaborated on the six impact changes—Horn used direct quotes from coaches, athletic directors, and presidents from across the country. It also was apparent that Horn had carefully studied all of the NCAA legislation. In fact, he spent more time gathering the written records than he did conducting his many interviews. Without this background, he would not have been able to conduct intelligent interviews with his sources.

Horn ended his piece by outlining pressing future issues—academic advising and payment to college athletes—and by relying on quotes from President Coor to tie back to the theme of the article: the increasingly major role being assumed in college athletics by presidents:

> Clearly, college presidents will play a critical role in any future reform. But that shouldn't surprise anyone, Coor said. The NCAA is run by presidents.
> University of Iowa President Hunter R. Rawlings III agreed.
> ''Narrow athletic interests are powerless in the face of presidential will and consensus,'' Rawlings wrote in *Sports Illustrated*.
> ''Well, they're not powerless,'' Coor said, ''but they're certainly tempered fairly substantially.''

Exercises

1. Clip major in-depth sports articles or a series from area newspapers. Dissect the writing strategies apparent in the stories. What types of leads are most common? What kinds of transitions are employed? Are the stories well organized? Do you have suggestions for improvements?

2. Content analyze the sports section of an area daily newspaper for a one-week period. How many in-depth stories are published during that time? Are most of the stories written by staff or are they written by syndicated writers?

3. Clip a major in-depth article from an issue of *Sports Illustrated*. Compare the *Sports Illustrated* story with the articles published in daily newspapers.

4. Select an issue about which you would like to write an in-depth story. Conduct research. Write a lead block. Conduct multiple interviews.

Working the Sports Desk

Action photos often become the focal point of well-designed sports pages.

(Photo by Irwin R. Daugherty)

CHAPTER NINETEEN

Designing Pages

T he sports section should be the design showcase of a newspaper. Editors can blend game stories, feature pieces, columns, ratings, results, and photos to create an aesthetically pleasing package.

Indeed, as the authors of *Electronic Age News Editing* wrote:

> Sports pages are tailor-made for bright, brisk design. Sports editors need not feel inhibited by the stoic overtones of historical political events or world crises. Sports elements literally beg for innovative treatment. In no other section of the paper is there such a consistent flow of dramatic photos: pole vaulters stretching and straining eighteen feet in the air; distance runners struggling through the final yards of an exhausting race; sinewy basketball players driving the lane through a forest of arms, legs, and torsos; 255-pound linebackers crushing backpedalling quarterbacks; gymnasts gracefully performing their poetic routines; and sleek hurdlers gliding over barriers. In addition, game stories, league round-ups, analysis pieces, feature stories, ratings, predictions, columns, and statistics compete for space on sports pages.
>
> The editor who designs sports pages has a unique challenge: he must fit a variety of writing styles, photos, and statistics into a neat, readable package. But he also has an advantage over an editor who designs news pages. On most days, sports editors can plan well in advance the contents of a given page; late-breaking, unexpected news is the exception rather than the rule. News and makeup judgments are often made well in advance of actual events.
>
> Well-designed sports pages are bright—as crisp as a line drive. Outstanding sports pages are often built around large, dramatic, well-cropped photographs. In fact, action photos should be the staple of well-designed sports pages.

Howard I. Finberg, assistant managing editor at *The Arizona Republic* and coauthor of *Visual Editing,* said that it is important to understand the function of the sports section as a whole and the design needs that follow that function. The function of the section is to convey a great deal of information to the reader quickly and easily. The design of the section should convey the excitement and drama of athletic contests.

"The potential for good design is just tremendous on sports pages," Finberg said. "But, taking advantage of that potential requires the same planning, direction, and enthusiasm necessary in other sections of the newspaper, such as news, features, or business."

The person designing the sports section should understand the overall design goals of the newspaper. "It is important that readers have a sense of belonging to the same newspaper as they read through each section," Finberg said. "However, that should not be a handicap to the designer in terms of being creative. There always is room for creativity in any design style."

A good designer looks at each page as a unit and finds dominant and visual elements, Finberg said. Sports page designers, for example, have the opportunity to be creative when planning Sunday pages during college football seasons.

"You can pack a lot of information about the previous day's games and you can, with photos and graphics, give your readers a sense of what went on during those games," Finberg said. "You can use large, dynamic photographs and informational graphics to get behind the players and the games."

Bob Clark, sports editor of the *Eugene* (Ore.) *Register-Guard,* said the sports page "should make a statement. . . . Let the reader know what you have decided is the important story of the day. Draw the reader to the story with graphics. But always keep it simple. Our photos are chosen to go with our stories. It is a rare occasion when we run a picture that does not complement a story."

Organization is the key to the attractive *Register-Guard* sports pages. "There cannot be enough planning," Clark said. "I spend an awful lot of time checking schedules to see what sports events are coming up. I talk to reporters about what angles their stories might take. Certain feature stories can be planned well in advance. We find out the approach the writer is going to take; we then bring in the photography department to plan appropriate photos to accompany the story."

During football and basketball seasons, there never is a shortage of good story and photo possibilities. Planning takes on added importance, however, during summer months and other slow news times. "We compensate for slow news days with good planning," Clark said. "If you plan ahead, you are never backed into a corner on slow days. You owe it to your readers to give them something fresh and visually exciting every day.''

Readers profit immensely from well-designed pages. Good newspapers strive to make reading an enjoyable, simple task. This is particularly important in our visually oriented society. Paul Borden, sports editor of the *Clarion-Ledger* in Jackson, Mississippi, emphasized the importance of designing pages to help readers find information. The sports desk at the *Clarion-Ledger* concentrates on packaging related items. "We try to group elements by sport or issue," said Borden. "That makes it easy for the reader. If the reader has to hunt for a story, we are doing the reader a disservice."

The *Clarion-Ledger*, for example, generally puts scores and summaries in agate type on a single page. Reference lines are inserted in stories to direct readers to the agate page for complete results. "We think the agate page—when it is well organized—is an excellent service to the reader," Borden said.

Most contemporary newspapers that do well in design competition have a light, airy appearance; a limited number of pictures and stories are featured on lead pages and there is ample white space.

Characteristics of Well-Designed Pages

Attractive design is in the eye of the beholder. Still, the following characteristics are common to award-winning newspapers:

- *Modular elements.* Stories and photos on the page are modular in shape (squares and rectangles).
- *Clean, simple, well organized.* Well-designed pages are not crowded. Often, the lead sports page will contain six or fewer elements (stories, digests, and photos). Lead stories often are accompanied by art work. Related items are packaged. For example, a football game story would not be featured at the top of the page and the accompanying photo buried in the bottom right corner.
- *White space.* White space, effectively used, adds a sense of organization to the page. Designers should not use white space simply for the sake of using it, however. Effective use of white space breaks the monotonous grayness of a page laden with type.
- *Dominant photos.* Large, well-conceived photos, often in color, adorn the sports pages of some of the country's best-looking newspapers. These photos are most effective when they accompany a story.
- *Informational graphics.* "How it works" and "how it happens" infor-

mational graphics have become increasingly common. For example, an informational graphic could detail the steps in an NCAA investigation with more clarity and conciseness than a long story.

- *Variation in column widths.* Most contemporary newspapers have six-column formats of 12 to 14 picas each. Odd-measure type (columns of type set more or less than the standard column width) puts the spotlight on certain stories. It also provides a break from the monotony of six columns of equal-width type.

- *Borders.* Borders should not be overused, but they are extremely effective in calling attention to particular stories or columns. They also are used to tie together related stories or related stories and photos.

- *Digests.* When newspapers started to feature fewer elements on their lead pages, some good stories were moved to inside pages of sections. At about the same time, more newspapers started to run digest columns, usually set off with borders, that provided a one-paragraph synthesis of a story, with the page number on which the complete story was published. Some digest columns do not refer the reader to complete stories on other pages; they are a series of short (three or four paragraphs) stories that are crisply written, each with a separate headline and sometimes accompanied by a mug shot.

- *Standing headlines.* These headlines, which remain the same each day, usually are found on the agate page. They do not change because readers grow accustomed to them. They are convenient signposts to readers' searching eyes. Standing headlines for the NFL, NBA, or Major League Baseball are common. In addition, some newspapers carry standing heads for bowling, horse racing, statistical leaders in various sports, and the like.

- *Special headlines.* Special headlines such as *kickers, hammers, side-saddles,* and *reverse kickers* serve both functional and aesthetic purposes. They are functional because they transmit more information to the reader than a normal one-line headline; they are aesthetic because they create white space. A kicker—a headline that is one-half the point size of the main headline—provides additional information about the story it appears over. Kickers generally stretch halfway across the top of the main headline. Hammer headlines—sometimes called slammers—grab the attention of the reader with a single word or short phrase. This word or short phrase will either be placed flush left above the main headline (which usually is half the point size of the hammer) or it will be flush left on the same line as the main head and separated by ellipses. Side-saddle headlines are placed to the left (the side) of a story. Side-saddles normally are three lines deep and fill one column. Reverse kickers are headlines in which the kicker is twice the type size of the main headline.

It is one thing for an editor who designs pages to know *how* they ideally should look; it is another thing for an editor, working under deadline pressure, to adroitly weave elements into a coherent, meaningful page. In the next section. Dave Lumia, sports editor of *The Mesa* (Ariz.) *Tribune,* describes the decision-making process that went into the design of the *Tribune*'s lead sports page on the Sunday of the first big college football weekend of the 1991 season.

Preparing a Page at *The Mesa Tribune*

"The fundamental elements of effective page design are no different for a sports section than for any other section of the paper. We strive for clean, modular layout that's well-organized and easy on the reader. That means a clearly dominant headline and dominant lead photo to tell the reader where to look first (often these will be part of the same package, but not always), a large number of 'entry points,' and frequent use of informational-type graphic devices that can be absorbed at a glance.

"At the *Tribune,* we have recently incorporated a Digest-type column that runs the length of the left-hand side of the sports front. This allows for a quick scan of sports news, upcoming events, and short items that we hope are appealing to the average reader. Our package is called 'Sidelines' and always includes the day's major sports scores, TV listings, and local sports events. It will normally also include references to the day's top inside stories and newsy stand-alone briefs, as well as a quote-of-the-day and trivia question when space allows.

"We've found, as expected, that Sidelines can be both a blessing and a curse. It's allowed us to include more quick-hitting items on the section front; it's eliminated the problem of where to fit in score lists, and it's given us a vehicle for promoting the best stories that don't make the sports front.

"On the downside, it's taken up fully one-fifth of our cover space each and every day—and that's caused a number of concessions in terms of layout and design. We've had to reduce our story count and downsize the play of photos. It's also taken away a prime location for our local sports columnist (his column ran down the left side probably 80 percent of the time prior to Sidelines) and necessitated more jumps. The jump problem is twofold: (1) study after study indicates that a large portion of readers don't follow a jump inside; (2) in an era of declining newshole, more space needed for jumps means fewer stories inside.

"For this Sunday page, Sidelines is a given down the left column at 15 picas wide, leaving 62 picas to work with. A typical *Tribune* sports front will include four or five stories, a dominant photo, and often, but not always, a secondary photo, plus as many graphic devices as are appropriate.

"On weekends, we lean heavily toward a five-story front, because we generally see more stories worthy of the cover than during midweek. This day was no exception. This particular September weekend marked the first full week of the college football season, the second week of the NFL, and the wrapup of the U.S. Open tennis tournament. It also came at a time when baseball's pennant races were heating up.

"Our story selection process generally occurs as follows: The sports editor keeps a running daily budget in the computer files—listing all local copy expected for each day's edition, plus the major national events. Working from this budget, the sports editor and layout chief will sort through the dummies and determine how much space to allot for the various elements and sketch out which stories will go on which pages. On the weekends, if the sports editor will not be working, he typically goes through this sorting and sketching out process on Friday night, with the understanding that things quite often have to be adjusted because of breaking news.

"The particulars for this Sunday edition were these:

■ "Though it was the first big week of college football, the local university, Arizona State, would not open until the following week. We did have budgeted a season overview of the Sun Devils, plus ASU's archrival, the University of Arizona, was opening its season on the road against Ohio State. Ohio State just happened to be coached by former Sun Devil coach John Cooper, who just happened to be embroiled in a slew of controversy regarding his lack of success, his personality and his alleged lukewarm commitment to academics.

■ "Our local NFL team, the Phoenix Cardinals, had surprised the Los Angeles Rams in their opener and were now in Philadelphia to play the Eagles as underdogs again. Our coverage plan included an advance and a column, plus an at-a-glance box.

■ "That day's U.S. Open play included the women's finals between Monica Seles and Martina Navratilova and the men's semifinals. Where normally we might handle this by playing the women on the front and referring inside to the men, this was an exceptional year in that thirty-nine-year-old Jimmy Connors had captured universal public interest with his totally unexpected and incredible charge into the semis.

■ "The baseball races had four weeks to go—but only one, the NL West, was especially compelling. Given everything else going on and the lack of any extraordinary individual achievements, baseball would have a hard time cracking our front-page lineup. In this instance, the Sidelines score list would serve a very valid purpose for our baseball fans.

"For the front-page, we considered both the Cardinals advance and column as must-haves. The team had won five in a row, including exhibitions, and the interest level was unusually high. Had we been later in the season and had the Cardinals been struggling, we would strongly consider only one Cardinals item on the front.

"We also felt that both the men's and women's tennis belonged— women's because it was the championship match and men's because of the compelling Jimmy Connors saga, even though he would lose his semifinal match. Connors was the story of the week, and to pull him off the front now did not make sense.

"With four must-have items already in the mix, we decided we definitely needed a fifth story—simply from the standpoint of wanting to have a college football presence on the page. We considered running the ASU overview but decided it would be best to run a game story and tentatively decided on Arizona–Ohio State, particularly because of the intrigue surrounding John Cooper. I say this was a tentative decision because we left open the possibility of subbing out the Arizona game for one of national impact, should it develop. For instance, had Tulane knocked off No. 1 Florida State, that would have bumped Arizona inside. Therefore, we arrived at a lineup of: (1) Cardinals advance, with graphic box; (2) Cardinals column; (3) U.S. Open women's final; (4) U.S. Open men's semifinals; (5) Arizona–Ohio State football.

"Our next question was what to play as the lead story. Had Arizona State been playing its opener, it would have been an obvious choice, but with the Devils idle, Arizona did not rate as a suitable substitute. That left Cardinals and tennis, and obviously we chose the tennis. Though we will occasionally lead the section with an advance, our general rule of thumb is we'd prefer leading with live news. Had a playoff berth been on the line or had the rest of the lineup been weak, then we would have played the advance as the lead, but that was not the case.

"We decided on the women's story over the men's simply because a final carries more weight than semifinals. Had Connors won his match, it might have changed our thinking and left us open to charges of male bias. With that decision made, we went on to select a Seles celebration shot as our lead art.

"We did want to display the Cardinals prominently, since it was our top local story, so we packaged the column and advance on the top of the page, but without the lead headline. This technique, which we often use in similar situations, left us with bumping heads, but they were different typefaces, plus we had the graphic box to keep the copy from flowing together.

"By playing the Cardinals package in such a way, it enabled us to position our lead art and headline in the center of the page, which gives the page good balance. The men's story was stripped underneath the women's package to give us a cushion of type between the lead tennis photo and the secondary football shot on the bottom of the page.

"We would have preferred an Arizona–Ohio State photo in that spot, but due to production difficulties, we had to punt and settle for a Michigan-Boston College photo, which was put in a box to distinguish it from the game story. We ended up jumping the three football stories and holding the tennis stories to the cover. This was done not necessarily because the tennis stories didn't warrant greater length, but because a heavy load of football and baseball coverage ate up much of our inside space. It was a tough call, but the fact that we were able to get both the men's and women's stories prominently displayed on the cover made it a decision we could live with.

"As with every other day of the week, these news judgments were purely subjective. Someone else could look at the day's events and make an equally logical case for displaying them entirely differently. When making our choices, we strive for balance (we wouldn't want a page with nothing but college football, for example), consistency (the Cardinals advance shouldn't be on C1 one week and C5 the next), and attractive design, all the while trying to give our readers what we think they're most interested in. (This is an important distinction—providing what we think the readers are interested in, rather than what we're interested in as journalists.) There are many different ways to piece together the puzzle, but on this particular day at least, I think we were successful."

A Look at Well-Designed Pages

While Dave Lumia is working diligently to give the *Tribune* a clean, readable look, his counterparts at other aesthetically pleasing newspapers are striving for the same goal. Some of these newspapers include *The Dallas Morning News, The Arizona Republic, The Orange County Register,* and the *Austin American-Statesman.*

Lead sports section pages, as well as some inside pages, from the September 8, 1991, editions of these newspapers are reproduced on pages 272–79 (figures 19.1–19.7).

Preparing a Special Page at *The Dallas Morning News*

Some of the nation's daily newspapers offer full-page color graphics to their readers. *The Dallas Morning News* has earned a reputation for doing so as well as any newspaper in the country. Ben McConnell, assistant art director/

graphics editor at the *Morning News,* likes his job. "It combines the writing, editing, and reporting skills I learned in journalism school along with the computer design sensibilities I've always been interested in," he said.

After a pencil sketch of the graphic is approved by appropriate department heads at the *Morning News,* McConnell "babysits" the graphic during its production. "I check in with the artist every so often and offer ideas, comments, and direction," he said. "I'm often a liaison between the artist and the originating desk, and vice versa." In the next section, McConnell describes the steps in creating a full-page color graphic on fishing, from idea to final proofing.

Creating a Full-Page Color Graphic

"1. *Tell a story.* An idea for a full-page graphic can come from casual curiosity as well as from full-blown projects. An off-the-cuff 'I wonder what kind of fish I can catch in this area' can be as suggestive as wanting to illustrate how athletes perform optimally in each event. Just like a good read, a graphic should tell a story simply and succinctly.

"2. *Is it timely?* Just like a story, a graphic should have a good peg. If the Olympics are a year away, put that graphic in the futures file. But the fish page idea was a good one, because fishing season was set to open soon. It's good to run the idea for a graphic by a few colleagues. (One person, for example, suggested including the best lures for the fish. Another said she wanted information about fishing licenses. Everyone said to include a map of where the lakes are.)

"3. *Tell the art department.* This is the most important step. Without the graphic editor's or art director's enthusiasm and input, a sportswriter's or editor's graphic idea is history. 'You have to convince the art department that the idea is visually and informationally viable,' said *Dallas Morning News* art director Ed Kohorst. 'Include the art department editors early in your idea process. If they like your idea, then work with them on sketching out the graphic's architecture. This includes art ideas, a headline, and how the information should be structured and written.'

"4. *Get a guarantee on the space and color.* This usually involves convincing the managing editor of your idea, so be prepared. You don't want to have an artist commit a lot of time to illustrating a full-page color graphic and not be able to run it or lose the color position. And by all means, avoid spot color; today's newspaper readers are visually savvy and look down on spot color. (Spot color is a block of one or more colors that accents a visual or placement of a story. Sometimes, it is referred to as a tint block.)

"5. *Assemble your information.* For our fish page, we called the fish and wildlife office for a list of fish in the area. We asked if they had pictures

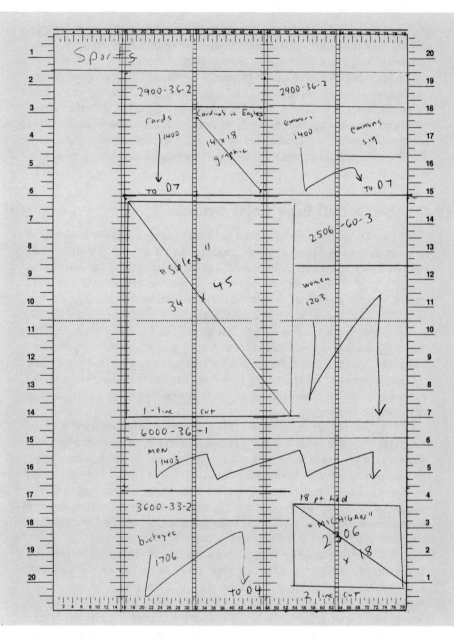

Figure 19.1. This dummy page prepared by editors at *The Mesa* (Ariz.) *Tribune* tells composing room personnel where to place stories and photos. Photo sizes, column widths, and placement of headlines are carefully marked. (Courtesy of Tribune Newspapers of Arizona)

Figure 19.2. The relationship between the dummy sheet and the finished page is apparent. (Courtesy of Tribune Newspapers of Arizona)

Figure 19.3. Scores, inside story summaries, and an index stretch across the bottom of this modular, clean page of *The Dallas Morning News*. (Courtesy of *The Dallas Morning News*)

Figure 19.4. A dominant photo of Monica Seles grabs readers' attention on this attractive, easy-to-read page from *The Arizona Republic*. (Courtesy of *The Arizona Republic*)

Figure 19.5. Tennis, baseball, and football stories are packaged effectively on this page of *The Orange County Register*. (Courtesy of *The Orange County Register*, copyright 1991)

SECTION

D

INSIDE

SPORTS

Sunday, September 8, 1991 Austin American-Statesman

Baseball, D4-5
Pro football, D13-14
High school football, D14-15

Seles sweeps past Navratilova

Teen-ager dominates final

By Thomas Bonk
Los Angeles Times Service

NEW YORK — Monica Seles, who pounds tennis balls with utter disregard for the laws of average, speed laws and law and order, completed a wild weekend at the United States Open.

One day after beating 15-year-old Jennifer Capriati in the semifinals, Seles knocked the wheels from under the handwagon of 34-year-old Martina Navratilova and won her first U.S. Open title 7-6

(7-1), 6-1 in bright sunshine Saturday.

Seles, 17, thus completed a sweep of the Grand Slam events she played in 1991 the Australian Open, French Open and U.S. Open.

You might notice that Wimbledon is missing. So does Seles.

"You know, winning this one, it's going to be hard to live with

(because) you always think, 'What if I would have played Wimbledon?'" she said.

"I might not have done well at sort of a Grand Slam or a flat. It is the Triple Crown without the Preakness or a hat track one goal short. Seles forfeited her chance at the Grand Slam when she withdrew from Wimbledon three days before it began, citing an underlying

champions to win the Grand Slam by capturing all four of the world's major tennis events in the same year. It has been done by Maureen Connolly in 1953, Margaret Court in 1970 and Steffi Graf in 1988.

So what Seles accomplished is

Women's tennis will have to wait a little longer for another

See Seles, D2

Perils of Sherrill: UT drops opener

Sluggish Horns stunned 13-6 by Miss. State

By Rick Cantu
American-Statesman Staff

Peter Gardere — chased by Mississippi State's Nate Williams (left), Kevin Henry (91) and Marc Woodard — had nowhere to run and nowhere to hide most of the afternoon.

STARKVILLE, Miss. — For the sixth straight time, Jackie Sherrill has found a way to beat the University of Texas football team.

This one, though, was his most surprising conquest yet.

Mississippi State 13, Texas 6. And perhaps no one in the Scott Field crowd of 34,123 Saturday was more surprised than the Bulldogs' first-year coach.

"Our players weren't afraid of Texas as much as I was," said Sherrill, his long-sleeved shirt soaked with sweat and Gatorade.

Many observers predict Sherrill, the former Texas A&M coach, will turn around Mississippi State's program. Even the staunchest critics, though, were baffled by the Bulldogs' upset of Texas.

They blitzed Texas with a vicious defense. Their offense, led by quarterback Williams "Sleepy" Robinson, was simple, effective and nearly error-free.

"There is no question that we don't have the same talent Texas has," Sherrill said. "But that really has nothing to do when you're trying a football game."

More Texas-Mississippi State coverage D10-11

Mississippi State relied on a simple plan: It used a powerful defensive front to harass Texas quarterback Peter Gardere. The Longhorns, ranked 13th in the country, were victims of their own mistakes.

A team that inspired the Horns with a Cotton Bowl berth last season suddenly is trying to regain its winning touch. And by losing Saturday, the Longhorns have lost their season opener five times in six years.

"The biggest surprise is that we didn't play the way we're capable of playing," defensive tackle James Patton said. "I'm surprised we would do that to ourselves."

This was certainly a team loss. No one asserted himself. An offense that scored more than 20 points nine times last season melted in the hot and muggy stadium. Texas offered no excuses.

"Mississippi State had more want-to than we did," Texas cornerback Mark Berry said.

"Every reporter in here is asking if we underestimated them," offensive tackle

See Sherrill, D9

Sherrill deserves credit for victory

John Maher

STARKVILLE, Miss. — Please, don't blame all of Texas' shocking 13-6 loss to Mississippi State on quarterback Peter Gardere.

"I didn't play a good game," Gardere understated after a day in which he passed for less than 100 yards and threw two crucial interceptions. Yes, Peter the Late played the whole afternoon the way he usually handles the first quarter. He never got in any kind of groove after getting off to his customary slow start. But he wasn't the only reason Mississippi State shocked Texas.

Start with Coach Jackie Sherrill. He's not the most likable guy in the world, but Sherrill does know how to orchestrate events. He had pumped-up fans here ringing their cowbells constantly. The woofers,

keep up with him, it was the sixth straight time that he'd left with a win over Texas.

Sherrill's team had just enough new wrinkles to worry the Longhorns.

They ran some defenses we hadn't seen," Saxton said. "They rolled their coverages over right before the snap."

Sherrill also elected not to blindly challenge Texas' offensive line with his less impressive defensive line.

"My guy wouldn't rush all the time," Texas tackle Chuck Johnson said. "About three times he played back and tried to play basketball. He tried to jump up and tip the ball."

The rest team bothered Gardere. Two passes were deflected at the line of scrimmage.

See Sherrill's, D9

guys barking like dogs, were turned way up, too.

"It was pretty dadgum loud," said backup quarterback Jimmy Saxton, who directed the only halfway effective drive of the day.

The sound effects helped Sherrill's undermanned squad play over its head for the entire game in the Mississippi heat and humidity. And, face it, Sherrill just has Texas' number. When he sprinted off the field with two Mississippi patriots trying to

SWC standings

Team	Conf.	Ovrl.
Arkansas	1-0	1-1
Houston	0-0	1-0
Baylor	0-0	1-0
Texas Tech	0-0	1-0
TCU	0-0	1-0
Texas A&M	0-0	0-0
Rice	0-0	0-0
Texas	0-0	0-1
SMU	0-0	0-1

Saturday's results
Houston 73, Louisiana Tech 3

Saturday's games
Mississippi State 13, Texas 6
New Mexico 97, Texas 47 Pano 7
Arkansas 17, SMU 0
Texas Christian 80, New Mexico 7
Texas Tech 41, Cal St. Fullerton 7

Fullback, defense key SWT victory

By Brad Owens
American-Statesman Correspondent

SAN MARCOS — Fullback Scott Smith and a savage Southwest Texas State defense teamed on the Texas A&I Javelinas on Saturday night, winning 29-14.

Coach Dennis Franchione said last month that last year's star fullback, Denver Bronco Reggie Rivers, would have to be replaced "by committee." After gaining 117 yards on 17 carries in his first game as the starter, Smith can hold his committee meetings up a phone booth.

Franchione said Smith, a sophomore, closed in emulations for Rivers' replacement with inspired play in Saturday's two-a-days.

"He was on a mission from the first moment he got here that he was going to be our starting fullback," Franchione said. "He made me feel good on that decision tonight."

The Bobcats gained 201 yards on the ground, controlling the ball for 11 minutes more than Texas A&I. The relentless, patient approach was made possible by a

predatory defense.

The Bobcats like to treat onto their home field to the accompaniment of the power chords of Guns 'N' Roses' Welcome to the Jungle. The Bobcat defenders welcomed Texas A&I to their home turf with open arms and cold hearts.

The defense, led by safety Rod Woodard and cool John Douglass, held the Javelinas to 72 yards in the first half and nailed Javelina runners for losses at times.

That pressure allowed the Bobcats to start five of their seven first half possessions in Javelina territory.

The offense ate up ground throughout the half, but snorted out near the goal line on the first three drives. After a missed field goal, an interception, a fumble and a punt, the Bobcats had 96 yards and zero points.

But the defense kept delivering the ball, and in the middle of the second quarter, the offense got its act together. Smith and slotback Todd Scott carried the load on a 13-play, 62-yard drive, with Scott diving over from the 1-yard line.

See Fullback, D6

Breach boys

Foes have bad, bad vibrations

By Randy Riggs
American-Statesman Staff

The Oilers and Bengals just don't get along, as Boomer Esiason and Johnny Meads (91) will readily admit.

Houston destroys a supposedly good Los Angeles Raiders team by 30 points, which is one point less than Cincinnati's humiliation by a supposedly average Denver Broncos team. Houston now plays Cincinnati, so the favorite is obvious.

The Bengals, of course.

Anyone who wonders why hasn't followed the bizarre histories of these two National Football League teams. Just when you think you've got them pegged as a Super Bowl contender or an expansion team, they do something to change your mind.

"It's crazy," Bengals quarterback Boomer Esiason declared. "Both teams are mirror images of each other. When you look at both rosters, you see a lot of outstanding players. You wonder why these teams can't stay consistent.

"I really don't have any theories for

why it's that way. If I had the answers, I'd sure as hell sell them to the owners of both clubs."

The Bengals are at their most dangerous the week after being whipped. Since Sam Wyche assumed coaching duties from Forrest Gregg in

See Oilers, D14

Oilers vs. Bengals

When: 7 p.m. today
Where: Riverfront Stadium, Cincinnati
Crowd: 59,755 (sellout)
Series: Oilers lead 21-16
Favorite: Bengals by 2
TV: TNT (Cable 16)
Radio: KLBJ-AM (590), WOAI-AM (1200), KSPL-AM (1470)

■ Emmitt Smith, Cowboys' workhorse		D12
■ NFL report: Week 2		D13

Figure 19.6. This *Austin* (Texas) *American-Statesman* page provides readers with statistical information, a variety of sports coverage, and action photos in a clean, modular design. (Courtesy of the *Austin American-Statesman*)

Figure 19.7. Readers are treated to dominant photos, informational graphics, game story sidebars, analysis, and quick facts on these attractive facing pages in the *Austin American-Statesman*. (Courtesy of the *Austin American-Statesman*)

tent on offense until the fourth quarter and,

l too long'

a ball on an incomplete pass in the fourth quarter of the Longhorns' 13-6 loss to Mississippi State. Luster made several big plays to stifle Texas.

Grading the Longhorns

Quarterbacks
F Peter Gardere looked as if he was playing in his first college game. Many of his passes were thrown high, leaving his receivers exposed for brutal hits. He didn't lead Texas on any touchdown drives. When the offense fails, the quarterback must be held accountable.

Running backs
C When the passing game failed, Mississippi State was able to key on Texas running backs. Butch Hadnot managed to run for 75 yards, but their longest run from scrimmage was only 22 yards.

Receivers
C Derrick Duke provided some clutch catches and the receivers did a good job of holding on to most of Gardere's throws. On several occasions, the receivers stopped their routes short of the first-down marker. On other plays, the receivers got bunched together.

Offensive line
D Gardere was given decent pass protection. Texas running backs didn't have many big holes to run through. The Mississippi State defensive line dominated the trenches, stopping many Texas rushing attempts at the line of scrimmage.

Defensive line
B- The Texas line rushed the passer well and helped limit Mississippi State to just 249 total yards. Shane Dronett provided pressure from

left end, but Bulldog quarterback William Robinson slipped many tackles. No one could contain fullback Michael Davis, who ran straight through Texas' gut for 70 yards on eight carries.

Linebackers
B+ Mical Padgett and Anthony Curl combined for 20 tackles. Padgett kept Texas' hopes alive with a 48-yard interception return in the fourth quarter. Mississippi State was able to keep drives alive with short passes over the middle.

Secondary
B Texas allowed just eight pass receptions. Cornerbacks Grady Cavness and Mark Berry played well, but the secondary didn't make any big plays. No great hits. No interceptions.

Special teams
C Jason Ziegler made both his field goals and surprise starter Kelly McClanahan did a decent job punting. However, Texas didn't break any good runs on punts or kickoff returns. The Longhorns didn't apply much pressure to Mississippi State kickers.

Overall
D The offense looked like a rudderless ship. Texas will not win many games unless the passing game improves. Texas runners are good, but they can't carry the whole load. Texas has many good players, but where are the leaders? They have two weeks to find some answers.

— **Rick Cantu**

The numbers game

Horn's taunting comments work Bulldogs into frenzy

By Kirk Bohls
American-Statesman Staff

STARKVILLE, Miss. — Five minutes before Saturday's kickoff, the Mississippi State Bulldogs were given a stirring pep talk by Mike Davis.

Texas' Mike Davis.

State fullback Michael Davis ran for a career-best 70 yards, but it was his comments with the Longhorns who may have had the most profound effect in the Bulldogs' 13-6 upset, even though the Texas player didn't get into the game.

State Coach Jackie Sherrill showed his team a film clip in which the Texas wide receiver said of the 15th-ranked Longhorns didn't score at least 30 points on State, they didn't deserve to be ranked.

"That was an indicator of what they thought about us," State defensive coordinator Bill Clay said. "At least, that's how we interpreted it. It was ill-advised for him to say it."

Not that Clay would want him to take it back. An aroused State defense that ranked eighth in the Southeastern Conference last season put the clamps on Davis' teammates, holding Texas to 211 yards and 13 first downs.

Davis' stinging words riled the Bulldogs, who Sherrill concedes were outmanned.

"We don't have any first-round draft choices," Sherrill said. "We do not have the same talent as Texas. You can put this in all caps. But Texas didn't give us enough credit for our speed in front. Our players have played Alabama, Auburn, LSU. They weren't as scared of Texas as I was.

It showed. In the second half, the Longhorns managed only 83 yards and four first downs and never drove closer to their 40-yard line than the 19-yard line, save for Mical Padgett's interception return to the 6 when Texas settled for a field goal.

The other deep penetration came on Texas' first possession of the game, when quarterback Peter Gardere threw three incompletions — all three passes were deflected, two by linemen — and was sacked by end Rodney Stowers on fourth down.

"Our defense came together," Stowers said. "I don't think we surprised ourselves. We just let the light shine through."

Texas running back Butch Hadnot saw little daylight, finding or making — his own creases for 75 yards. "He's a nice back," Stowers said.

Niceties aside, the Bulldogs largely kept to their basic defense, seldom blitzing. From State's standpoint, its defensive front simply overpowered Texas' offensive line.

Stowers swarmed inside linebacker Daniel Boyd's 12 tackles, and Kevin Henry had seven tackles and broke up two passes, and nose tackle Nate Williams had seven stops.

"I think we jolted them a little bit," Williams said. "They were trying to knock us off the ball, but we have a great defense. I could see panic in their eyes in the latter part of the third quarter, and they fell apart.

Texas seemed intent on establishing the ground game with twice as many runs (24) as passes (12) in the first half, but State established that Texas couldn't run. Consequently, the Longhorns frequently found themselves in third-and-longs, which they converted eight of 19 times.

"Our defensive line may not look as good as Texas guys in uniforms," strong safety Lance Aldridge said. "But they got up the field well and made Gardere run around."

A rugged hit by UT's Shane Dronett jars the ball from quarterback William Robinson. The Bulldogs recovered.

Texas-Mississippi State quick stats

What they had to say

"No, I don't think Jackie's a god yet. Probably more like a minor deity."

— **David Murray, editor of Dawgs' Bite magazine**

279

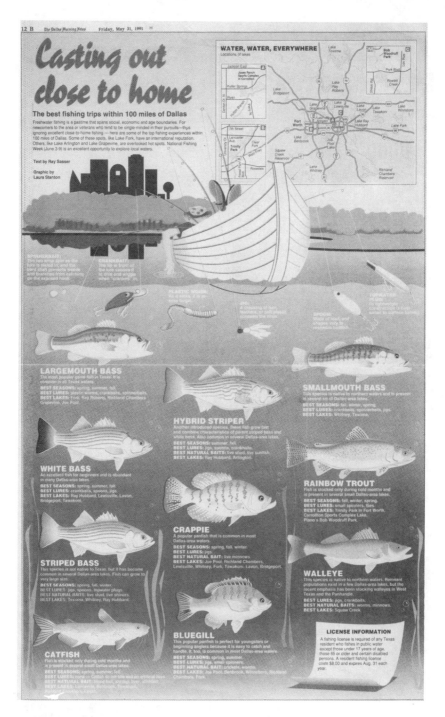

Figure 19.8. This full-page color graphic is the result of hard work and precise planning on the part of staffers at *The Dallas Morning News*. (Courtesy of *The Dallas Morning News*)

that we could have or borrow. We also asked for maps, bulletins, everything there was to know about fishing in the area.

"6. *You're an editor—start to edit.* We focused on our original intent: to show what the fish look like, what lures look like, where the lakes are, and how you get a license. We edited out information about spawning habits, water temperature, and boating regulations (a different graphic, perhaps). 'It's important that the editor prioritize the information because he or she may not be here when I have to decide whether something doesn't work and has to be cut from the graphic,' said Laura Stanton, *Morning News* artist and creator of the fish graphic. When you're done editing, 20 inches of copy may look like it's hardly going to fill 126 inches of news hole, but remember, this is a graphic. Premium space is devoted to illustration, not type. Write a catchy headline. 'Fish and their locales in the region' doesn't work. You'll need a nut graph summarizing the graphic.

"7. *Be organized.* In assembling materials for the art department, we had: pictures representing ten fish (all, hopefully, illustrated at the same angle), pictures of lures (or the lures themselves), a map of the area's lakes, a brief how-to on getting a license, a headline, a brief introduction, and a list of our sources.

"8. *Set a run date.* Giving an art department a day or even a few days to design and illustrate a full-page color graphic is setting yourself up for disappointment. A full week should be the minimum amount of time for the artist.

"9. *Be available but don't butt in.* Don't go on vacation. Do answer questions or requests for more information. Do make suggestions or comments on the artwork, but don't insist on them. The graphics editor and the artist will work together on visual presentation: how big the fish should be, how big the map should be, whether or not to use a photo of a wooden or aluminum boat, and so forth.

"10. *Proof carefully.* Proof, then have a colleague proof. Then proof again. The artist should make all necessary corrections in one session. (Nothing will raise the ire of an art department more than having to go back into a full-page color graphic at deadline because an editor missed a typo. Or worse, an editor wants to refine the writing. Getting into a graphic, making the corrections, and re-outputting separations takes much more time than, say, changing an electronic version of a story and outputting a correction.) After corrections, the graphic goes to press. What you'll have: a high-impact version of a well-told story.''

Exercises

1. Compare tear sheets of the lead sports section pages of at least six daily newspapers. Which pages contain the most effective informational graphics? Which pages contain the most dynamic photographs? Which pages are the easiest to read?

2. Read the lead stories published in one day's sports section of a metropolitan daily. Would some of the stories be more informative if they had been supplemented with informational graphics? If so, what types of informational graphics would you suggest?

3. Invite the person responsible for designing sports pages at an area daily to class. Discuss the design philosophy of the newspaper and how the designer attempts to facilitate the philosophy.

Sports coverage isn't all fun and games. Writers also must possess an understanding of the freedoms they enjoy under the First Amendment.

(Photo by Henri Cohen)

CHAPTER TWENTY

Legal Considerations

S ports reporters and editors sometimes are confronted with legally ticklish situations:

- Should they report that a football player had been indicted for illegal drug use if the athlete's attorney threatens a libel suit?
- Should they report that a high school basketball player is being benched because he violated training rules? What would happen if the young man's parents brought a libel suit?
- Should they write a column about the inept way a volleyball tournament was conducted? Can opinions that cause embarrassment to officials be freely expressed?
- Should they publish information provided by an anonymous source? If the information is published, would a reporter have to reveal the source if called upon to do so in court?

These are some of the situations that might confront sportswriters. This chapter, which will examine the basics of libel, privacy, and journalist's privilege, is not meant to be a comprehensive overview of these sometimes complex areas. It is presented to provide sportswriters with a working knowledge of the basics.

Libel

Libel has been defined as a defamatory falsehood that holds a person up to public hatred, ridicule, or scorn. In a libel suit, a plaintiff must show that he or she was identified in the article (though not necessarily by name), that the article was communicated to a third party (publication in a newspaper certainly satisfies that requirement), that he or she was harmed by the article, that the information in the article was false, and that the defendant was at fault. All five requirements must be met or the plaintiff (the individual bringing the suit) has no chance of collecting damages.

Just because these requirements are met, however, does not mean the plaintiff will collect damages. A number of defenses are available to the person or publication being sued.

Robert H. Phelps and E. Douglas Hamilton, coauthors of an authoritative book, *Libel: Rights, Risk, Responsibilities,* list several defenses that flow from statutory and common laws. Some defenses are absolute (if proved, they effectively ward off libel damages regardless of the circumstances): consent or authorization; privilege of a participant; and the statute of limitations. Some are conditional (depending upon the circumstances, they may or may not be a bar to damages being assessed): truth; fair comment and criticism; neutral reportage; and privilege of reporting.

In addition, the "actual malice" defense (which was articulated in *New York Times Co. v. Sullivan* in 1964 and will be discussed below) provides protection when the plaintiffs are public officials or public figures.

Overviews of the statutory and common law defenses discussed by Phelps and Hamilton follow:

> *Consent or authorization.* Seldom does a subject who knows he or she is going to be criticized in a newspaper give consent to the publication. Let's assume a sportswriter calls a coach and reveals some damaging information he or she had heard about him. The coach confirms the information and says, "Go ahead and publish it. I don't care." The reporter would have a privilege to do so. Obviously, reporters seldom will find themselves with such permission.
>
> *Privilege of a participant.* This privilege has evolved to give protection to those who testify before governing bodies. A U.S. senator, for example, has an absolute privilege to make any allegations he or she wants while standing on the floor of the Senate. A person testifying at a trial cannot be sued for libel for what he or she says about the accused. Sportswriters will not find much use for this defense, but it is available if the circumstances justify it.
>
> *Statute of limitations.* Sportswriters never want to get sued, but if they are, this can be an ironclad defense. If suit is not brought within a specified period after publication, the plaintiff does not have standing to sue. The statute of limitations for libel in most states is one, two, or three years.

Truth. Phelps and Hamilton emphasize that, in some states, truth is a defense only (these are the *conditions*) when published with good motives and for justifiable ends.

Fair comment and criticism. This defense can be used by columnists who express opinions. The defense applies only when words clearly are expressions of opinion—not statements of fact. Also, the opinions must be concerning a matter of general or public interest.

Privilege of reporting. This conditional defense gives journalists the right to report what transpires at public meetings, hearings, and in courts of law. According to Phelps and Hamilton, the reporting must be accurate, and there can be no extrinsic facts introduced. If John Jones testifies in court that coach Henry Smith gave him drugs before a game, the journalist can report the allegation with immunity even though the statement turns out to be false. It must be emphasized, however, that this privilege applies only to statements made in most public meetings, in courts, or in documents filed as part of the public record. The privilege does not extend to off-the-cuff remarks made by sources in private settings.

Neutral reportage. This defense protects writers when they accurately report accusations made by one responsible party against another if the subjects are involved in a public controversy. The conditions are that the story must be an accurate report of what was said, and it must pertain to a public controversy. This defense has not been accepted in all jurisdictions. Some jurisdictions have rejected it. Reporters should check to see if it applies to their states.

Clearly, these common law and statutory defenses give journalists some protection. Still, it is the "actual malice" defense that is most widely and effectively used.

The "Actual Malice" Test

Prior to 1964, there was no national libel defense standard applicable when public persons were plaintiffs. Most states adhered to the common law precedent that public officials did not have to meet a heavier burden to collect libel damages than did private persons. Legal scholars occasionally contended that, since the press was the watchdog for the public, the press should have more legal leeway to discuss public persons.

In a landmark decision in 1964, the U.S. Supreme Court made it much more difficult for public officials to recover damages for libel. L. B. Sullivan, a county police commissioner in Alabama, sued the *New York Times* and others. Sullivan contended that he had been libeled by a full-page advertisement published in the *Times* under the heading "Heed Their Rising Voices."

The thesis of the advertisement—which was signed by scores of prominent Americans and clergy—was that the civil rights movement was being met by resistence by some southern officials. The ad incorrectly stated the number of times Dr. Martin Luther King, Jr., had been arrested and erroneously said that demonstrating college students in Montgomery, Alabama, had been starved into submission. Sullivan, who was not named in the ad, contended that he had been libeled. Because he was a county police commissioner, he said persons would think of him when reading the ad. The Alabama courts awarded Sullivan $500,000 in damages.

The U.S. Supreme Court considered whether public officials should be able to collect libel damages simply by showing that published statements were false. Justice William Brennan wrote:

> The constitutional guarantees require, we think, a federal rule that prohibits a public official from recovering damages for a defamatory falsehood relating to his official conduct unless he proves that the statement was made with "actual malice"—that is, with knowledge that it was false or with reckless disregard of whether it was false or not.

Brennan said the press needed "breathing space" to discuss public issues and public officials. Thus, it is not enough for a public official to prove that an allegation is false—the public official must show that the statement was made in reckless disregard for the truth. That, obviously, is difficult. As a result of *Sullivan*, the press enjoys freedom to discuss public officials with relative immunity. Still, if a reporter knowingly lies—and the plaintiff is able to prove it in court—the reporter can be held liable for damages.

The Supreme Court, in 1967, extended the "actual malice" protection to defendants accused by *public figures*—not just public officials—of libel. Because so many sports page articles focus on public officials or public figures, the *Times* rule has been of great benefit to sportswriters.

In 1968, for example, the 9th U.S. Circuit Court of Appeals affirmed a lower court decision in favor of *Look* magazine. *Look* had been charged with libel by baseball star Orlando Cepeda. An article published in the magazine had questioned Cepeda's ability.

The circuit court noted that, when the U.S. Supreme Court held that public figures had to meet the heavy actual malice burden in order to collect libel damages, Cepeda had to overcome "important obstacles." The majority wrote:

> Because of the Supreme Court's protective attitude toward freedom of the press, the burden of proof was rightly placed on Cepeda to prove, if he could, actual malice as defined in New York Times, or extreme departure from the standards of investigation and reporting.... The court instructed the jury three times on the subject of actual malice, including in that term wanton recklessness and heedlessness of the plaintiff's rights. It also included in the concept of malice reckless or heedless failure to check sources of information, or such failure to check, for the purpose of avoiding finding the truth.

The court said Cepeda clearly was a public figure, as evidenced by "his fame as an extraordinary baseball player."

Two years later, the 5th U.S. Circuit Court of Appeals handed down a similar opinion in a libel suit brought by Bon Air Hotel, Inc., Augusta, Georgia, against Time, Inc., publisher of *Sports Illustrated,* and sportswriter Dan Jenkins. Jenkins had relied on interviews and personal observation to write an article about the Bon Air Hotel, a Masters Golf Tournament institution that apparently had seen better days. Jenkins, who had covered the tournament thirteen years, wrote that the staff included waiters who "tumbled drowsily through the dining room"; he wrote that the rooms were "wide enough so that by turning sideways a guest can walk between the bed and the dresser"; he wrote that hotel management's attitude toward guests was "stay-at-your-own-risk"; and that "sleeping at the Bon Air has long been difficult for reasons other than the heat or cold. It is noisy. Not the least amount of noise sometimes is created by the clacking of high-heeled shoes going down the fire escape outside a guest's window at 4:00 A.M."

The hotel objected also to a drawing that accompanied the article in *Sports Illustrated;* it showed, among other things, three braces supporting the outer hotel wall and some trash around the swimming pool.

The circuit court held that the district court was correct in finding for the magazine and writer. According to the circuit court opinion, the hotel had contended that merely because it long had been a fixture of the Masters tourney did "not make an inconspicuous and little-known hotel a matter of such public interest." The court determined, however, that the tournament was of public interest and the hotel would have to meet a heavy burden to recover damages. The *New York Times* test was applied; the court concluded that Jenkins and *Sports Illustrated* had not acted in reckless disregard for the truth.

The circuit court found that Jenkins had drawn from his extensive background of covering the tournament and that a magazine researcher carefully had checked the article for accuracy "by telephone conversations, by personal interviews, by consulting Time, Inc., files and by reading relevant published sources on golf tournaments and Augusta." The researcher had even sent a list of questions to be verified by the magazine's Atlanta correspondent. Clearly, the court said, the article had not been published in reckless disregard for the truth.

The press enjoys considerable protection from libel when discussing public officials and public figures, but the U.S. Supreme Court tightened the definition for a public figure in a 1974 decision (*Gertz v. Robert Welch, Inc.*). The court said a well-known Chicago attorney who had been reasonably active in civic affairs nevertheless had not achieved a "level of especial prominence" and had not thrust himself voluntarily into the "vortex of a controversy." Thus, he did not merit public figure status for purposes of libel suits. The court said that private persons who become involuntarily involved in events of public interest need only show negligence on the part of the defendant—a failure to exercise reasonable care in preparing the story—rather than actual malice.

Sometimes it is difficult for the press to know in which category the courts will place their subjects—public or private. When the subject clearly is in the public category, journalists can publish stories knowing that they can rely on the actual malice defense so long as they are not heedlessly reckless. If the subject clearly belongs in the private person category, however, journalists cannot depend upon the actual malice defense.

Writing Opinion Columns

A libel decision handed down by the U.S. Supreme Court in 1990—one that Bruce W. Sanford, a well-known First Amendment lawyer, said was laden with "broad and troubling implications"—opened a can of worms for sports columnists. In *Milkovich v. Lorain Journal Co.,* the court ruled that the First Amendment does not make the news media totally immune from libel suits based on statements of opinion. The trick, of course, lies in determining whether statements are "pure opinion" or are "sufficiently factual to be susceptible of being proved true or false."

The *Milkovich* suit, which was tangled within the judicial system for fifteen years, grew from an Ohio high-school wrestling match between Maple Heights and Mentor. A brawl erupted at the match; several were injured. Not surprisingly, the Ohio High School Athletic Association (OHSAA) conducted a hearing to determine facts and, if necessary, to dole out punishment. After hearing testimony, OHSAA placed Maple Heights' team on probation for a year and declared it ineligible for the state tournament. In addition, Maple Heights coach Mike Milkovich was criticized for his actions during the altercation.

Shortly after OHSAA's ruling, a group of parents sought a restraining order, contending that the Ohio governing board had denied Maple Heights due process. Milkovich and Superintendent H. Donald Scott were among those who testified in court. The court overturned the OHSAA ruling, thus prompting journalist Ted Diadiun to write and publish a column in the *News-Herald,* which is owned by the Lorain Journal Co. In essence, the columnist said that Milkovich had perjured himself.

Diadiun's column, which included his picture, carried this headline: "Maple beat the law with the 'big lie.'" Diadiun wrote that "when a person takes on a job in a school, whether it be as a teacher, coach, administrator or even maintenance worker, it is well to remember that his primary job is that of educator." The columnist went on to say that school officials naturally leave their marks on the students and that the young people learn not just from books but from personal experiences and through observations of their superiors and peers. Diadiun wrote:

> Such a lesson was learned (or relearned) yesterday by the student body of Maple Heights High School, and by anyone who attended the Maple-Mentor wrestling meet of last Feb. 8.
>
> A lesson which, sadly, in view of the events of the past year, is well they learned early.
>
> It is simply this: If you get in a jam, lie your way out.
>
> If you're successful enough, and powerful enough, and can sound sincere enough, you stand an excellent chance of making the lie stand up, regardless of what really happened.
>
> The teachers responsible were mainly head Maple wrestling coach Mike Milkovich and former superintendent of schools H. Donald Scott.
>
> Last winter they were faced with a difficult situation. Milkovich's ranting from the side of the mat and egging the crowd on backfired during a meet with Greater Cleveland Conference rival Mentor, and resulted in first the Maple Heights team, then many of the partisan crowd, attacking the Mentor squad in a brawl which sent four Mentor wrestlers to the hospital.

Diadiun then contended that Milkovich and Scott had misrepresented "the things that happened" when they testified before OHSAA's Board of Control and that they "apparently had their version of the incident polished and reconstructed" when testifying in court. Diadiun wrote that "the judge bought their story, and ruled in their favor."

Diadiun concluded his column with these four paragraphs:

> Anyone who attended the meet, whether he be from Maple Heights, Mentor, or impartial observer, knows in his heart that Milkovich and

> Scott lied at the hearing after each having given his solemn oath to tell
> the truth.
> But they got away with it.
> Is that the kind of lesson we want our young people learning from
> their high school administrators and coaches?
> I think not.

Milkovich sued for libel. The lower courts, though, holding for the
newspaper company, based their decisions, in part, on the grounds that the
article constituted an "opinion" that was protected by the First Amendment.

The U.S. Supreme Court, however, reversed and remanded the case,
holding that because Diadiun's statements were "sufficiently factual to be
susceptible of being proved true or false," it was up to a jury to decide
whether the column was libelous.

Chief Justice William Rehnquist wrote that when the court, in 1974,
said that "under the First Amendment there is no such thing as a false
idea," such an assertion was not intended "to create a wholesale defamation
exemption for anything that might be labeled 'opinion.' " Rehnquist used
this example: If a speaker says, "In my opinion, John Jones is a liar," the
speaker has implied a knowledge of facts that would lead to that conclusion.
"Simply couching such statements in terms of opinion does not dispel these
implications," Rehnquist wrote.

Rehnquist also noted that "at common law, even the privilege of fair
comment did not extend to 'a false statement of fact, whether it was
expressly stated or implied from an expression of opinion.' "

The chief justice contrasted the statement, "In my opinion Mayor Jones
is a liar," with the statement, "In my opinion Mayor Jones shows his
abysmal ignorance by accepting the teachings of Marx and Lenin." Rehnquist
said the latter would not be actionable because it "does not contain a
provably false factual connotation." Rehnquist wrote that "public debate
will not suffer for lack of 'imaginative expression' or the 'rhetorical
hyperbole' which has traditionally added much to the discourse of our
Nation."

Very simply, Rehnquist said that Diadiun's assertions were "not the
sort of loose, figurative or hyperbolic language which would negate the
impression that the writer was seriously maintaining [Milkovich] committed
the crime of perjury. Nor does the general tenor of the article negate this
impression. We also think the connotation that [Milkovich] committed
perjury is sufficiently factual to be susceptible of being proved true or
false."

Justice Brennan, in dissent, said that it was plain to him that "Diadiun's
assumption that Milkovich must have lied at the court hearing is patently

conjecture." Brennan also noted that "the tone and format of the piece notify readers to expect speculation and personal judgment. The tone is pointed, exaggerated and heavily laden with emotional rhetoric and moral outrage. Diadiun never says, for instance, that Milkovich committed perjury. He says that 'anyone who attended the meet . . . knows in his heart' that Milkovich lied—obvious hyperbole as Diadiun does not purport to have researched what everyone who attended the meet knows in his heart."

David A. Schulz, writing in *Editor & Publisher* magazine, said the case primarily complicates "the determination over which statements can and cannot be actionable." Schulz concluded that "*Milkovich* in no way alters existing safeguards for opinion contained in state constitutions and in the common law 'fair comment' privilege, and to this extent does not dramatically alter the protection for statements of pure opinion."

Attorney Sanford predicted "a litigation boom" as a result of *Milkovich*. Writing in *presstime*, Sanford said: "What seems clear is that *Milkovich* puts a new premium on precision in language. Stories that slosh through swamps of confusion or vagueness or simply seem to imply more than they're prepared to state will be problematic. Stories that reasonably imply a false factual connotation—even if unintended by the writer—will be newly vulnerable to a lawsuit."

Invasion of Privacy

It has become more fashionable during recent years for persons who think they have been wronged by the media to file suit for invasion of privacy. Privacy has been defined most simply as "the right to be let alone." Dean William Prosser of the Hastings College of Law divided privacy into four branches:

- *Appropriation,* which involves taking the name or likeness of someone and converting it to personal gain.
- *Intrusion,* which involves intruding either physically or by electronic means into the solitude of another.
- *Publication of embarrassing private facts,* which involves publication of private information that, according to the courts, violates a sense of common decency.
- *False light,* which involves publication of a non-defamatory falsehood. This branch is related to libel, which involves publication of a defamatory falsehood.

Consideration of cases will place each of these branches in better perspective.

Appropriation

A Cleveland television station filmed the county fair routine of Hugo Zacchini, who was shot from a cannon into a net two hundred feet away. Zacchini had requested that the station not film his act. He said that if people could watch his performance on television, they would not pay to watch him live. In other words, he contended that the television station had appropriated his act for the station's economic gain. The station countered that the act—which fair goers did not have to pay extra to see once they were inside the grounds—was a matter of public interest.

Naturally, television stations show film clips of sports events regularly. Justice Lewis F. Powell, in a U.S. Supreme Court dissenting opinion, said showing film of Zacchini's act on the evening news was a "routine example of the press fulfilling the information function so vital to our system."

Justice Byron White, who wrote the majority opinion, did not view it that way. He said "the broadcast of a film of (Zacchini's) entire act poses a substantial threat to the economic value of that performance." White said Zacchini had a right to "exclusive control over the publicity given to his performance." This decision turned on the fact that Zacchini's entire 15-second act had been shown on the news.

The decision (*Zacchini v. Scripps-Howard*, 1977) shows that the electronic media need to be careful when filming entire acts or events. Sportswriters are not likely to run afoul of this privacy branch. Generally, sportswriters are reporting on performances to enlighten or inform the public—not for any personal economic benefit. The only defense when accused under this branch is consent—preferably in writing.

Intrusion

Reporters need to carefully consider procedures for gathering news. A federal circuit court of appeals in 1972 said that photographer Ronald Galella had to maintain a certain distance from Jacqueline Kennedy Onassis and her children. The court recognized that Galella had a right to take photos of public persons in public places—but said there is a limit. Galella made a habit of popping from behind bushes and from beneath tablecloths to take photos of the unsuspecting Onassis. The circuit court said: "The First Amendment has never been construed to accord newsmen immunity from torts or crimes committed during the course of newsgathering. The First Amendment is not a license to trespass, to steal or to intrude by electronic means into the precincts of another's home or office."

The courts have made clear that the First Amendment does not protect journalists who commit crimes when *gathering* the news, but, at the same time, the courts occasionally have extended journalists a privilege to publish information that has been gathered illegally by others. A case decided by the circuit court of appeals for the District of Columbia in 1969 illustrates this (*Pearson v. Dodd*).

Some disgruntled employees and former employees of a U.S. senator approached syndicated columnists Drew Pearson and Jack Anderson. The employees said they had proof that the senator was converting public campaign money to private use. Pearson and Anderson asked for documentation. The employees made copies from the senator's files but returned the originals. The columnists published a series of columns based upon the information. The senator sued for invasion of privacy under the intrusion branch.

The circuit court said there was no defense for the actual physical intrusion, but the postintrusion publication was protected if the information was newsworthy. In this instance, information about a U.S. senator who was apparently misusing public money was indeed of interest to the public. Pearson and Anderson were not held liable for damages.

Publication of Embarrassing Private Facts

Mike Virgil, an extraordinary body surfer, sued Time, Inc., for an article written about him that was published in *Sports Illustrated*. Virgil claimed the article, which he said contained embarrassing private facts, was an invasion of his privacy. *Sports Illustrated* writer Curry Kirkpatrick interviewed Virgil and several of the surfer's acquaintances in Southern California. Virgil also consented to being photographed by a free-lancer who had been hired by the magazine.

Kirkpatrick's 7,000-word article painted a vivid picture of Virgil the surfer and Virgil the man. Kirkpatrick wrote:

> Virgil's carefree style at the Wedge (a surfing area) appears to have emanated from some escapades in his younger days, such as the time at a party when a young lady approached him and asked where she might find an ashtray. "Why, my dear, right here," said Virgil, taking her lighted cigarette and extinguishing it in his mouth.

Kirkpatrick quoted Virgil who described a trip to Mammoth Mountain:

> "I quit my job, left home and moved to Mammoth Mountain. At the ski lodge there one night I dove headfirst down a flight of stairs—just because. Because why? Well, there were these chicks all around. I thought it would be groovy. Was I drunk? I think I might have been."

The article also quoted Virgil as saying that he sometimes would purposely injure himself while working in order to collect compensation so he could devote more time to surfing. Virgil's wife was quoted: "Mike also eats spiders and other insects and things."

Before the article was published, a *Sports Illustrated* researcher checked it for accuracy. She talked to Virgil, who said he had decided that he did not want the story to be published. He said he thought the article was going to focus on surfing—not on his personal habits and his personality.

Sports Illustrated, convinced that the facts of the article were accurate, published it despite Virgil's request. The 9th U.S. Circuit Court of Appeals in 1975 vacated the case to a lower court. The circuit court said the district court should consider "whether (and, if so, to what extent) private facts respecting Virgil, as a prominent member of the group engaging in body surfing at the Wedge, are matters in which the public has a legitimate interest." The circuit court said the district court should determine "whether the publicizing of these facts would prove highly offensive to a reasonable person—one of ordinary sensibilities."

The circuit court also quoted from a legal source that said:

> In determining what is a matter of legitimate public interest, account must be taken of the customs and conventions of the community; and in the last analysis what is proper becomes a matter of the community mores. The line is to be drawn when the publicity ceases to be the giving of information to which the public is entitled, and becomes a morbid and sensational prying into private lives for its own sake, with which a reasonable member of the public, with decent standards, would say that he had no concern.

Taking this into consideration, the lower court held that the article indeed was newsworthy, which was *Sports Illustrated*'s defense, and the magazine was not liable for damages.

The *Virgil* case shows, however, that the line between newsworthy information that is not "morbid and sensational" and information that is written only because it would appeal to the morbid curiosity of readers can be a fine one.

Sportswriters should move with caution on stories that contain embarrassing private facts. Newsworthiness is a broad—yet somewhat vague—defense. Consent from the subject is the safest course.

False Light

Reporters must paint realistic pictures of their subjects. To portray a subject in a false—untruthful—light could lead to an invasion of privacy suit.

An Ohio woman became upset when the *Cleveland Plain Dealer* published a story about how her family was holding up one year after the death of her husband who had died in a bridge collapse. The story exaggerated the poverty of the family; the reporter fabricated quotes and attributed them to the mother. The article painted a sympathetic picture of the family. It did not libel them; the implication was that the family was coping with adversity. The woman filed suit under the false light branch (*Cantrell v. Forest City Publishing Co.,* 1974).

Defenses available when sued under the false light branch are truth and actual malice. The U.S. Supreme Court said the woman was entitled to recover damages. The story was not true; it was, in part, exaggerated fiction. And, since the reporter realized he was exaggerating the plight of the family, he had acted with reckless disregard for the truth.

Journalist's Privilege

Many journalists contend that they should have a right to not reveal names of confidential sources or information that has been given to them in confidence. The courts, however, have not conferred this absolute privilege upon the press.

The U.S. Supreme Court in 1972 (*Branzburg v. Hayes*) held that reporters do not have an absolute First Amendment privilege to withhold information that could aid a grand jury investigation. Justice Byron White said that it was not better to write about crime than to do something about it by testifying in legal proceedings. The Supreme Court, however, made clear that reporters could not be harassed by law enforcement officers and that journalists still could appeal to the courts if they felt requests for information were not proper.

In a concurring opinion, Justice Powell said the requested information should be relevant to the case and should go to the heart of the matter. The implication was that journalists should not be subjected to "fishing expeditions" by law enforcement officials.

Also, Justice White said that states were free to pass laws giving journalists testimonial privileges under certain circumstances. About half the states have what are commonly referred to as "shield laws." Basically, these laws exempt journalists from revealing confidential sources and information. Because of hostile judicial interpretations, however, reporters have found themselves in jail for refusing to reveal information even in those states that have shield laws.

The common law does not give journalists absolute protection from revealing confidential information. The common law extends such privilege under some conditions to doctors, lawyers, and clergy. On occasion, however, lower courts have held, particularly when requests from officials did not seem germane to the case and did not go to the heart of the matter, that journalists did not have to reveal information. Still, journalists gamble when they think shield laws or the First Amendment always will protect them from being cited for contempt if they refuse to provide requested information to courts of law or to grand juries.

Exercises

1. Invite an attorney or a communication law professor from your school to class. Ask the expert to discuss recent court opinions that have an impact on working journalists, in general, and on sportswriters and editors, in particular.

2. Invite a sportswriter or editor who has been involved in a lawsuit to class. What strategies were used by the newspaper to defend against the suit?

3. Clip sports articles that you have read that you think raise legal questions. Bring them to class to discuss.

APPENDIX

Associated Press Sports Guidelines and Style

Here is a summary of selected sports guidelines and rules from *The Associated Press Stylebook and Libel Manual*. Additional rules can be found in the stylebook, which journalists refer to constantly.

A

All-America, All-American The Associated Press recognizes only one All-America football and basketball team each year. In football, only Walter Camp's selections through 1924, and the AP selections after that, are recognized. Do not call anyone an *All-America* selection unless he is listed on either the Camp or AP roster.

   Similarly do not call anyone an *All-America basketball player* unless an AP selection. The first All-America basketball team was chosen in 1948.

   Use *All-American* when referring specifically to an individual: *All-American Pat Ewing*, or *He is an All-American.*

   Use *All-America* when referring to the team: *All-America team*, or *All-America selection.*

Americas Cup (golf) **America's Cup** (yachting)

archery Scoring is usually in points. Use a basic summary. Example:

> (After 3 of 4 Distances)
> 1. Darrell Pace, Cincinnati, 914 points.
> 2. Richard McKinney, Muncie, Ind. 880.
> 3. Etc.

AstroTurf A trademark for a type of artificial grass.

athletic club Abbreviate as *AC* with the name of a club, but only in sports summaries: *Illinois AC*. See the **volleyball** entry for an example of such a summary.

athletic teams Capitalize teams, associations and recognized nicknames: *Red Sox, the Big Ten, the A's, the Colts*.

B

backboard, backcourt, backfield, backhand, backspin, backstop, backstretch, backstroke Some are exceptions to Webster's New World, made for consistency in handling sports stories.

badminton Games are won by the first player to score 21 points, unless it is necessary to continue until one player has a two-point spread. Most matches go to the first winner of two games.

Use a match summary. See **racquetball** for an example.

ball carrier

ballclub, ballpark, ballplayer

baseball The spellings for some frequently used words and phrases, some of which are exceptions to Webster's New World:

backstop	home run	RBI (s.,pl.)
ballclub	left-hander	rundown (n.)
ballpark	line drive	sacrifice
ballplayer	line up (v.)	sacrifice fly
baseline	lineup (n.)	sacrifice hit
bullpen	major league(s) (n.)	shoestring catch
center field	major-league (adj.)	shortstop
center fielder	major-leaguer (n.)	shut out (v.)
designated hitter	outfielder	shutout (n.,adj.)
doubleheader	passed ball	slugger
double play	put out (v.)	squeeze play
fair ball	putout (n.)	strike
fastball	pinch hit (v.)	strike zone
first baseman	pinch-hit (n.,adj.)	Texas leaguer
foul ball	pinch hitter (n.)	triple play
line	pitchout	twi-night double-
foul tip	playoff (n.,adj.)	header
ground-rule double		wild pitch
home plate		

NUMBERS: Some sample uses of numbers: *first inning, seventh-inning stretch, 10th inning; first base, second base, third base; first home run, 10th home run; first place, last place; one RBI, 10 RBI. The pitcher's record is now 6-5. The final score was 1-0.*

LEAGUES: Use *American League, National League, American League West, National League East,* etc. On second reference: *the league, the pennant in the West, the league's West Division,* etc.

BOX SCORES: A sample follows.

The visiting team always is listed on the left, the home team on the right.

Only one position, the last he played in the game, is listed for any player.

Figures in parentheses are the player's total in that category for the season.

Use the *First Game* line shown here only if the game was the first in a doubleheader.

One line in this example—*None out when winning run scored*— could not have occurred in this game as played. It is included to show its placement when needed.

First Game

PHILADELPHIA	ab	r	h	bi		SAN DIEGO	ab	r	h	bi
Stone lf	4	0	0	0	Flannry 2		3	0	1	0
G Gross lf	0	0	0	0	Gwynn rf		4	0	2	0
Schu 3	4	1	0	0	Garvey 1		4	0	0	0
Samuel 2b	4	0	1	2	Nettles 3b		3	1	1	0
Schmdt 1	4	0	0	0	Royster 3		0	0	0	0
Virgil c	4	2	2	1	McRynl cf		4	0	1	1
GWilson rf	4	0	0	0	Kennedy c		4	0	1	0
Maddox c	3	0	0	0	Martinez lf		4	1	1	0
Jeltz ss	2	0	0	0	Templtn ss		4	0	2	1
KGross p	3	0	1	0	Dravcky p		2	0	0	0
Tekulve p	0	0	0	0	Bmbry ph		1	0	0	0
					Lefferts p		0	0	0	0
Totals	32	3	4	3			33	2	9	2

Philadelphia	010 200 000-3
San Diego	000 200 000-2

Game Winning RBI - Virgil.
E. Templeton, G. Wilson, DP - Philadelphia 2. LOB - Philadelphia 3. San Diego 6.2B - Templeton, Gwynn, HR - Virgil (8).

	IP	H	R	ER	BB	SO
Philadelphia						
KGross W,4-6	7 1-3	9	2	2	0	3
Tekulve S,3	1 2-3	0	0	0	1	0
San Diego						
Dravecky L,4-3	7	4	3	1	1	2
Lefferts	2	0	0	0	0	1

HBP—Flannery by KGross. T—2:13. A-17,740.

LINESCORE: When a bare linescore summary is required, use this form:

Philadelphia	010 200 000—3 4 1
San Diego	000 200 000—2 9 1

K. Gross, Tekulve (8) and Virgil; Dravecky, Lefferts (3) and Kennedy. W - KGross, 4-6, L. Dravecky, 4-3. Sv - Tekulve (3). HRs - Philadelphia, Virgil 2 (8).

LEAGUE STANDINGS:
The form:

All Times EDT
NATIONAL LEAGUE
EAST

	W	L	Pct.	GB
Pittsburgh	92	69	.571	-
Philadelphia	85	75	.531	6½

WEST

	W	L	Pct.	GB
Cincinnati	108	54	.667	-
Los Angeles	88	74	.543	20

(Night games not included)
Monday's Results
Chicago 7, St. Louis 5
Atlanta at New York, rain.
Tuesday's Games
Cincinnati (Gullett 14-2 and Nolan 4-4) at New York
(Seaver 12-3 and Matlack 6-1) 2, 6 p.m.
Wednesday's Games
Cincinnati at New York
Chicago at St. Louis, night
Only games scheduled.

In subheads for results and future games, spell out day of the week as: *Tuesday's Games,* instead of *Today's Games.*

basic summary This format for summarizing sports events lists winners in the order of their finish. The figure showing the place finish is followed by an athlete's full name, his affiliation or hometown, and his time, distance, points, or whatever performance factor is applicable to the sport.

If a contest involves several types of events, the paragraph begins with the name of the event.

A typical example:

> 60-yard dash—1, Steve Williams. Florida TC, 6.0 2, Hasley Crawford, Philadelphia Pioneer, 6.1. 3, Mike McFarland, Chicago TC, 6.2. 4, Etc.
> 100—1, Steve Williams, Florida TC, 10.1. 2, Etc.

Additional examples are provided in the entries for many of the sports that are reported in this format.

Most basic summaries are a single paragraph per event, as shown. In some competitions with large fields, however, the basic summary is supplied under a dateline with each winner listed in a single paragraph. See the **bowling** entry for example.

For international events in which U.S. or Canadian competitors are not among the leaders, add them in a separate paragraph as follows:

Also: 14, Dick Green, New York, 6.8. 17, George Bensen, Canada, 6.9. 19, Etc.

In events where points, rather than time or distance, are recorded as performances, mention the word points on the first usage only:

1. Jim Benson, Springfield, N.J., 150 points. 2. Jerry Green, Canada, 149. 3. Etc.

basketball The spellings of some frequently used words and phrases:

backboard	free-throw line	jump shot
backcourt	frontcourt	layup
backcourtman	full-court press	man-to-man
baseline	goaltending	midcourt
field goal	half-court pass	pivotman
foul line	halftime	play off (v.)
foul shot	hook shot	playoff (n., adj.)
free throw	jump ball	zone

NUMBERS: Some sample uses of numbers: *in the first quarter, a second-quarter lead, nine field goals, 10 field goals, the 6-foot-5 forward, the 6-10 center. He is 6 feet 10 inches tall.*

LEAGUE: *National Basketball Association* or *NBA.*

For subdivisions: *the Atlantic Division of the Eastern Conference, the Pacific Division of the Western Conference,* etc. On second reference: *the NBA East, the division, the conference,* etc.

BOX SCORE: A sample follows. The visiting team always is listed first.

In listing the players, begin with the five starters—two forwards, center, two guards—and follow with all substitutes who played.

Figures after each player's last name denote field goals, free throws, free throws attempted and total points.

Example:

LOS ANGELES (114)
Worthy 8-19 4-6 20, Rambis 4-6 0-0 8, Abdul-Jabbar 6-11 0-0 12, E. Johnson 8-14 3-4 19, Scott 5-14 0-0 10, Cooper 1-5 2-2 4, McAdoo 6-13 0-0 12, McGee 4-7 4-5 14, Spriggs 4-7 0-2 8, Kupchak 3-3 1-2 7. Totals 49-100 14-21 114.
BOSTON (148)
McHale 10-16 6-9 26, Bird 8-14 2-2 19, Parish 6-11 6-7 18, D. Johnson 6-14 1-1 13, Ainge 9-15 0-0 19, Buckner 3-5 0-0 6, Williams 3-5 0-0 6, Wedman 11-11 0-2 26, Maxwell 1-1 1-2 3, Kite 3-5 1-2 7, Carr 1-3 0-0 3, Clark 1-2 0-0 2. Totals 62-102 17-25 148.
Three-point goals - Wedman 4, McGee 2, Bird, Ainge, Carr. Fouled out - None. Rebounds - Los Angeles 43 (Rambis 9), Boston 63 (McHale 9).

Assists - Los Angeles 28 (E. Johnson 12), Boston 43 (D. Johnson 10).

Total fouls - Los Angeles 23, Boston 17. Technicals - Ainge. A-14,890.

STANDINGS: The format for professional standings:

Eastern Conference
Atlantic Division

	W	L	Pct.	GB
Boston	43	22	.662	-
Philadelphia	40	30	.571	5½
Etc.				

In college boxes, the score by periods is omitted because the games are divided only into halves.

UCLA (69)
Jackson 1-6 2-2 4, Maloncon 4-7 2-2 10, Wright 4-7 1-5 9, Gaines 4-6 1-2 9, Miguel 5-10 0-0 10, Butler 2-3 6-8 10, Hatcher 3-8 0-0 6, Immel 2-2 1-1 5, Haley 1-1 4-4 6, Miller 0-2 0-0 0, J. Jones 0-3 0-0 0, Dunlap 0-0 0-0 0. Totals 26-55 17-24 69.
ST. JOHN'S (88)
Berry 10-14 3-5 23, Glass 4-5 3-6 11, Wennington 5-9 4-4 14, Moses 5-6 0-0 10, Mullin 6-11 4-6 16, Jackson 1-3 5-5 7, Stewart 0-3 2-2 2, S. Jones 1-2 2-2 4, Bross 0-1 0-0 0, Rowan 0-2 0-0 0, Shurina 0-0 1-2 1, Coregy 0-0 0-0 0. Totals 32-56 24-32 88.
Halftime - St. John's 48, UCLA 35. Fouled out - none. Rebounds - UCLA 25 (Wright 9), St. John's 39 (Mullin 9). Assists - UCLA 18 (Gaines 5), St. John's 21 (Moses 8). Total fouls - UCLA 22, St. John's 20.
A-15, 256.

The format for college conference standings:

	Conference			All Games		
	W	L	Pct.	W	L	Pct.
Missouri	12	2	.857	24	4	.857

betting odds Use figures and a hyphen: *The odds were 5-4; he won despite 3-2 odds against him.*

The word *to* seldom is necessary, but when it appears it should be hyphenated in all constructions: *3-to-2 odds, odds of 3-to-2, the odds were 3-to-2.*

bicycle

bowl games Capitalize them: *Cotton Bowl, Orange Bowl, Rose Bowl,* etc.

bowling Scoring systems use both total points and won-lost records.

Use the basic summary format in paragraph form. Note that a comma is used in giving pinfalls for more than 999.

Examples:

ST. LOUIS (AP)—Second-round leaders and their total pinfalls in the $100,000 Professional Bowlers Association tournament:

1. Bill Spigner, Hamden, Conn., 2,820.
2. Gary Dickinson, Fort Worth, Texas, 2,759.
3. Etc.

ALAMEDA, Calif. (AP)—The 24 match play finalists with their won-lost records and total pinfall Thursday night after tour rounds - 26 games - of the $65,000 Alameda Open bowling tournament:
1. Jay Robinson, Los Angeles 5-3, 5,937.
2. Butch Soper, Huntington Beach, Calif., 3-5, 5,932
3. Etc.

boxing   The three major sanctioning bodies for professional boxing are the World Boxing Association, the World Boxing Council and the International Boxing Federation.

box office (n.)   **box-office** (adj.)

bullpen   One word, for the place where baseball pitchers warm up, and for a pen that holds cattle.

C

coach   Capitalize only when used without a qualifying term before the name of the person who directs an athletic team: *General Manager Red Auerbach signed Coach Tom Heinsohn to a new contract.*

If *coach* is preceded by a qualifying word, lowercase it: *third base coach Frank Crosetti, defensive coach George Perles, swimming coach Mark Spitz.*

Lowercase *coach* when it stands alone or is set off from a name by commas: *The coach, Tom Heinsohn, was charged with a technical.*

The capitalization of *coach* is based on the general rule that formal titles used directly before an individual's name are capitalized.

colt   A male horse 4 years and under.

courtesy titles   On sports wires, do not use courtesy titles in any reference unless needed to distinguish among people of the same last name.

cross country   No hyphen, an exception to Webster's New World based on the practices of U.S. and international governing bodies for the sport.

Scoring for this track event is in minutes, seconds and tenths of a second. Extend to hundredths if available.

Use a basic summary. Example:

National AAU Championship
Cross Country
Frank Shorter, Miami, 5:25.67 2. Tom Coster, Los Angeles, 5:30.72. 3. Etc.

Adapt the basic summary to paragraph form under a dateline for a field of more than 10 competitors. See the **bowling** entry for example. See also the **track and field** entry.

cycling Use the basic summary format.

D

decathlon Summaries include time or distance performance, points earned in that event and the cumulative total of points earned in previous events.

Contestants are listed in the order of their overall point totals. First name and hometown (or nation) are included only on the first and last events on the first day of competition; on the last day, first names are included only in the first event and in the summary denoting final placings.

Use the basic summary format. Include all entrants in summaries of each of the 10 events.

An example for individual events:

Decathlon
(Group A)
100-meter dash - 1. Fred Dixon, Los Angeles, 10.8 seconds, 854 points. 2. Bruce Jenner, San Jose State, 11.09, 783. 3. Etc.
Long jump - 1. Dixon, 24-7 (7.34m), 889, 1,743. 2. Jenner, 23-6 (7.17m), 855, 1,638. 3. Etc.
Decathlon final - 1. Bruce Jenner, San Jose State, 8,524 points. 2. Fred Dixon, Los Angeles, 8,277. 3. Etc.

discus The disk thrown in track and field events.

diving Use a basic summary.

E

ERA Acceptable in all references to baseball's *earned run average*.

F

figure skating

filly A female horse 4 years old and under.

football The spellings of some frequently used words and phrases:

ball carrier	end line	field goal
ballclub	end zone	fourth-and-one (adj.)
blitz (n.,v.)	fair catch	fullback

goal line	lineman	quarterback
goal-line stand	line of scrimmage	runback (n.)
halfback	out of bounds (adv.)	running back
halftime	out-of-bounds (adj.)	split end
handoff	pitchout (n.)	tailback
kick off (v.)	place kick	tight end
kickoff (adj.)	place-kicker	touchback
left guard	play off (v.)	touchdown
linebacker	playoff (n.,adj.)	wide receiver

NUMBERS: Use figures for yardage: *The 5-yard line, the 10-yard line, a 5-yard pass play, he plunged in from the 2, he ran 6 yards, a 7-yard gain.* But: *a fourth-and-two play.*

Some other uses of numbers: *The final score was 21-14. The team won its fourth game in 10 starts. The team record is 4-5-1.*

LEAGUE: *National Football League,* or *NFL; United States Football League,* or *USFL.*

STATISTICS: All football games, whether using the one- or two-point conversion, use the same summary style.

The visiting team always is listed first.

Field goals are measured from the point where the ball was kicked—not the line of scrimmage. The goal posts are 10 yards behind the goal lines. Include that distance.

Abbreviate team names to four letters or less on the scoring and statistical lines as illustrated.

The passing line shows, in order: completions-attempts-had intercepted.

A sample agate package:

```
Birmingham-Houston, Stats
Birmingham                                    7 16 0 7—30
Houston                                       14 7 0 6—27
                        First Quarter
Hou—Harrell 23 pass from Dillon (Fritsch kick), 1:00
Bir—Jones 11 run with lateral after Mason 12 pass from Stoudt
(Miller kick), 5:57
Hou—Harrell 6 run (Fritsch kick), 8:07
                       Second Quarter
Bir—FG Miller 47, 1:13
Bir—Caruth 6 run (Miller kick), 5:49
Hou—Johnson 36 pass from Dillon (Fritsch kick), 12:12
Bir—FG Miller 43, 14:33
                       Fourth Quarter
Bir—FG Miller 20, 3:42
Bir—Stoudt 1 run (kick failed), 9:09
Hou—Dillon 8 run (pass failed), 13:58
A-13,202
```

	Bir	Hou
First downs	21	15
Rushes-yards	46-209	12-70
Passing yards	109	260
Return yards	75	112
Comp-Att	13-24-0	17-33-2
Sacked-Yards Lost	4-23	2-24
Punts	3-38	3-41
Fumbles-lost	1-1	2-0
Penalties-yards	3-25	12-69
Time of Possession	35:57	24:03

INDIVIDUAL STATISTICS

RUSHING—Birmingham, Caruth 23-84, Coles 14-59, Stoudt 8-50, Gant 1-5. Houston, Harrell 4-34, Fowler 5-26, Dillon 3-10.

PASSING—Birmingham, Stoudt 13-24-0 133. Houston, Dillon 17-33-2 283.

RECEIVING—Birmingham, Toler 4-53, Jones 3-15, McFaddon 2-38, Coles 2-12, Mason 1-12, Caruth 1-4. Houston, Johnson 5-108, McGee 3-59, McNeil 3-36, 2-27, Sanders 3-29, Verdin 1-24.

MISSED FIELD GOALS—Houston, Fritsch 32.

The rushing and receiving paragraphs for individual leaders show attempts and yardage gained. The passing paragraph shows completions, attempts, number of attempts intercepted, and total yards gained.

STANDINGS: The form for professional standings:

American Conference
East

	W	L	T	Pct.	PF	PA
Baltimore	10	4	0	.714	395	269
New England	9	5	0	.643	387	275
Etc.						

The form for college conference standings:

	Conference				All games				
	W	L	T	Pts.	OP	W	L	T	Pts.	OP
UCLA	6	1	0	215	123	8	2	1	326	233
Etc.										

In college conference standings, limit team names to nine letters or fewer. Abbreviate as necessary.

fractions Put a full space between the whole number and the fraction. Do not separate with a *thin* symbol.

G

game plan

gelding A castrated male horse.

golf Some frequently used terms and some definitions:

Americas Cup No possessive.

birdie, birdies One stroke under par.

bogey, bogeys One stroke over par. The past tense is *bogeyed.*

eagle Two strokes under par.

fairway

Masters Tournament No possessive. Use *the Masters* on second reference.

tee, tee off

U.S. Open Championship Use *the U.S. Open* or *the Open* on second reference.

NUMBERS: Some sample uses of numbers:

Use figures for handicaps: *He has a 3 handicap; a 3-handicap golfer; a handicap of 3 strokes; a 3-stroke handicap.*

Use figures for par listings: *He had a par 5 to finish 2-up for the round; a par-4 hole; a 7-under-par 64; the par-3 seventh hole.*

Use figures for club ratings: *a No. 5 iron, a 5-iron, a 7-iron shot, a 4-wood.*

Miscellaneous: *the first hole, the ninth hole, the 10th hole, the back nine, the final 18, the third round. He won 3 and 2.*

ASSOCIATIONS: *Professional Golfers' Association* (note the apostrophe) or *PGA. PGA Tour* is the official name. Use *tour* (lowercase) on second reference.

The same principle applies to the *Ladies Professional Golf Association* (no apostrophe, in keeping with *LPGA* practice).

SUMMARIES—Stroke (Medal) Play: List scores in ascending order. Use a dash before the final figure, hyphens between others.

On the first day, use the player's score for the first nine holes, a hyphen, the player's score for the second nine holes, a dash and the player's total for the day:

First round:
Jack Nicklaus	35-35—70
Johnny Miller	36-35—71
Etc.	

On subsequent days, give the player's scores for each day, then the total for all rounds completed:

Second round:
Jack Nicklaus	70-70—140
Johnny Miller	71-70—141
Etc.	

Final round, professional tournaments, including prize money:

| Jack Nicklaus, $30,000 | 70-70-68—278 |
| Johnny Miller, $17,500 | 71-70-69—280 |

Use hometowns, if ordered, only on national championship amateur tournaments. Use home countries, if ordered, only on major international events such as the British Open. If used, the hometown or country is placed on a second line, indented one space:

Arnold Palmer	70-69-68-70—277
United States	
Tony Jacklin	71-70-70-70—281
England	

The form for cards:

Par out	444 343 544-35
Watson out	454 333 435-34
Nicklaus out	434 243 544-33
Par in	434 443 454-35—70
Watson in	434 342 443-31—65
Nicklaus in	433 443 453-33—66

SUMMARIES—Match Play: In the first example that follows, the *and 1* means that the 18th hole was skipped because Nicklaus had a 2-hole lead after 17. In the second, the match went 18 holes. In the third, a 19th hole was played because the golfers were tied after 18.

Jack Nicklaus def. Lee Trevino, 2 and 1.
Sam Snead def. Ben Hogan, 2-up.
Arnold Palmer def. Johnny Miller, 1-up (19).

Grey Cup   The Canadian Football League's championship game.

Gulfstream Park   The racetrack.

gymnastics   Scoring is by points. Identify events by name: *sidehorse, horizontal bars,* etc.

Use a basic summary. Example:

Sidehorse—1, John Leaper, Penn State, 8.8 points. 2. Jo Tumper, Ohio State, 7.9. 3. Etc.

H

halfback

handball   Games are won by the first player to score 21 points or, in the case of a tie breaker, 11 points. Most matches go to the first winner of two games.

Use a match summary. Example:

Bob Richards, Yale, def. Paul Johnson, Dartmouth, 21-18, 21-19.
Tom Brenna, Massachusetts, def. Bill Stevens, Michigan, 21-19, 17-21, 21-20.

handicaps Use figures, hyphenating adjectival forms before a noun: *He has a 3 handicap, he is a 3-handicap golfer, a handicap of 3 strokes, a 3-stroke handicap.*

hit and run (v.) **hit-and-run** (n. and adj.) *The coach told him to hit and run. He scored on a hit-and-run. She was truck by a hit-and-run driver.*

hockey The spellings of some frequently used words:

blue line	goal post	power-play goal
crease	goaltender	red line
face off (v.)	penalty box	short-handed
faceoff (n., adj.)	play off (v.)	slap shot
goalie	playoff (n., adj.)	two-on-one break
goal line	power play	

The term *hat trick* applies when a player has scored three goals in a game. Use it sparingly, however.

LEAGUE: *National Hockey League* or *NHL.*
For NHL subdivisions: *the Patrick Division of the Campbell Conference, the division, the conference,* etc.

horse races Capitalize their formal names: *Kentucky Derby, Preakness, Belmont Stakes,* etc.

I

IC4A See **Intercollegiate Association of Amateur Athletes of America.**

indoor (adj.) **indoors** (adv.) *He plays indoor tennis. He went indoors.*

injuries They are *suffered* or *sustained,* not *received.*

Intercollegiate Association of Amateur Athletes of America In general, spell out on first reference.
A phrase such as *IC4A tournament* may be used on first reference, however, to avoid a cumbersome lead. If this is done, provide the full name later in the story.

J

judo   Use the basic summary format by weight divisions for major tournaments; the match summary for dual and lesser meets.

K

Kentucky Derby   *The Derby* on second reference. An exception to normal second-reference practice.

L

lacrosse   Scoring in goals, worth one point each.

   The playing field is 110 yards long. The goals are 80 yards apart, with 15 yards of playing area behind each goal.

   A match consists of four 15-minute periods. Overtimes of varying lengths may be played to break a tie.

   Adapt the summary format in **hockey.**

Ladies Professional Golf Association   No apostrophe after *Ladies.* In general, spell out on first reference.

   A phrase such as *LPGA tournament* may be used on first reference to avoid a cumbersome lead. If this is done, provide the full name later in the story.

left hand (n.) **left-handed** (adj.) **left-hander** (n.)

M

marathon   Use the formats illustrated in the **cross country** and **track and field** entries.

match summary   This format for summarizing sports events applies to one vs. one contests such as tennis, match play golf, etc.

   Give a competitor's name, followed either by a hometown or by a college or club affiliation. For competitors from outside the United States, a country name alone is sufficient in summaries sent for domestic use.

   Example:

   Jimmy Connors, Belleville, Ill. def. Manuel Orantes, Spain, 2-6, 6-3, 6-2, 6-1.

N

National Association for Stock Car Auto Racing Or *NASCAR*.

National Collegiate Athletic Association Or *NCAA*.

numerals

O

odds See **betting odds.**

P

pingpong A synonym for *table tennis.*
The trademark name is *Ping-Pong.*

platform tennis See **tennis.**

play off (v.) **playoff, playoffs** (n. and adj.) The noun and adjective forms are exceptions to Webster's New World Dictionary, in keeping with widespread practice in the sports world.

postseason, preseason No hyphen.

R

racket Not *racquet,* for the light bat used in tennis and badminton.

racquetball Games are won by the first player to score 21 points, unless it is necessary to continue until one player has a two-point spread. Most matches go to the first winner of two games.
Use a match summary. Examples:

> John Smith, Rutgers, def. Paul Giroux, Harvard, 21-8, 17-21, 22-20.
> Frank Tivnan, Columbia, def. Tim Leland, Princeton, 21-17, 21-19.

record Avoid the redundant *new record.*

right hand (n.) **right-handed** (adj.) **right-hander** (n.)

runner-up, runners-up

S

scores Use figures exclusively, placing a hyphen between the totals of the winning and losing teams: *The Reds defeated the Red Sox 4-3, the*

Giants scored a 12-6 football victory over the Cardinals, the golfer had a 5 on the first hole but finished with a 2-under-par score.
Use a comma in this format: *Boston 6, Baltimore 5.*
See individual listings for each sport for further details.

sports editor Capitalize as a formal title before a name.

sports sponsorship For general style see main section. For the titles or names of sports events use the commercial sponsor's name of the event on first reference. Example: *Buick Mr. Goodwrench Open.*

stadium, stadiums Capitalize only when part of a proper name: *Yankee Stadium.*

swimming Scoring is in minutes, and if appropriate, seconds and tenths of a second. Extend to hundredths if available.
Most events are measured in metric units.
Identify events as *men's 440-meter relay, women's 100-meter backstroke*, etc., on first reference. Condense to *men's 440 relay, women's 100 backstroke* on second reference.
See the **track and field** entry for the style on relay teams and events where a record is broken.
Use a basic summary. Examples, where qualifying heats are required:

> Men's 200-meter Backstroke Heats (fastest eight qualify for final Saturday night) heat 1 - 1, John Nabor, USC, 2:03.25. 2, Zoltan Verraszio, Hungary, 2:03,50 3. Etc.

T

table tennis See **pingpong.**

tennis The scoring units are points, games, sets and matches.
A player wins a point if his opponent fails to return the ball, hits it into the net or hits it out of bounds. A player also wins a point if his opponent is serving and fails to put the ball into play after two attempts (*double faults,* in tennis terms).
A player must win four points to win a game. In tennis scoring, both players begin at *love,* or zero, and advance to 15, 30, 40 and game. (The numbers *15, 30* and *40* have no point value as such—they are simply tennis terminology for *1 point, 2 points* and *3 points.*) The server's score always is called out first. If a game is tied at 40-all, or *deuce,* play continues until one player has a two-point margin.
A set is won if a player wins six games before his opponent has won five. If a set becomes tied at five games apiece, it goes to the first player to win seven games. If two players who were tied at five games

apiece also tie at six games apiece, they normally play a tie-breaker—a game that goes to the first player to win seven points. In some cases, however, the rules call for a player to win by two games.

A match may be either a best-of-three contest that goes to the first player or team to win two sets, or a best-of-five contest that goes to the first player or team to win three sets.

Set scores would be reported this way: *Chris Evert Lloyd defeated Sue Barker 6-0, 3-6, 6-4.* Indicate tie-breakers in parenthesis after the set score: *7-6, (11-9)*

SUMMARIES: Winners always are listed first in agate summaries. An example:

> Men's Singles
> First Round
> Jimmy Connor, Belleville, Ill., def. Manuel Orantes, Spain, 2-6, 6-3, 6-2, 6-1.
> Bjorn Borg, Sweden, def. Jim Green, New York (default).
> Arthur Ashe, New York, def. James Peters, Chicago, 6-3, 4-3 (retired).

track and field   Scoring is in distance or time, depending on the event.

Most events are measured in metric units. For those meets that include feet, make sure the measurement is clearly stated, as in *men's 100-meter dash, women's 880-yard run,* etc.

For time events, spell out *minutes* and *seconds* on first reference, as in *3-minutes, 26.1 seconds.* Subsequent times in stories and all times in agate require a colon and decimal point: *3:34.4.* For a marathon, it would be *2 hours, 11 minutes, 5.01 seconds* on first reference, then the form *2:12:4.06* for later listings.

Do not use a colon before times given only in seconds and tenths of a second. Use progressions such as *6.0 seconds, 9.4, 10.1,* etc. Extend times to hundredths, if available: *9.45.*

In running events, the first event should be spelled out, as in *men's 100-meter dash.* Later references can be condensed to phrases such as *the 200, the 400,* etc.

For hurdle and relay events, the progression can be: *100-meter hurdles, 200 hurdles,* etc.

For field events—those that do not involve running—use these forms: *26½* for *26 feet, one-half inch; 25-10½* for *25 feet, 10½ inches,* etc.

In general use a basic summary. For the style when a record is broken, note the mile event in the example below. For the style in listing relay teams, note 1,600-meter relay.

> 60-yard dash—1, Steve Williams, Florida TC, 6.0 2, Hasley Crawford, Philadelphia Pioneer, 6.2 3, Mike McFarland, Chicago TC, 6.2 4. Etc.
> 100—1, Steve Williams, Florida TC 10.1. 2. Etc.

Mile—1, Filbert Bayi, Tanzania, 3:55.1, meet record; old record 3:59, Jim Beatty, Los Angeles TC, Feb. 27, 1963. 2. Paul Cummings, Beverly Hills TC, 3:56.1. 3, Etc.

Women's 880—1, Johanna Forman, Falmouth TC, 2:07.9. 2. Etc.

1,600-meter relay—1, St. John's Jon Kennedy, Doug Johnson, Gary Gordon, Ordner Emanuel, 3:21.9. 2. Brown, 3:23.5. 3. Fordham, 3:24.1. 4. Etc.

Team scoring—Chicago TC 32. Philadephia Pioneer 29. Etc.

Where qualifying heats are required:

Men's 100-meter heats (first two in each heat qualify for Friday's semifinals): Heat 1—1, Steve Williams, Florida TC, 10.1. 2. Etc.

V

volley, volleys

volleyball Games are won by the first team to score 15 points, unless it is necessary to continue until one team has a two-point spread.

Use a match summary. Example:

National AAU Men's Volleyball
First Round
New York AC def. Illinois AC 15-7, 12-15, 19-17.
Vesper Boat Club, Philadelphia, def. Harvard 15-7, 15-8.

W

World Series Or *the Series* on second reference.

wrestling Identify events by weight division.

Y

yard lines Use figures to indicate the dividing lines on a football field and distance traveled: *4-yard line, 40-yard line, he plunged in from the 2, he ran 6 yards, a 7-yard gain.*

Index